# Anthropology of Contemporary Issues

A SERIES EDITED BY

## ROGER SANJEK

# Praying for Justice

## FAITH, ORDER, AND COMMUNITY
## IN AN AMERICAN TOWN

### *Carol J. Greenhouse*

*Cornell University Press*

Ithaca and London

Copyright © 1986 by Cornell University

All rights reserved. Except for brief quotations in a review, this book, or
parts thereof, must not be reproduced in any form without permission in
writing from the publisher. For information, address Cornell University
Press, 124 Roberts Place, Ithaca, New York 14850.

First published 1986 by Cornell University Press.
First published, Cornell Paperbacks, 1989.

International Standard Book Number 0-8014-1971-9 (cloth)
International Standard Book Number 0-8014-9708-6 (paper)
Library of Congress Catalog Card Number 86-47642
Printed in the United States of America
*Librarians: Library of Congress cataloging information
appears on the last page of the book.*

*The paper in this book is acid-free and meets the guidelines for
permanence and durability of the Committee on Production Guidelines
for Book Longevity of the Council on Library Resources.*

To Fred

# Contents

# Preface

A major finding of empirical studies of the use of law in the last decade is that, in spite of a popular image of the United States as a litigious society, Americans seem to prefer avoidance to other modes of dispute resolution. This book attempts to contribute to that body of scholarship by examining the premises and quality of avoidance in a community and cultural context. The place is "Hopewell,"* Georgia, a white, moderately affluent, newly suburban town, where family, work, and religion form the core of people's concerns.

I went to Hopewell in September 1973 to study dispute settlement in an American community, and my assumption, or hope, was that the role of the court in the social fabric of a town would be thrown into relief if the community was in the process of change. The rest of the book should make it clear why such a legal study was not possible in this community and also how it is that one can begin a study of an American community by looking for conflict and end by considering questions of a person's relationship to God. The following discussion briefly outlines the nature of the field work that led, in circuitous ways, to this book.

I chose Hopewell for a variety of reasons that might interest others who plan to study American communities. Primary among them was the fact that it was a county seat with its own court. Some courts of the same level (superior and inferior state courts) have

*All names of the local persons and places that formed the community in this study are fictitious.

jurisdiction over more than one county in Georgia; the fact that "Hopewell County" was a single jurisdiction would facilitate follow-up and record searches. Secondary was Hopewell's proximity to Atlanta, which is the site of state and federal courts; my thought was that I would be able to follow disputes up and out of the judicial ladder. The concentration of relevant records at the Hopewell courthouse did turn out to be extremely convenient, though not because I was tracking litigants. The proximity to the city became a dimension of the study in an entirely different sense than I anticipated then. My search for a field site took place at long distance, and my only resources were an atlas and the state register. Hopewell County looked promising as a dynamic and diverse community because it was represented as being "half green" and "half brown"—half rural and half industrial—and because the county and town were divided by a railroad track. Later, before I began the field work proper, I visited the town on a detour from another errand in the area and what I saw confirmed my sense of the town as a feasible place to undertake ethnographic work.

By the time I settled in Hopewell, I had been in contact with the Historical Society, whose existence I guessed at and whose response to my interest in the town's current history was gracious and generous. The group offered me hospitality, work space, and a task: reviewing and completing genealogical records of important townspeople. The experience of working with genealogies was extremely rewarding. The first stage of the research was with those records and, coincidentally, with the other people at the commercial office that doubled as the society's headquarters. On days when I was not involved there, I perused court dockets and surveyed other records held by the court clerk's office. These are public records and readily available.

Meanwhile, I was getting to know my neighbors at the apartment complex I had chosen as a place to live. It was a fortuitous choice, since it was a "respectable" place whose tenants were "like" me: single "career girls" in their early twenties. (The quotation marks indicate local speech.) One woman in particular became a good friend, and as an act of friendship she introduced me to her friends, who were the core of the "college and career group" at the Baptist church. (Voluntary activities at the church are age-graded; this group was eighteen and over—by no means all college students—

and single.) I am not a Baptist but welcomed their invitations to join them at church as a gesture of inclusion and as a chance to sample the town's social life. I did attend the church as a guest. At that point, I thought of my work with the Historical Society and at the courthouse as my study and participated in the evenings with my neighbor's friends as a somewhat peripheral social activity. I soon realized that my real study was there at the church, that what I wanted to know about conflict and courts and the law in general was being answered in sermons, in prayer, and in a growing number of conversations. I was not prepared for this turn of events because I was already involved with the church on a different basis. I had friends there, and as a way of acknowledging their generosity in what I hoped would be a nonreligious, inconspicuous, but meaningful role, I joined the church choir.

I was "caught"—to borrow Favret-Saada's (1981) term—long before I knew it. I later learned that singing is considered a ministry among Baptists and, as I hope the text makes clear, that friendship and witnessing are inseparable. A Baptist "witnesses" for Jesus by introducing a non-Baptist, or lapsed Baptist, to the idea of salvation. Witnessing involves no urging or importuning but rather an explication of what Jesus has accomplished in the believer's life. It is an invitation by way of autobiography, and I found these invitations—when I realized what they were—challenging, respectful, and loving. To a believer, witnessing is a gift. To a nonbeliever, it is many privileged conversations, which I hope I have not dishonored in this book. The implicit invitation of the witness is mirrored in the explicit invitation during the Baptist church service. The hymn of invitation accompanies a prayerful moment when "prospects," as they are called, become the objects of prayer. When a prospect decides that he has been visited by the Holy Spirit and wishes to signal his acceptance of Jesus, he walks down the aisle of the church to the altar to give his pledge to the minister and rejoicing congregation. I know that many people expected me to take this step, which I could not; my steady presence at the church seemed to suggest that I was engaged in an unusually long ("thoughtful," my friends later said) struggle with the Holy Spirit. I never did join the church, although I believed the minister when he told me that if I did, there would be an "instant revival." "A thousand people would follow you to the altar," he said.

[11]

Seven months of intense involvement at the church were punctuated at intervals by interviews on the subjects of Christianity and conversion. "Interview" somewhat misstates the case, since the inquiry was in both directions. Many members of the church, but particularly the minister, were generous with their time and patience. I was anxious not to deceive, but I also knew that my questioning might be taken as a sign of my "conviction" (wrestling with the Holy Spirit). I cannot recall ever asking a question that was not fully answered, and I did not have to ask many: people were so glad to discuss their faith and their discovery of it that, as word of my interest spread, people sought me out. I was moved by their confidences, which were offered selflessly, and this book represents my effort to accept and understand them.

Once I understood that my continued presence at the church was being interpreted as a prolonged spiritual crisis by those who knew me or knew of me, I decided that I could no longer participate in church activities. I knew that I had become troubling, and I feared becoming an affront. Although my friends assured me that they saw my delay as being due to my desire to be convinced intellectually, I also knew that my failure to join the church had by itself caused tears and doubt among people I cared about. At that point, I turned my attention back to the courts and to the development of the county and finally moved to the city in late 1974. I commuted to Hopewell for social visits, interviews, and archival research through the fall of 1975. I did not return until the fall of 1980, when I collected the data reported in Chapters 4 and 5.

Apart from originating in activities in and around the church, the court, and the Historical Society, which I have already described, my data come from countless conversations that were largely unplanned. Since my "job" left me as free as the unemployed housewives I came to know, many mornings or afternoons were spent touring sites around the county, at work with other women on craft projects (a local passion), or just in conversation over coffee or Coca-Cola (another passion). The book has acquired its bias toward women's words in this way. Relationships between men and women or, from my perspective, men and unmarried women were formal and impersonal by comparison. My sense of men's lives comes partly from their wives and sisters. I knew some, of course, and talked with them—most extensively with my own "peers" (age-mates) at the church. I also heard men pray, read news of them in the papers, and witnessed their separate lives at the courthouse or simply in stores and on the street. I rarely carried a note pad but kept a journal in which I recorded daily events and scenes and, when I thought I knew enough, wrote biographical essays describing to myself individuals whose stories seemed especially vivid or salient. These records along with files full of news clippings, church programs, and other mementoes form the basis of what follows.

In their explanations of how society functions, the people of Hopewell have much to say about the law; most Americans do not use the courts to process their personal complaints, so the widespread lack of experience with the courts in Hopewell is not surprising or especially significant. As the text makes clear, however, the people who manage to avoid the courts in Hopewell fall into two categories. Baptists form one of them, in that they avoid not only the courts but also the adversarial concepts of conflict and remedy that the law entails. The other category, which includes everyone else, expresses attitudes about conflict that are congenial to the law (that is, in adversarial terms, oriented toward remedial awards) but prefers to settle disputes out of court. I have written about these differences and their significance elsewhere (Greenhouse 1982a, 1982b, 1983, and 1986), but two points remain that might appear counterintuitive in the American context. First, it appears that law use in general and litigation in particular prerequire a world view that is not universal among even affluent white Americans, such as the people in Hopewell are. At the very least, that world view must include both the legitimacy of the state's institutions and a sense that the human condition can be meaningfully changed by human action. The Baptists in Hopewell do not believe in the second of these things: the state merits our obedience, but only God can change the conditions of life, they say.

The second point is that the people of Hopewell demonstrate for us that rights are not larger than culture. The Baptists of Hopewell are not powerless by any stretch of the imagination, and their aversion to using the law in their interpersonal affairs appears to impose few measurable costs on them. I cannot accept the questions—which I have heard many times—that attempt to test the credibility of the Baptists' patience with hypothetical justiciable problems (What if someone were murdered? What if there were a major theft?). Such things did not happen while I was in Hopewell, and at any rate, Baptists there speak of the *need* for salvation precisely because they recognize that such temptations can occur. They do not pray to avoid such confrontations, but for strength in dealing with them. In writing about them, I cannot help exposing Hopewell's Baptists to such cynicism but no more so than their daily lives do. I would answer in return that if the Baptists in Hopewell do not endure much that others would consider hard, the rest of the world does not give us much assurance that greater pain than theirs enables people to overcome a view of society that defeats them long before they exercise the rights to which their law entitles them. Just as individualism is a promise and a burden, praying for justice is at once an act of faith and despair.

CAROL J. GREENHOUSE

*Ithaca, New York*

# A Note to Readers in Hopewell

One of the realities of anthropological writing in the current age is the presence of a very special audience of readers: the ones whose lives form the subject of the research. Although every anthropologist welcomes the participation of "informants" as collaborators during the months or years of field work, few would honestly say they relish the scrutiny of their former hosts when it comes to the finished text. In our books and monographs, we prove ourselves to have been very bad guests, or so it would seem. When I began my work in the town I call Hopewell, I promised you, my hosts, a copy of whatever book might come from my labors there, and this is it. Here I want to explain the connection between the things you showed me and the things I have written about, so that if you do not like the book, at least you will know that its source is the same respect and affection that I hope were evident in my regard for you when I lived in Hopewell.

I am sure that you will not like the book, not least because if you did, it would be the first recorded instance in the United States of a population appreciating the anthropology visited upon it. Americans do not seem to like being written about for the most part, and they do not like being analyzed at all. J. P. Marquand's novel *Point of No Return* captures the aching sense of personal violation that is the consequence of an anthropologist's field research in a New England town. The ambiguity of the analyst/confidante's role has devastating consequences in that book's plot. In this book, I have tried to avoid committing that kind of harm by writing not so much about your lives but about the people you told me about and especially the *way* you told me about them. The book is about love, faith, remorse, and hope. My hope is that no single person will recognize himself or herself here. Those of you with whom I spent the most time will not find yourselves portrayed on the following pages, although you may recognize the sound of your own voices. I did not consider that I had the right to single out individuals for description or analysis, when all of the people I knew presented themselves to me as ordinary, even typical.

As the introduction explains, this book is the product of a long series of conversations. These conversations were a privilege and a pleasure, and I have tried to preserve their integrity by writing about their whole sense, not dissolving them into bits of information to be reshuffled like so many cards. The mood of an evening's talk or the flow of a morning's conversation—these were among the things that enter into the analysis on the following pages, along with the things that we talked about or did not talk about. I hope you will understand that if I have written about these conversations, it is not because I stand in judgment of my interlocutors but because these conversations made me want to write. I suspect that this will be another source of your displeasure with this book: it includes so many things that were never quite put into words and, so you may feel, never should be. In particular, you may feel that conflict, which is central among the themes of this book, should not be given air and a voice.

So let me say this: this book is not about *conflicts;* it does not pick and probe at the relationships among people—relationships that, in any case, seemed more like art than sociology. It *is* about conflict in that the more I listened in Hopewell and the more I read, the more I understood what I took to be your feeling that social life should have a certain grace. For many of you, the grace is God's; for all of you, the grace is southern. What was special in my experience with you was the way you opened doors of hospitality and friendship, the way you taught newcomers to belong by treating them as if they already belonged, and the way you believed in Hopewell's future. There is much more—or much else. Ordinarily, these things, which when added together we might call the "quality of life," do not have to be put into words. But anthropology is not ordinary. Its hungry pen wants to put things into words so that as we struggle to imagine all the forms of human experience on earth, we can imagine them for their own specialness, not just as a sequence of comings and goings, of "doings." My hope is that readers of this book will learn something of your way of life, since I believe deeply that you have something to teach them about the American soul.

I have not yet said what grace has to do with conflict. My sense is that, for you, being a lady or a gentleman has to do with (among other things) letting the awkward moments pass and letting the bright moments shine. In the Baptist church, I learned the same message in a different way: being Christian means focusing on God's will, not one's own, and on letting one's own soul reflect the bright light of faith, not the dim light of self-vaunting. My own way of putting this—and hence to say in this book—is that men and women find it important to learn to live together by setting their self-interest and anger aside. This is the point where the book begins. It ends by suggesting that this idea—about grace, or faith, or the silencing of conflict—has a history. I have had to reopen that history in a way that will sound unfamiliar to you, to make the point to readers that your own ethic is a powerful one.

Whatever else it is, this book is a testimony to my debt to you. I have tried to discharge that debt in a number of ways in the text itself. Primary among them is my commitment to protecting your privacy, both from the world beyond Hopewell and within Hopewell. First, there are no maps or illustrations, and I have changed the names of your town and county and of every person I cite from there. Some local citizens have published books about Hopewell, and I have quoted them without giving them credit (I do use quotation marks but no names or book titles), so that they do not give the game away. The history I have written is as accurate as I know it, but I have written it in a way that makes your town indistinguishable from a handful or two of others in the region. I have written about the novel that was written about your town (actually, there were several), but I have left it to you to give out its author and title, if you prefer. My goal was to make it possible for any one of you to deny successfully that this book is about your town. That way, we can all be *sure* that no one will take my word over yours about anything that matters to you.

Another part of my debt is reflected in the decisions I have made about the directions this book takes. You often wondered what

[17]

anthropologists *do;* this is a sample. I have decided not to present your town as some quaint backwater (it is not), with a past but no future. In the years I have known your town, it has grown beyond what I could have imagined in 1973. I lament the loss of some of your exotic scenery (there is nothing like it in upstate New York), but I am glad for you that the malls and subdivisions have brought Hopewell so much capital and energy. This leads me to my next point: I have decided to present your town as part of the process of current American history. Finally, I have written about your town in the language of anthropology, so that as we ponder the nature of social and cultural life, we can have your witness at hand as one testimony of the shape Western civilization has taken in our modern era.

One of my fears is that you will think that I have written about Hopewell because it is odd, unique, or flawed. This is not the case. Hopewell is, to me, as unique as a familiar face, but I am able to write about the town as an anthropologist precisely because of its parallels, on innumerable points, to other American communities and other human communities. Some of these points of comparison are mentioned and discussed in the footnotes to each chapter. By becoming the subject of a work of anthropology, a community does not become a laboratory animal strapped to the table but—far different—a companion in the mind, an unseen teacher. This would be the place to write at length about what anthropology is and how its long tradition of field work has developed throughout the century—this would be the place if this were that kind of book. Because it is not, I will end this note to you by offering all readers in Hopewell a suggestion that will reveal me to be the pedant you may have suspected I am: *if* you read this book, please read at least one other volume of anthropology—*then* you will taste for yourselves the comparative questions about social life that brought me to your doorsteps.

C. G.

# Acknowledgments

This volume reflects the light of a bright sky of personal thanks to many individuals and agents. If I named them all and explained my debt in every case, this small book would be utterly overwhelmed, and it would look like small thanks indeed. As it is, I must use some other channel to express my thanks to the many people whose conversation, whose direct or indirect encouragement, or, simply, whose life of good witness inspired the development of the study and the manuscript. It will be a pleasure to express my debt to them, and the debt will in no way be discharged with the thanks. That is also true of the following sources, to whom I give thanks for intellectual or material support of the most essential and formative sort: two teachers, Evon Z. Vogt and the late Klaus-Friedrich Koch; the National Institute of Mental Health for the training grant that funded my graduate training, including the original research for this volume, through the Department of Anthropology at Harvard University; my colleagues and students in the Department of Anthropology at Cornell University; the College of Arts and Sciences at Cornell University for a study leave and faculty research grant in 1980; and Peter Agree, at Cornell University Press. Portions of the following pages have evolved from earlier published versions. The two paragraphs on local conceptions of family life on pages 48 and 49 appeared in earlier form as part of my article on American individualism and anthropology (cited in the Bibliography as Greenhouse 1985b) and are used here with permission from *Human Organization*, copyright © 1985 The Society for Applied

Anthropology. An earlier version of Chapter 3, part 2, addressed related themes in my contribution to George Marcus's edited volume on elites (cited in the Bibliography as Greenhouse 1983). An earlier version of Chapter 5 was published in *Symbolizing America*, edited by Hervé Varenne, copyright 1986 University of Nebraska Press.

I also thank my family, all of whom helped in ways that may surprise them to learn. Again, here I can only sketch the essential outlines of my debt, and they will signal the shape of my acknowledgment to those whom I do not name in these pages. I borrow themes from the book to specify my thanks in relation to this project: In the memory of my father, I found a model of humor, wisdom, and forbearance that made the subject of this book—an ethic of restraint—plausible. In my conversations with my mother, I learned early the joys of enthusiasm and questioning. In addition to everything else she is for her daughters (and that is much), she is an apt and eager intellectual partner and a tireless supporter. My sister's creative gifts have opened universes of the imagination to me from the time of my earliest memories. Not only did she teach me to read and write, she also taught me the pleasures of narrative, both giving and receiving.

Finally, I dedicate this book to my husband, Alfred C. Aman, Jr., who has shared in very immediate ways every day of this project's life with me, all but the earliest months in Hopewell. The breadth of his mind and the warmth of his heart are the roof and hearth of his own scholarship, and they gave ample shelter to this work too. It is not only for this that he has my gratitude; there is so much more. This book is about concepts of faith and order in a town that I call Hopewell. Some time after Fred and I met, someone from Hopewell who knew me well told me of her certainty that it was God who had made Fred's path cross with mine. Ordinarily, as an auditor in such conversations, I maintained a fairly steady inner dialogue, a murmur of skepticism. But on this occasion, I could not bring myself to rouse that inner voice when it did not speak of its own accord.

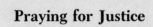

**Praying for Justice**

# Introduction

## The Book: Scope and Aims

This book is written roughly in the order of its discovery in that it begins with a contemporary conception of social order and concludes with a discussion of the historical referents of that conception. It begins and ends in the community that I call "Hopewell," a suburban town near Atlanta, Georgia. The population of 4,000 within the town limits now forms part of an urban sprawl that makes "Hopewell" difficult to define, both as a place and as an idea. The county's population was about 100,000 when I completed most of the field work for this study (1973 to 1975); Hopewell is 98 percent white. At the time of the study, the town's suburbanization was still relatively recent. The interstate highway had extended past the town's edge only a few years before, making large-scale commuting feasible and attractive. When I arrived, the townspeople perceived themselves to be in the midst of intense social change, and that fact forms part of the background of this book.

The central focus of this book is the religious doctrine and praxis of Hopewell's Baptists and the relationship of the Baptists' understanding of their faith to the general community's understanding of itself. The link between the two is the Baptists' ethic of avoidance in actual and potential conflict situations and the selective ahistoricism of the community at large. The ultimate argument of the book is that avoidance in interpersonal relationships is the stuff of which ahistoricism is made: looking too closely at the past—"opening

[23]

closets," "looking for skeletons," are some native expressions—risks the renewal of past controversies. The local concept of the past is implicitly one of conflict, and the community's studied ahistoricism is—again, implicitly—an avoidance of conflicts that once divided the town profoundly. These same conflicts gave meaning to the social classifications that are the Hopewell Baptists' metaphors of salvation. Thus the Baptists' sociology of faith and the community's theory of history can be approached with the same map.

In developing these ideas, I have made some choices and compromises and resisted some temptations of which the reader should be aware. First, the book is concerned primarily with people's *ideas* about conflict and, much less, with conflicts themselves. For example, I am less certain about what people in Hopewell actually do with their problems than what they believe they *should* do with their problems. Thus I intend the book as an explication of the cultural framework within which they understand conflict, remedies, and justice. It is above all a cultural analysis, or an analysis of the relationships among ideas (Durkheim 1965: 463, Weber 1954: 1). Although my findings support those of other scholars studying community processes of dispute resolution in the United States (Baumgartner 1980, Buckle and Thomas-Buckle 1982, Engel 1984, Merry 1979, Nader 1980, Perin 1977), they also differ in that they are not so concerned with patterns of choice making as with the perception of choices and their ramifications.

This book entails implications for legal anthropologists and others interested in cultural aspects of disputes, dispute resolution, and remedial choice making in the United States. First is the reiteration of the point that overt disputes were relatively difficult to find in this community context. Had I chosen to focus on disputes, there would have been public matters in the newspapers and enough interpersonal tension to report, but to do so would have been a serious misrepresentation of the community I knew. Thus the anthropologists' conventional reliance on the case method, to show rules in action (see Gluckman 1973) or the relationship of normative breaches to their social context (see Collier 1975, van Velsen 1969), was not an especially effective resource in this study. I found that my analytical assumptions erred in conceptualizing the dispute as having universal significance in structural terms; the research taught me that the structural preconditions of disputing do not exist everywhere, even among affluent Americans (see Greenhouse 1982b). (For a related theoretical critique of the case method, see Cain and Kulscar 1981–1982.) The people of Hopewell do not consider order to be a matter of complying with rules, nor do they consider that human intervention can accomplish any constructive purpose. They are not remedy oriented; they seek no satisfaction except that of prayer. There are lapses, of course; however, their understanding of conflict and its social significance is not built on the lapses but on other terms.

The point about disputes and their relative lack of importance leads to the second implication of the study: that a cultural conception of order does not consist first or only of rules but—in this case—of social classifications understood in normative terms. The norms are not commands, or requirements, but explanations and justifications (Greenhouse 1982a). A person chooses one explanation over another and thereby identifies with one group over another. Thus Hopewell's Baptists, at least, have managed to accomplish something of what Tocqueville described as the American dream: a society without overt applications of human authority, a society built not on obedience but on participation. Huizinga's study of the United States, originally written between 1918 and 1926, develops this theme more generally. In his discussion of individualism, he cited an American political scientist's definition of the state as an example of Jeffersonian thinking: "'The State,' says W. Y. Elliott, 'is ultimately a pluralistic arrangement of group forces.' This is really only a modern way of expressing the denigration of government which was already present in Jefferson" (1972: 275). Huizinga went on to explain that Americans' conception of the basis of groups is "feeling"— "we-feeling" (1972: 277). Indeed, Varenne's (1977: 34–35) study of the farmers of "Appleton"—standing together to recite the Farm Bureau's Creed, accomplishing the "we" by pronouncing "I" in unison—is a vivid example of Huizinga's observation. Hopewell conforms to this representation.

Thus a theory of social order inevitably underlies any particular instance of group participation. In Hopewell, as Chapters 1 and 2 explain, the theory of order is very much as other scholars have described American society: individualism in Tocqueville's sense of withdrawing from authority, preferring to imagine a society built up of voluntary acts of association and cooperation. The extension, or corollary, of this preference is an insistent egalitarianism, that is, not only is human authority inappropriate, it is also illegitimate. Bailey captured the essence of the idea that is at work here: "Equality comes about through the mutual cancellation of supposed efforts to be unequal" (1971: 19–20). The symbolic *process* of equality involves the selection and cancellation of specific markers of inequality, and that is exactly what Hopewell's Baptists do in elaborating their equation of Christianity and harmony. Harmony and equality are two elements of a larger idea (and ideal) of society in nature and the cosmos. Bailey developed the image of individuals who exempt themselves from social competition, as the Baptists of Hopewell do: "They want harmony—or say they want it: if people quarrel, that is because people are sinful. Consequently, there are certain figures who stand outside the competition and symbolize the common desire for communal harmony" (1971: 21).

The question of how the *desire* for communal harmony can be effectively symbolized raises the final point. In Hopewell, Baptists and non-Baptists alike share an image of elite status that explicitly focuses on the elite individual's ability to resolve conflict, both personally and structurally. In the personal sense, conflicts might be disputes or potential disputes, but in the structural sense, the conflicts are the particular contradictions that the groups feel most keenly. For Baptists, it is capitalism; for others, it is other things (see Chapter 3). In the contemporary society, then, conceptions of elite status, symbolically expressed, articulate the desire for communal harmony by dissociating value from prestige and by dissociating value from power. This symbolic process also has a historical dimension, and that is in a selective attention to those aspects of the past that show the resolution of profound conflict in these terms. Gorer (1948: 200) described in compelling terms the therapeutic historical amnesia the South has suffered since 1865. Hopewell, in this case, is no exception. It is not Cherokee removal that is "remembered" but "progress"; it is not the Civil War that is remembered but the kindness of a few Yankee soldiers to southern families; it is not poverty or the Populists who are remembered but the political reunification of the town in the twentieth century. The selective ahistoricism that consists of silencing old disputes is inseparable from the ethic of harmony that silences new ones. The one demands the other. The book travels a full circle.

Hopewell is perhaps not a typical community, but it is not unique either.

The formation of the county and its development to the present day are a continuous demonstration of the ways in which a small community can be molded by and participate in regional and national issues. Although the focus of the study is local, I found that my research was continually drawn outward to the state, region, and nation. I have resisted the temptation to attempt a complete history of Cherokee removal, state's rights, and populism in this area from the local perspective; instead, I have confined the historical discussion to the critical problems of historical consciousness generated by the ethnography. One implication of this discussion is that it is meaningful to conceive of cultural continuities even in communities like Hopewell, where the population has been unstable and where the original families have been overwhelmed by newcomers. Once newcomers adopt the language of local social classification, they effectively join Hopewell's cultural system and subscribe to its theory of history.

Finally, the aim of this book is twofold. The ethnographic problem in general is the exploration of conceptions of order in a single American community. Specifically, I must account for the central, negative place that conflict holds in that system of ideas. Second, I must account for the terms in which that centrality and negative value are expressed. The intellectual context of the study is addressed in the remainder of this introduction; additional implications (beyond those raised in the course of the central argument in the text) are developed in the brief postscript.

## Hopewell in the Anthropology of Law

As readers move through the following chapters, my hope is that they will find a useful study of how one group of Americans thinks about order in their social universe. Here, I briefly address its context in the anthropology of law or legal anthropology with nonspecialists in mind, or readers who want to contextualize my analysis of Hopewell in the anthropological and social science literature.

*Legal anthropology* is the cross-cultural study of social ordering. I write "ordering" rather than "order" because the emphasis of scholars in this field is on the social and cultural processes by which people organize their normative expectations and accountabilities. In the fifty years in which there has been an identifiable scholarship in the anthropology of law, it has been enlivened by a number of debates, all of which are relevant to the analytical choices that sculpt the present volume. I discuss these things while introducing the concerns of legal anthropology from a developmental perspective.

There are two principal modes of research and analysis in legal anthropology. The older of these modes converges at major points with the development of the academic legal profession and its jurisprudential tradition. The other one derives from classical social science, from Weber in particular. If legal anthropology has relied more on the former mode, the signs are that it is becoming increasingly tied to the latter one (for example, Geertz 1983: 167–234).

Anthropological conceptions of law can be traced to Montesquieu, whose principal tenet held that legal systems can and must reflect the differences among the social systems of which they form a part. This relativism charters legal anthropology's comparative agenda. A century later—a century of new liberal theories—Maine's *Ancient Law* examined the development of contract law in Rome, contextualizing questions of law (strictly speaking) in the wider normative system embedded in kinship and status. It is from Maine, even more directly than from Montesquieu, that the anthropology of law inherits its energy to find the connectedness between what courts do and what people think. Maine's concern was to examine the pristine development of a complete legal system, and his hypothesis concerning the transformation on the basis of legal accountability from status to contract had analogies in the European late Middle Ages. As a general hypothesis of alternative legal foundations, Maine's work is cited by ethnographers of law today. (For a complete study of Maine's legal thought and his antecedents in legal evolutionary approaches, see Stein 1980).

In the English-speaking anthropological world, the philosophical genealogy from Montesquieu to Maine reached the twentieth century in parallel projects on both sides of the Atlantic. In England, Max Gluckman (1940) analyzed a case study of social tension among indigenous elites and British colonial administrators in South Africa and argued for the case method in that work and in his subsequent research in Zambia (then Rhodesia; the book was published in 1955). In his book on the Barotse, Gluckman elaborated on the extended case analysis of his 1940 article, building his investigation around compact descriptions of cases of dispute together with their outcomes at the native court or elsewhere. Meanwhile, two Americans, Llewellyn and Hoebel (1941), analyzed "the Cheyenne Way" by means of memory cases, narratives of disputes dated fifty or more years. The historical aspect of their method has not proved to be influential, but their use of "trouble cases" or "law jobs" as units of analysis had an enormous impact on the field. These early writers, much influenced by academic law (Gluckman by Maine, Gray, and Salmond; Hoebel by Hohfeld and Llewellyn himself), found in their method a link to legal audiences who, in the Anglo-American system, were used to the case method of the common law. For Gluckman and for Llewellyn and Hoebel, the legal audience had a special importance—to Gluckman because he hoped his ethnographic work would help preserve for the Barotse some of their precolonial jural autonomy; to Llewellyn and Hoebel because they sought to demonstrate the emergence of well-formed legal ideas among the tribal Cheyenne.

Yet the case method, to these and subsequent analysts, was not merely a means of reaching audiences outside of anthropology (although that was surely one result). The case method was held out as the most feasible means of discovering the rules—both literally and figuratively—that govern a population. This claim is simple enough on the surface but is actually profoundly problematic. (We will return to it momentarily.) Cases were understood by the many anthropologists who used the method to embody reasons—reasons for disputing, reasons for deciding on one outcome or another—and these reasons attached directly to the cultural concerns that brought anthropologists to the field in the first place. Through reasons, scholars gained a point of access to the larger culture, to the extent that "legal" reasons also applied in the wider social arena. Thus Bohannan (1967) referred to "double institutionalization," and Nader (1965) proposed case studies as one basis of a cross-cultural examination of law.

The case method guided a large corpus of anthropological literature on law from the 1930s through the 1960s and early 1970s. (For synoptic reviews covering these years, see Collier 1975, Moore 1970a, Nader 1965, and Snyder 1981.) Anthropologists working in virtually every part of the world returned with extensive accounts of conflict and its resolution. Outside of anthropology, the legal realists and, later, the law and society movement turned toward anthropological data and research techniques to accomplish their own comparative agendas. The achievement of the case method in legal anthropology is primarily in its detailed display of problematic social relations in cultural contexts—at best, with verbatim accounts of trouble, preference, strategy, rationalization, and perhaps reconciliation. Perhaps ironically, the case method stimulated an enormous amount of empirical research but offered relatively limited comparative possibilities. Since the 1970s, legal anthropologists have developed comparative studies around questions of dispute processing, that is, around the organizational processes (negotiation, mediation, arbitration, and adjudication, to take one set; see Koch 1974: 37, Moore 1978) by which disputes reach their outcomes and the "ecology" of those processes in society (Collier 1975). Outside of anthropology, the focus on mediation and alternatives to adjudication has been very widespread; indeed, the original model for American "mediation centers" came from Gibbs's (1963) article on the Kpelle moot (Danzig 1982). In short, the domination of the field by the case method has generated a large body of data whose impact is widely felt; yet commentators suggest with increasing certitude that cases in and of themselves do not accomplish the comparative enterprise that is the hallmark of anthropology (Abel 1980).

The critique of the case method—and no one suggests abandoning it—comes from two directions. On the one hand, it is a critique of the virtually exclusive focus on disputes. Cain and Kulscar's (1981–1982) extensive critical review argues convincingly that all disputes are not of equal significance, that different social structures lend significance to different sorts of problems. This is a losing-the-forest-in-the-trees argument; the critique is a highly constructive one that concludes with some recommended priorities. Another sort of critique challenges the interpretive assumption of the case method that reasons offered in argument are the same ones that motivate and/or rationalize a society at peace. In other words, the question is: is what people say and do in dispute situations the same as in other contexts? Legal anthropologists interested in language suggest that the answer to this question is no (Mather and Yngvesson 1980–1981). A case of dispute resolution is not simply a magnifying glass for everyday life; it is something in itself.

At issue here is the question of the extent to which social life is organized by rules. Legal anthropologists have tended to obscure the important distinctions to be made between implicit and explicit rules on the one hand (Comaroff and Roberts 1981) and between rules and other normative formulations on the other hand (Greenhouse 1982a and 1985a). The case method and its rationale of revealing "legal" ideas in social context rests on the assumption that social life is constituted by its rules. Its critics argue that, if anything, the situation is the other way around, that rules are constituted as such by social groups. The latter approach, which is more or less tied to Wittgenstein's (1958) work on language and meaning (see also Pitkin 1972), deems unacceptable the assumptions that (a) rules ordinarily motivate behavior or that (b) there can be rules in the absence of rule makers. As anthropologists become increasingly aware of the vectors of power and hierarchy in their research settings (for example, Moore 1970b), the latter point in particular emerges as a strong plea for intellectual caution.

The alternative to imagining rules at the heart of every positive act is to see society's heart in its mind, that is, to probe not rules but the ideas that people find compelling and on which they base (or try to base) their conduct as a matter of course. This is the relevance of Weber's "value-rational conduct" (1954: 1) in the anthropology of law. Value-rationale conduct derives from the "conscious faith in the absolute worth of the conduct as such, independent of any aim" (1954: 1). Weber specifically contrasted this type of action from "purpose-rational conduct," which is undertaken for some self-interested purpose. His (1954: 5) definition of *law* as physical or psychological coercion applied by a specialized staff has tended to overshadow the importance he placed on normative ideas apart from those backed coercive threats. Much of the ethnography of law maps systems of coercion and their means of securing legitimacy; value-rational conduct is perhaps left as the domain of religion. Indeed, Geertz's (1973: 90) famous definition of *religion* serves just as well, word for word, as a definition of a *normative*

[31]

*order* in general: "A religion is: (1) a system of symbols which acts to (2) establish powerful, pervasive, and long-lasting moods and motivations or even by (3) formulating conceptions of a general order of existence and (4) clothing these conceptions with such an aura of factuality that (5) the moods and motivations seem uniquely realistic" (original emphasis omitted). Durkheim avoided this ambiguity by tying his definition of *religion* to that of a church (1965: 62); Weber embraced it by contextualizing his consideration of law on wider issues of validity, legitimacy, and culture. There is nothing to be gained in subsuming these wider concerns under the rubric of some broadly construed "law"; there is everything to be gained by exploring the relevance of these other domains to *law*, narrowly defined. The risk in defining *law* too broadly (to be synonymous with *order*, for example) is in losing the possibility of studying the power that the law generates in social systems. The benefits of examining the cultural context of law are in the discoveries of culture's intrinsic order (extended examples can be found in Bentley's [1984] discussion of the Maranao and in Rosen's [1984] study of Islam in Sefrou).

In this spirit, in this book, my subject is the anthropology of law but not law. My premises are that although the Baptists of Hopewell order their community, it is not a legal order but one based on deeply held values. I take it that the fact that these values are widely enunciated does not constitute psychological coercion, nor, as I show in Chapter 3, is there a specialized staff to see to their enforcement. Since my ethnographic problem requires that I pay particular attention to concepts of order and their social referents, I do not offer trouble cases for the most part, lest individual behavioral choices be assumed congruent with collective cultural representations. My hope for this book is that it contributes to the anthropology of law both in the way it frames the cultural problem (how is order conceptualized?) and by its approach to that problem (by exploring the sociocultural referents of systems of ideas over time). Although the present volume is not directly comparative, I have tried to make clear in the text where comparative implications might emerge.

Some readers will finish the book and want to know: "So that's what they think in Hopewell (maybe). What do they do about conflicts when they occur?" That is a legitimate question and one whose answer would have to range much more widely than this book. This book touches on conflict behavior, but I readily confess to being more concerned with the terms of people's relief and remorse than in the improvised behavioral responses to inconvenience, trouble, cheating, and even tragedy. If I were to study Hopewell again with an eye to people's conflict behavior, my hypothesis would be that the cultural logic outlined here represents the limits people place on their interpretations of their own and others' actions. At various points in this book, I conclude that the logic of the "life of good witness" does motivate a certain pattern of restrained action, but I never mean to suggest that people in Hopewell cannot conceive of other possibilities. Culture is not the script of their daily lives but the logic behind the choice of one script among many of which they are well aware.

These same readers—and perhaps others—will want to know if the cultural explication that follows can be used as a basis for predicting behavior. I have been asked by lawyers, for example, if it would be strategic to prefer or bar a Hopewell Baptist from a jury in this or that circumstance. The Hopewell Baptists I knew all considered themselves to be good citizens and, I am sure, would discharge their duties responsibly. As it happened, I did not know of anyone who had served on a jury. In any case, I doubt that the following pages are much of a guide to prediction of anything except a current of yearning and regret in people's private lives. The book concerns people's understandings of their personal responsibilities in their social relationships. To the extent that people feel free, or are free, to act on their understandings, perhaps there is a degree of predictability that emerges out of this ethnography. The question of the extent to which predictability, or behavior in general, tests the analysis presented in this book is another matter. A cultural investigation is testable in its own terms—its coherence and logic; its anticipation of contradiction (and no cultural system is without contradictions); its priorities, clarity, and ambiguity.

This book is very much influenced by the jurisprudential tradition outlined above, and I acknowledge that long tradition as the source of many of my own questions. My analytical priorities came from the data themselves; in Hopewell, to understand conflict I had to understand first the issues raised in this book. This point is not one of personal intellectual preference but one that refers to the

[33]

particular significance of ideas about law in the cultural system of this American town.

## Hopewell and the United States

Readers are justified in wondering to what extent they are reading about the rest of the United States. My answer lies somewhere between that of Warner (1949: xv and 1952: 33) or Gorer (1948: 5–6), who claimed to write on America as a whole, and that of Henry (1974: 7–8), who found in the United States a vast collection of cultures consisting of individuals and moments. Varenne (1984a) analyzed this conceptual diversity in American anthropology and accounted for it in a compelling cultural argument. Indeed, the basis for my answer flows directly from the book's underlying premises, described earlier. Specifically, a concept of culture as constituted by the logic of symbols and their connected meanings could be neither universally shared nor particularly unique. The human imagination is too varied, too responsive to private and public experience, to be so transparent or opaque. Thus I take a certain level of generalizability to follow from the concept of culture as the set of relations among ideas. Ideas—no matter how private or idiosyncratic—are *about* something or someone (to choose two out of many possible examples). Men and women may be solitary thinkers, in other words, but the fact of their thinking places them in a social, or shared, universe. To be specific, my argument in this book is that people in Hopewell think the way they do about conflict because they have available to them a language and a set of images that give conflict certain (negative) meanings. These images are collective representations (Durkheim 1965: 488) that acquire their social character in the social process itself. The availability of these representations in Hopewell has a long history; indeed, philosophical antecedents of American Protestant anabaptist sentiment can be found early in the European Middle Ages, when theologians and kings argued over the question of whether there could be any secular legitimacy to a monarch's regime.[1] At the same time, most writers (and readers) of

1. The specific importance of silence in Hopewell's response to conflict may be related plausibly to old Protestant traditions of stilling the tongue so as to hear the Holy Spirit speak, of symbolizing restraint from fleshly excesses with silence (Weber 1958: 149, Bauman 1983).

America have been absorbed in the implications of its individualism and its egalitarian rhetoric. These ideas, too, have long roots in the American past and in the cultural traditions of the West. From these perspectives, the portrait I draw of Hopewell is undoubtedly recognizable to many American readers, even if Hopewell's faces are not the face in the mirror.

This is not at all to say that Hopewell is a typical place—there can be no such thing. In the immediate past, people in Hopewell used the idioms of fundamentalism and individualism to frame their local responses to critical social issues. The historical sections of the book describe these responses and show their connections to the contemporary ethnographic problem. What gives Hopewell its meaning as a place? The synergy of the social processes in this region, which was for so long the frontier, is not separate from the individual lives of its inhabitants but, in part, constitutes them. These same processes, and others, make Hopewell and many other places "communities" in that they are valid as loci of study and as analytic units (see Dollard [1957: 1] on the rootedness of the individual in community). This is perhaps what *community* means: a group of people who may share nothing except the assumption that the question "where are you from?" inevitably has an answer that is both relevant to and revealing of an individual's nature (see Varenne forthcoming). In anthropology, as in ordinary life, we easily use the word *community* without thinking of the chain of cultural premises that lie behind questions linking person and locale. It is important to remember that as the following pages show Hopewell people thinking about society, they themselves are generalizing from concepts of society that they have learned from experience. To borrow Rousseau's language, "society" is, to them, Hopewell writ large.

The problematics of what it means *to be* from some particular place have long held particular interest among anthropologists of the United States. The verb alone suggests the extent to which *local* identity has existential value for individuals. Warner's work in Yankee City and Jonesville (1949 and 1952) argues for dominance of occupation and ethnicity in defining status membership; importantly, however, the referents and context of status membership are the towns themselves. Singer's (1977 and 1984) reanalysis of Yankee City elaborates on Warner's treatment of emblems of being and belonging among residents of Yankee City. Then, as now, people define *belonging* as autochthony; a family might have to wait five or six generations before being considered "insiders." At the same time, *belonging* in the most general sense is tied to culture over nature: "Americans differ from the rest of the world in their belief that nationality is an act of will, rather than the result of chance or destiny" (Gorer 1948: 146). It is chance or destiny, however, that accounts for family. These two strands—autochthony (nature, birth) and will (culture, the polity)—reiterate the two strands Schneider (1968) identified in his cultural account of American kinship: blood (nature) and law (culture). Thus the semiotics of personal and family identity merge with those of collective, community identity—both, as it were, braiding together the consequences of one's birth and one's contracts. On another level, the convergence of various forms of belonging in the dual imagery of nature and culture (blood and law, birth and contracts) dissolves any contradiction between the individual and community. Varenne (1977) has demonstrated this point with ethnographic data from "Appleton" (see also Varenne 1984b). In any case, *individualism*—the withdrawal from society for the sake of private interests—implies community; this is Varenne's finding (1977: 40).

A final point shows not only that locale draws on the fundamental components of personal and collective identity by virtue of the emblematics of belonging but that these components have sacred meaning. The sacred aspects of personal and collective systems of meaning were detailed by Warner (especially 1949 and 1963, Singer 1984). Perin (1977) adopted Turner's (1969) approach to account for the sacredness of the various categories of tenants (renters, owners, and so on) arrayed along "the ladder of life." In Hopewell, collective representations of the local sociology are sacred in that their idiom is that of salvation (we are saved; others are not, to offer a beginning example). In Yankee City, local meanings are sacralized in rituals of various sorts (Memorial Day, tercentenary processions); there are other rituals in Hopewell. What is key is that in raising issues of "place," one returns directly to questions of personal identity, sacredness, and the normative order; that is where this book begins.

Since Hopewell is in the South, some readers will expect to find the community analyzed in relation to something they would call "southern culture." I cannot do this for two reasons or sets of reasons. First, my research problem did not include the comparative ethnographic base that would have enabled me to conclude that the South represents a distinctive cultural area, in the anthropological sense of the term. Certainly, I had no basis for starting with the premise of the region's cultural separateness. The Civil War "created the concept of the South as something more than a matter of geography" (Cash 1941: 68), and although that creation has had a profound impact on the life of the nation, I found that its major relevance to this study was as a source of particular collective representations (see Chapters 3 and 4). In any event, Hill wondered whether the South is today more integrated in the nation than it was at the turn of this century and resolved the issue deftly: "[N]o one can doubt that there has been *a South*" (1967: 21; original emphasis). Second, my research problem focused on a community whose essential features differ in at least two respects from the dominant image of the South in anthropological literature and other commentary. One is in the fact that Hopewell is 98 percent white and exceptionally homogeneous economically. This means that dimensions of caste and class that have been so important to previous studies of southern towns are less identifiable here (Davis, Gardner, and Gardner 1941; Dollard 1957). I do not mean that racism and classism could not be found in Hopewell; they are refracted through the system of social classification (analyzed in this book) that transforms social differences into generic differences of nature. The second source of difference is in the extremely conservative position Hopewell's Baptists take on the question of the social gospel: they draw a thick line between the realm of the church and the realm of social action. Thus in important respects, this account reads differently from the accounts of Eighmy (1972), Hill (1966), and Marty (1976), whose works have been so influential. Readers who are interested in general works on the South might begin with Simkins (1963) and Tindall (1967 and 1972).

## In the Shadow of the Enlightenment

When the Enlightenment burst into the consciousness of the Europeans whose America was soon to become the United States,

[37]

the shape of American culture was permanently altered. Montesquieu, Hume, Burke, Rousseau—these were the authors whose work America's founding fathers devoured and debated. From this era modern Americans inherited a vision of the fundamental vitality of liberty and equality; of the reciprocal, contractual relationship between government and citizens; and of law in relation to the cosmos. Commentators on the America of this period—Cobbett, Crèvecoeur, and Tocqueville—sound familiar to American ears not only because of the depth of their insight but also because of the impact of their generation's ideas, then new, on the enduring shape of American understanding.

Some of these ideas form the subject of this book: individualism, equality, liberty, and the relationship of civil law to moral law. This book is a cultural study of a group of modern Americans in the suburbs of a major metropolitan center, and these ideas are very much their concerns. As the men and women I knew in Hopewell discussed their thoughts about their private and public burdens, responsibilities, opportunities, and dreams, they drew on the heritage of the Enlightenment in the nature of their questions about individual relationships to society and in their assurance that the social order and the natural order alike form systems whose mysteries yield to reason. They evoke Rousseau in viewing their own families as the bedrock of American society, even the very model of society. They are Southern Baptists. They believe in God, and they believe that God's plan is the history and the future of all creation, whose evolution is, to them, proof of God's supreme intelligence.

In equally important ways, however, the people I knew in Hopewell resisted central elements of these philosophical foundations. Not for them is Rousseau's "civil religion" (Bellah 1968, Rousseau 1952), which consists of public utterances about the supernatural and leaves the "inner worship" to the private individual (Rousseau 1952: 430). Bellah's description of this "religion" outlines "a collection of beliefs, symbols, and rituals with respect to sacred things and institutionalized into a collectivity. This religion . . . while not antithetical to and indeed sharing much in common with Christianity, was neither sectarian nor in any specific sense Christian" (1968: 10). Indeed, at the core of America's public religion, Bellah found a continual reiteration of the Revolution in the tenet that

[38]

"the rights of man are more basic than any political structure and provide a point of revolutionary leverage from which any state structure may be radically altered" (Bellah 1968: 6). The people I knew in Hopewell view this "civil religion" as hypocrisy, an inescapable hypocrisy that arises from the contradiction they see in the need for human governments to find legitimacy in the dominion of God.[2] That quest, they are certain, is futile, since justice is God's alone to know and to accomplish. Civil law is perhaps mandated by the frailty of human nature but not legitimated by it. What justice do people in Hopewell seek?

In his *Persian Letters*, Montesquieu, as "Usbek," wrote to "Rhedi" concerning his conviction that social justice can survive even when faith in God fails. *Justice*, which Montesquieu defined as "a relation of suitability," is a description of God's acts: since God (by definition) has no needs (he "is sufficient to himself"), he has no self-interest and is therefore incapable of committing an injustice. On the other hand, "[m]en are capable of unjust actions because it is in their interest to do them, and they prefer their own satisfaction to that of others." But since men are not "gratuitously wicked," they "make an effort to resemble this being of whom we have so exalted a conception, and who if he existed would be just necessarily" (1973: 162–163, Letter 83). From this point, Montesquieu concluded that "justice is eternal." His parable of the Troglodytes suggests the same idea (Montesquieu 1973: 53–61, Letters 11 through 14): that even without a commanding authority, men in a state of nature soon discover the virtues of collective interest. The justice Montesquieu proposed is a quality of relationships. Justice is not a property of God to be imitated by individuals but a kind of relationship of which God is readily capable—having no need for self-interest—and to which individuals can aspire by setting their self-interest aside. *Justice*, in this context, is an adverb; it defines the process by which human relations achieve order.

As part of the conceptual apparatus of religious tolerance in a secular state, Montesquieu's approach has been formative in the United States. The Baptists I knew, while assiduously maintaining

2. Marty contrasted evangelicals and fundamentalists to the civil religion on other grounds: the civil religion claims to speak to and for all Americans, whereas the fundamentalists "use [a] distinct mode of looking at reality in order to keep claims of others at a distance" (1976: 180–181).

the boundary between church and state, reject any implication that God's justice can be imitated successfully by humans. God's justice is his alone. Justice—to Hopewell's Baptists—is not an adverb but an attribute of God. Good men and women—Baptists—enact God's plan not by *understanding* it but by "opening their hearts" to it. This is a crucial distinction.

A parallel distinction was made by Rousseau, writing after Montesquieu. Rousseau proposed that all justice is from God: He is its only source. Did we but know how to receive Heaven's ordinance direct, then we should stand in need neither of government nor of law" (Rousseau 1952; 286, bk. II, chap. 6). Had Rousseau ended *The Social Contract* there, Hopewell's Baptists might well have found the description of their own convictions within its compass. But Rousseau's comment is made in passing, in a tone almost ironic. He proceeded from that point to an extended discussion of government, law, and the limits of human freedom in a civil society. Indeed, Rousseau concluded the volume with an argument against a Christian state, largely on the grounds that the needs of the state and the requirements of Christianity refer to different realms:

> Christianity as a religion is wholly spiritual. It is occupied only with the thought of Heaven. The Christian's country is no longer of this world. True, he does his duty, but he does it in a mood of profound indifference to the success or failure of his efforts. Provided he has nothing with which to reproach himself, it matters little to him whether things here below go well or ill. If the State flourishes he scarcely dares to enjoy his share of the public happiness, and fears lest the glory of his country may make him proud. If the State perishes, he blesses the hand of God for lying heavy on His people. (1952: 433)

Rousseau's solution to this problem is to recommend that all citizens be Christian, while leaving the administration of the state to the law—hence the salience of separating the "religion of the man as man" from the "religion of the citizen," or civil religion (1952: 430).

Hopewell's Baptists do not accept this dual religion, which is fundamental to the public organization of American society. The bland pieties of public rhetoric have, to them, sectarian meaning; they want public and private domains to run on the same principles. They pay their taxes and send their sons to war, but they insist that the domains of politics and law are conceits. They are not separatists, like the Amish (see, for example, Hostetler 1968 and 1984). They claim simply to be uninterested in the affairs of the world, by which they mean "disinterested." Hopewell's Baptists voice strong disapproval of activist fundamentalist groups in the United States on these grounds, the notable example being the Moral Majority, vocal in the 1980 and 1984 presidential election campaigns. They condemn the Moral Majority for misunderstanding the role of the church, which (they claim) should not be an avenue toward politics but away from it. They doubt the Christianity of the Moral Majority, and they doubt the group's sincerity. Hopewell's Baptists insist that the principal legitimate use of the pulpit (or, for a Christian, the media) is to call the unsaved to Jesus.

I introduce what is essentially an ethnographic problem with the vocabulary of the authors of the Enlightenment to make two points. First, in their rejection of the civil religion, Baptists in Hopewell respond to fundamental currents of contemporary American culture. Second, their response—as we shall see—is cast in the vocabulary the Enlightenment itself provided: a great love of liberty and a deep ambivalence about human authority. The South has been excluded for so long from studies of "mainstream" American culture (cf. Gorer 1948: 5–6), treated as a "subculture" by two generations of scholars (see Hill 1977), that this idiom of response has, perhaps, been relatively submerged by other themes. This book implicitly argues against the idea of a southern subculture on these grounds.

From another perspective the loud voices of the Moral Majority overwhelm the whispered qualifications that some fundamentalists bring to the very idea of the state. This book emphasizes the terms and significance of those qualifications. This theme provides another link to the world beyond Hopewell. Where the people in this book explicitly resist particular forms of human authority—in conflict, law, and prestige based on wealth—other Americans voice their resistance in other ways: "lumping" their disputes, worrying about litigiousness, and concerning themselves with the incremental markers of upward mobility. I write about Hopewell's Baptists not because they are "different," but because the oblique light of their interpretation of social experience illuminates so much more

[41]

than their own small town. To the extent that other Americans worry—with Rousseau—about the question of whether justice is possible in a society of "mere men" (Rousseau 1952: 330), the Baptists of Hopewell have something to say.

Most of the people I knew in Hopewell were Southern Baptists, although Southern Baptists are actually outnumbered by Methodists in town. Although the ethnographic chapters of this book focus centrally on people's understanding of their own faith, the book is not "about" Baptists in general. Southern Baptists number about 43 million in the United States today, and to the extent that this book contributes to the anthropology of American religion, perhaps it is in its argument that religious meanings are deeply embedded in local historical experience. This is an argument against generalization on the basis of religion; at least, it is an argument for caution.

Fundamentalism is the subject of a wide literature in the United States. The anthropological literature, which is by tradition rooted in local situations, paints a series of different pictures of the nature of religious experience among Americans who—nominally—"belong" to the same church. Thus this study adds yet another variation to the themes developed by Batteau (1982a and b), Bryant (1980), LaBarre (1969), Peacock (1975a and b), and Zaretsky (1974). Those studies are of rural or marginal groups; Hopewell's Baptists are—on very much the other hand—urbane, sophisticated, educated, affluent, and very much connected to the world. They welcome the suburbanization going on around them. They like the comfortable new houses, fashionable clothes, convenient services and amusements, and the advantages of disposable income that proximity to the city has meant for them. Wallace's (1978) study of urban Rockdale (Pennsylvania) offers a monumental social and cultural history of the partnership between evangelical Christianity and the capitalism of the early industrial revolution. To my knowledge, Baptists in Hopewell never preached a "social gospel," nor did they identify with the local elite—I refer here to two important dimensions of Wallace's study. What this book has in common with these other works is the point that American Protestantism readily absorbs a wide variety of secular referents. Thus, it is no accident that religious and secular meanings converge in individuals' explanations of social experience in Hopewell.

[42]

# [1]

# The Personal Role in Family and Friendship

## Four Families

Martha Jean was sure enough that she wanted to leave her husband Leonard to have sought legal advice, and she was sure enough of what the consequences would be to have wanted to guard the secret of her intended separation. So on the day that she collapsed on the street, no one knew that she had been on her way to a lawyer's office to end their marriage. Martha Jean does not remember blacking out. Her first memory is of waking herself in the hospital by imagining her husband and of realizing—barely conscious though she was—that she was seeing him in her mind without having consciously willed it. Then he was at her side. Seeing him, she says, she felt a flood of love for him, something she had not felt in a long time, perhaps never before.

After prolonged illness, she was finally well again. A miraculous recovery, the doctors said. Martha Jean struggled to comprehend what had happened to her, and she says she realized suddenly that miracles have only one author, Jesus. If Jesus had caused her recovery, then he had also caused her sickness, she reasoned. It was as if he had wanted to stop her in her tracks, to capture her attention, but not to harm her permanently. She thought again and again of waking to the imagined presence of her husband. It became clear to her that Jesus wanted to prevent her from separating, that he had caused the accident so that she could realize her love for her husband. She found Jesus, too, and credits him now with both her personal salvation and the salvation of her marriage.

Reflecting back to that day thirty years ago, Martha Jean says that her illness transformed her. Until then, she believes, she had not lived in a deliberate way but simply had let things happen to her without thinking about whether or not she wanted them to happen. Her marriage to Leonard was like that—something that had happened to her. They had had a child in their first year of marriage and then another. Martha Jean says now that Leonard, like all men, does not much like babies but did become interested in the children once they were in school. There was a third child and a fourth, and she felt crushed by the weight of her responsibilities and Leonard's demands. A quiet evening with supper on the table when he was ready for it was usually more than she could manage. She also says he was not interested in her problems any more than he was interested in her pleasures. Her friends, even now, must be out of their house by the time he returns from work, and her hobbies must be put away so that he can sit in the living room without looking at them. Sometimes there is enough time to work on her painting but not enough time to unpack and repack the canvases and paints, so Martha Jean generally spends whatever leisure time she has on extra household chores. When she decided she wanted to end her marriage, she knew she would have to leave town after the divorce, and she looked forward to that. She says she could not possibly have felt more alone.

When Martha Jean found Jesus, her attitude toward her problems changed but not the problems themselves. Her husband still dominated her, and she felt increasingly betrayed by her children, who seemed to prefer their playmate-father to their disciplinarian-mother. Leonard taunted her with their preferences. Martha Jean says that Jesus gave her the courage to face these problems and to confront Leonard. She began to explain her feelings to Leonard and asked him to take some initiative in caring for the family and in helping the children appreciate her. She says now that he improved and remembers with pleasure that he began to ask the children to kiss her goodnight, too, when they came to say goodnight to him. She says that her greatest hope was that Leonard, too, would find God. She decided that attending church once a week was important to her and that she would go whether or not the family came with her; they did not, but she continued to set the example. She never revealed to Leonard what her errand had been on the day of her collapse, but she did her best to explain what she understood of Jesus and what he might mean in their lives. But he was and is not interested in hearing about Jesus.

Martha Jean says that Jesus helped her see the differences between herself and Leonard and to accept them. Jesus returned her to her marriage, she says, to deepen her spiritual maturity and to help her grow. By her own account, her marriage is, as a result, better than it was during her period of wanting to end it. Her resources for tolerating her marriage have grown; she is comfortable with herself. In one sense, Martha Jean now has her marriage *and* her divorce. As she says, without malice, "Leonard is not saved, and I am. I'm going to heaven and he's going to hell."

Ted and Eileen, a local couple, had not been married for more than a year or two but were considering a separation. They both seemed unable to end their competition with each other and the arguing that resulted. Both were unhappy with this situation, which seemed to have no solution. One night as they were driving home, they were caught in a tornado—not uncommon in the early spring—and were paralyzed with fear. As the winds abated, they realized that they were clinging to each other, although neither had reached out consciously. Their survival without injury led them both to decide that Jesus had been the author of the storm and that he had brought them through it so that they could realize their love for him and each other. Their brush with death, they said, taught them that the things they had been arguing over were not important and that their marriage was a commitment to Jesus through each other. They say now that their marriage is a happy one; they have had children and are raising them as Christians.

Ellen followed her older sister to the altar to be born again as a Christian at the age of eight but at eighteen realized that she had never fully understood the meaning of her own faith. As her spirituality deepened, she says, she "felt the Holy Spirit" again and again and felt she was truly being reborn. She renewed her faith at church, offered testimony, and prayed for opportunities to show her new commitment. After some weeks of struggle with the question of how to dedicate her life to Christ, she sensed the Holy Spirit telling her to enter mission work overseas. Ellen was willing for her own part, but mission work would precipitate a major break with her parents, who were not saved and already felt ambivalent about the extent of their daughter's commitment to the church. She prayed for their salvation and for the strength to resist their opposition.

These developments initiated a critical period for Ellen, who felt grief that her own rebirth should have so alienated her parents and even deeper distress that her own parents should feel so little need for Jesus. She prayed by herself and with others over the question of whether her mission should be at home or abroad. Eventually, she felt that the Lord was telling her to witness to her parents. She enrolled in a local college and continued to live at home.

Lynn's mother was taken ill suddenly, and she lay in a hospital in Texas, perhaps dying. Her father had died years before, while Lynn was still a teenager. All of Lynn's siblings were settled in the West. The family had moved there from Hopewell just after Lynn's graduation from high school. Lynn stayed in Hopewell because she was in love with a boy from high school and refused to leave him. Thus she had not been with her father during his illness and death. It was after her father's death that she found Jesus. This new crisis, she believed, would be a challenge to her faith, since she was committed to witnessing to her mother before she died. Her greatest hope was to see her saved; her greatest fear was that her mother might die and be separated from Lynn forever. Later, she remembered these as her thoughts while she flew west.

Afterward, she remembered with particular pleasure her mother's welcome. Lynn had not seen her in years, but she still felt a strong bond; she says that she is her mother's favorite child. Lynn promised to pray for her, and she also promised that she would not leave her mother until she was well.

At her brother's house, where Lynn and the other siblings and their families were living until their mother's situation stabilized, Lynn found only aggravation. She had not expected that they would share her faith, but she had expected their respect. Their drinking, profanity, and continual arguing irritated her, and she began to feel that the real challenge to her ability to witness was there, not at the hospital. She started to pray for them and about them, that is, to pray for their salvation and also for the strength to deal with them without losing herself to anger. She kept trying to discount them—"Lord, I know this doesn't matter; I know you can handle this. Help me handle it please"—but, in spite of herself, frequently was bitter that her goodwill was being exploited. During her weeks there, she became the family cook, housekeeper, and chauffeur. She decided she would have to be a more aggressive witness and stopped the family before each meal to ask a blessing. Later, she found hope in the fact that the children began to accept this routine, looking toward her for a prayer before they would lift their forks.

Meanwhile, she was satisfied with her witness with her mother. Lynn asked her mother's permission to share her faith with her, to tell her what Jesus had brought to her life. Her mother listened sympathetically and promised Lynn that she would think over what she had said. Lynn believed that her mother was already a God-loving person, already a Christian in her heart, and that her salvation was not far away.

Her mother recovered almost as quickly as she had taken ill. Her sudden recovery after weeks of illness seemed nothing short of a miracle to Lynn. As she prepared to return to Hopewell, Lynn reflected that Jesus had perhaps caused this harmless illness to provide an opportunity for Lynn to confront and witness to her family. She was immensely relieved to be returning home and wondered if her witnessing had been effective. She decided that perhaps it had been for her mother and her nieces and nephews; the others "need the Lord" but, she said later, are too concerned with material things to look within themselves for God.

These women and men are not unusual, and their stories are not unusual. They form everyday conversation over coffee, sometimes with tears or laughter, sometimes as simple narrative—a comment on human nature or a small piece of autobiography for the information of a visitor. Their stories are the subjects of church sermons and personal testimony before the congregation (see Chapter 2). They are everywhere, available for the listening. These stories and the stories in them are the heart of this book: people living with others whom they love or are trying very hard to love, enmeshed in

[47]

relationships they consider themselves powerless to change, finding Jesus and praying for justice.

## Family and Society

Some understanding of family life in Hopewell is essential in all that follows in this book. The family is the crucial institution through which the people of this community understand all sociological forms. It is their link between nature and culture. It is their link between the world of humans and God's heaven. It is the standard by which they measure all legitimate authority, and all personal maturity. The family is by definition authentic: although other groups of people might feel "like" family, "family" itself is not qualifiable. Families, as we shall see, might be good or bad, but their very goodness and badness flows from the fact that a family is literally essential. Friendship is a different sort of compact, but it is related to the local sense of family in that one's selection of friends allows an individual to sketch out, or sculpt, his or her own particular characteristics. Friendship and family life never compete but rather complement and complete each other. All of these ideas are developed in this chapter.

The paradox of family life in Hopewell is that although the family is the primary link between individuals and the society around them, family life also isolates individuals.[1] This is because the family is understood by people not primarily as a set of relationships (as anthropologists might see the family, for example) but as a set of interlocking roles, or identities. Thus in the local view, family life becomes perfect not as individuals perfect their knowledge and appreciation of one another but rather as individuals perfect their senses of themselves. One often hears phrases like "he is such a good husband" or "she's a wonderful mother"; these phrases are complete in themselves. Nothing like "a good husband for Mary" or "a wonderful mother for that sort of child" enters into the evaluation. This is only one kind of evidence for the major point of this

1. Fitchen (1981) made this point about the poor families of "Chestnut Valley," where the isolation is not only conceptual but also practical, as families struggle to remain above the subsistence level largely on their own. From a symbolic perspective, Batteau (1982) examined this "contradiction" of kinship.

chapter, which is that family life, while all-important as a model for society itself, is also crucial to the cultural formation of individuals by isolating them within relationships over which they believe they have no control.

Mothers, fathers, husbands, wives, and so on are not created by families; rather, people in Hopewell see families as being made up of these roles. These terms are not the names given to linkages between people but rather are labels for sets of properties that individuals strive to attain, even before marriage and regardless of the partner's performance.[2] Many of the people whose lives this chapter is meant to reflect consider the family their greatest source of emotional satisfaction; at the same time, conflict within the family is excruciating precisely because the concept of family admits no, or few, remedies when problems arise. Martha Jean's account of her dissatisfaction with her marriage never referred to the possibility that the problem might lie *between* herself and her husband; rather, her efforts at improving her situation were entirely interior, in improving herself. She addressed this need eventually by joining the Baptist church. She explained her conflict with her husband entirely in terms of the extent to which she was herself a good wife or an inadequate wife. The meaning of the wife's role and other role identities are explored below.

Family life is considered "natural" in that human nature preordains it. Thus to be a wife is a natural manifestation of adult womanhood (and therefore marriage is expected early; see below); motherhood, too, is seen as the natural role of the wife. Moreover, to the extent that people believe that God directs the selection of a spouse and the nature of any children born to a marriage, family is not only natural but sacred. As we shall see, both of these aspects contribute to the individual's sense that family life is essentially unalterable except under very particular circumstances (primarily through accretion by birth and hospitality and attrition by death). Whether or not people cede so immediate a place to God in their concept of their own families, most people speak easily of the nature of wide categories: "daddies," "women," "teenage boys,"

2. Stack's (1974) discussion of American urban black kin ties constitutes an important comparison. In "the Flats," kin ties are continually renegotiated through exchange relationships. Inclusion depends considerably, although by no means exclusively, on performance.

[49]

and so on. These categories provide individuals with a sense of affinity to others. In the Baptist church, these groups provide the basis for the organization of all activities except the worship service (see Chapter 2).

The idea that a family is a group bound by nature is very widely shared in the United States. The fullest account is Schneider (1968). Schneider's analysis of Americans' concepts of kinship draws a distinction between "blood" and "law"—descent and marriage—in the formation of family ties. Importantly, blood symbolically conveys not only the genealogical relationship but also specific family traits. This idea is relatively implicit in Schneider's work but emerges in ethnographic examples, such as Blu (1980: 24–27), and in official public responses to problems of cultural identity. The "blood fraction" is still one standard test for identifying members of America's indigenous tribes. When the Japanese and Americans of Japanese descent were interned during World War II, their cultural identification was presented as a matter of "blood" mixtures. The widely held belief that blood in part constitutes the self perhaps contributes to an explanation of why the public policy examples are not descried as obsolete science.

The connection that Hopewell people draw between nature and the family is only the first part of a cultural syllogism whose second part is the association of family to society. Society is the family writ large (see Rousseau 1952). This idea has many ramifications, some of which are discussed in this book. First, the family is, apparently by definition, the smallest social unit, a unit that admits no subdivisions or any outside intervention. In this way, families have a political autonomy in the local conception; however, balancing that autonomy is the utilitarian view that families yield some of their autonomy to the community and, through communities, to the state for their own protection (broadly conceived). It should be noted that this is a very limited sort of concession to the community and that the question of what local governments and other governments can demand of private citizens is one that is frequently asked. The family is the traditional, if somewhat idiomatic, bulwark of the individual against the state: the local view is that no one, official or other, has the right "to tell a man how to run his family." That the argument should be framed as a question of authority rather than as a question of privacy is significant and is discussed further below.

Second, if the family is the sanctuary of the individual against the community, the community is also (and therefore) a confederation of families, just as the state is a confederation of communities, and so on, to form the union. This is the sense that people in Hopewell convey. Families remain inviolable within this system not so much because they are understood to have divergent interests (which is the logic of democracy) but because they have a natural right to be treated as discrete decision-making units. Families form micropolitical systems, and much of the local ambivalence about secular and civic authority is expressed in terms of preserving the natural and rightful autonomy of the family. Popular democracy is not the natural consequence of the local conception of the family; however, republicanism and clearly defined vertical systems of authority are. Thus the ideas that the people of Hopewell hold about the state and its institutions relate to a conception of family and natural law and, for some, God and the very nature of the universe.

Within the micropolitical systems that families constitute, authority and responsibility are carefully distributed. Within families, this is a subject of discussion and potential tension, although individuals seem to approach marriage with fairly well defined expectations of themselves and their future spouses and even children. The eldest male carries the greatest authority; he may or may not head the nuclear family but might be the grandfather or a great-uncle in another household. Within the nuclear family, the husband/father represents this authority. Importantly, the man conveys authority, but he does not create it. His wife, although subordinate to his protection and will, can be described fairly as his partner in decisions. Where partnership is the appropriate metaphor, though, the division of labor is carefully detailed. Men, for example, are considered experts in pragmatic worldly decisions, especially where money is concerned; women are presumed to be more spiritual and intuitive, more sensitive to emotion. For this and other reasons (below), although the man is understood to be the head of his family, his wife has direct charge of the children, except in major matters of discipline. The husband, then, mediates between his family and the world; the mother mediates between her husband

and her children. Children have equal status in the family until they are old enough to adopt by imitation the gender roles of their parents. Then the family divides into male and female sections for purposes of household work and ordinary recreation, although the family operates as a unit in all formal activities, including decision making and disciplining. The notion that individual members of a family might have divergent interests is unthinkable or at the very least an abnormality to be corrected by whatever means possible (counseling, for example, but see below).

Thus to say (as people in Hopewell do) that society is the family "writ large" carries with it the stipulation that the component elements of the larger unit, too, are united in their interest, which can be loosely referred to as the common good. The image of society—and other social units larger than the family—as family is not only a call for loyalty, trust, and feelings of mutual identity and commitment but a claim that these things already prevail. Just as families solve their own problems by coming to terms with their natural roles, people believe that communities should solve their problems from within, by a process of clarifying their purpose, which is—by definition—consensually based. Just as families are bound by the sacrament of acceptance, so communities should be bound together by consent of their members—and so on. Such imagery imposes some strict limits on the forms debate can take: disputes almost inevitably become watersheds where groups are defined and redefined. Chapters 4 and 5 show this logic in action during a period of 150 years. My purpose now is merely to suggest that there are important connections to be made between the local conception of the structure and function of family life and ideologies of conflict among larger groups who are not kin.

The point has already been made that people in Hopewell conceive of families as naturally harmonious composites of individuals whose role identities are highly individuated. Once organized in groups, interpersonal and intergroup relationships do seem to be narrowly relevant. Relationships take two ideal forms: the bond of affinity, mentioned above, or reciprocal arrangements between potential adversaries. Families, for example, enjoy (or rue) relationships, and certainly relationships such as town to state, state to nation, and church to state are familiar themes. This is yet another way of making the point that individuals are at the foundation of this system and that the smallest meaningful social unit is the family. The restriction of relational concepts to groups underscores their culturality in the local conception of such things. People in Hopewell imply that families are made by nature and/or God, but other social groups are made by men, this qualitative difference permits the greater sense of flexibility and control that seems to operate beyond the family. In other words, things made by men are capable of transformation, but things made by God are transformable only by God. This distinction becomes important in Chapter 2, where the capacity of men to change and to effect change is the focus of the Baptists' concerns with the normative order.

It is on this question of the source of the association (the work of God or the work of man, in the local lexicon) that friendship can be distinguished from kinship. As we have seen, God (or nature) builds families, but people make their own friendships (unless the friendship is exceptionally close or leads to marriage, in which case the authorship question arises again). Kin terms are readily extended to close friends, and phrases such as "he's like a brother to me" or "she's an older sister to me" have connotations of reciprocal loyalty and obligation that transcend specific situations, such as the workplace. Importantly, though, in these descriptive idioms of close friendship, the relational "to me" is included, unlike the "good mothers" and "good husbands" mentioned earlier. Friendship is personal in a way that family cannot be; this difference is explored later in this chapter.

In summary, the people of Hopewell conceptualize family organization and relationships in ways that potentially structure their relationships well beyond the family. First, family roles are understood as natural expressions of the self, as identities, not as relationships. Relationships are expressed as performances of duty, and successful performance gives satisfaction even if the relationship itself is not satisfactory, as we shall see in some of the cases in this chapter. Second, to the extent that family roles do provide a basis for relating to others, those others are the many categories of persons (known and unknown) in parallel roles. A woman who is a mother, for example, feels a natural kinship with all other mothers, and this felt bond is itself a basis for conversational intimacy on the subject of motherhood. (Women who are not mothers would be presumed uncomprehending and uninterested.) In more general

[53]

terms, conceptions of family roles form the basis of articulating gender relationships beyond the family. Relationships within the family tend to be entirely unarticulated. More generally still, since other organizations are understood in family terms, family provides a basis for larger regional and even national identities, since individual roles (for example, father and mother) are capable of infinite application to other categories, such as president and Congress or God and individuals, by virtue of their component normative structures.

## Family Roles

In theoretical terms, people in Hopewell see the bond between husband and wife as sacred and whole. At the same time, apart from incidents or epochs of overt conflict, as in the first two cases above, men and women assume that they do not understand each other either personally or categorically. Men especially are considered by women to be essentially ignorant of what they call "women's lives," however they might be defined. For example, I was visiting a woman from the community in the hospital immediately following her surgery when another woman arrived. She said to the patient, who was very much in pain, "Well, have a good rest, dear. When I had surgery I felt like it was a good lesson to the Daddies, to make them realize how much we really do around the house and to make them appreciate us." The effectiveness of the notion of "teaching the Daddies a lesson" as a rationale for accepting pain is a measure of a certain social distance even between spouses that adults readily recognize and acknowledge.

The domain shared by husbands and wives is in fact relatively narrow. They certainly have separate circles of friends, a situation that the division of labor facilitates. A man's friends at work or a woman's "girlfriends" are not generally the people they see socially when they are together (see Bott [1957: 60], who associates role segregation with network "connectedness"). In fact, the women I knew were unwilling—and thought it would be wrong—to take time away from their families to pursue activities with their friends. All of an individual's friendships are of his or her same sex; relationships with members of the other sex are highly patterned, although they might appear to be casual. At any rate, only the hours when their husbands were working and their children were in school were times when women thought they could visit freely. Visits to my house ended abruptly when supper needed to be prepared, and for the most part, when I was visiting, the conversation was over when the husband's car appeared. Other women confirmed this pattern as good manners. Similarly, most of the women I knew never visited their husband's offices even when they were in the neighborhood. That was a boundary that could not easily be crossed except under very special circumstances such as a Christmas party. But nonworking women did visit their employed female friends at their offices. Except at worship and Sunday school, men and women have separate activities even at church.

In the ordinary activities of the household routines, men and women share two meals a day with their children and, depending on their preferred leisure activities, potentially little else until they retire to sleep. A typical evening at home consists of television and/or hobbies: woodwork is popular among men, and crafts occupy many women's free time. If a couple is active in the church, church activities fill as many as four or five nights a week. Saturdays are devoted to household chores and errands; Sundays are almost entirely spent at church. Time spent away from home in Hopewell is most often devoted to visiting relatives who live out of town.

Men work for wages; women do not. Of the women who worked at the time of their marriage, few continued to work after their children were born. Hopewell's median income is higher than the state's and the nation's as a whole (ten thousand to twelve thousand dollars a family in the 1970 census), and families can afford to live reasonably well on one income. Most of the men's jobs are white collar or skilled blue collar. Two-thirds of the labor force in the county commutes to Atlanta; local or federal governments employ many men from Hopewell. Many women volunteer their skills in positions that often demand considerable time. The church, hospitals, clubs, and other organizations all require active members and administrators; each of these organizations defines a women's network in the community. In fact, women are expected to join clubs—"to meet people halfway"—as they become freed from the responsibilities of caring for very young children.

A mature woman is expected to maintain her household in cleanliness, style, and good health. Fastidious women iron even their children's playclothes and underwear. This is apparently not labor for labor's sake, since many kitchens have timesaving devices like microwave ovens, and women commonly use prepared foods and store-bought baked goods. Cooking, though, is an index of a woman's relationship to her own role. It is a theme of many conversations and some gentle competition; it is also a subject of gossip. When I returned to Hopewell after several years, during which time I had married, the most frequent question I was asked was: "Do you cook?" Working women are frequently the targets of joking by both men and women for what are presumed to be their domestic deficiencies.

The primary activity, or set of activities, that men and women share within the household is concern for their children. Although parents seek to conceal their differences in front of their children, the disciplining of children is a major source of discussion and dispute between spouses. Many men believe that their wives are, in their word, too "soft" to exact discipline from their children and that they share their children's tendency to make excuses. Women, on the other hand, seem to think that men are naturally hard and unfeeling and that they do not understand their own children since they are away from home so much of the time. If they yield to their husbands' designs for rearing children, it is because they consider men to be more expert in the normative order, not because they concede them any particular expertise in child training.

In fact, the division of tasks is less important than the more fundamental distinctions men and women in Hopewell draw between the kinds of knowledge that each possesses. Male and female sexuality represents only one aspect of such knowledge, albeit an important one. Sexuality is understood not only as a means of producing a family but as a basis for unity within a couple before and after their children are born. This is not a topic easily raised between relative strangers in conversation, especially if one of them is unmarried.

Essentially, men and women are expected to know different sorts of things and to act on these different sets of knowledge. Men seem to consider themselves (and are considered by women) to be pragmatic, rule oriented, and capable of defining and controlling situations. Men are seen as having been endowed with a kind of natural authority that they exert within the family as well as in the public institutions of the community, state, and nation. A certain degree of competitiveness and well-channeled aggression is expected and condoned in men (these things are considered inappropriate—unfeminine—in women). Men find an outlet for these emotions in hunting and in team sports, both of which are very popular activities. Individual sports, such as tennis and swimming, are not popular; there are no public facilities for these activities in town.

The characteristics that people take to be natural to men are also credited with making men good at business. Although many women are knowledgeable about their husband's businesses and financial affairs in general, many claim to be mystified or intimidated by business. Here, the crucial element that divides men and women seems to be what women at least consider to be the lack of emotion they see as natural to men. Apparently, a hard heart is necessary to success in public. Men are not considered unemotional as much as they expect and are expected to have a narrow emotional range. Pride, anger, loyalty, and sorrow are acceptable in men; rage is understood, if not approved, although tears are not. Regret, shame, sympathy, fear—these emotions belong to women. One woman said, "Women need to accept men, because men are strong and have ideas. Women just have feelings."

Women's knowledge involves what is assumed to be a natural intuitiveness with regard to people and situations. Women's fuller emotional lives and natural sympathy for others makes them (they say) impressionable and vulnerable to exploitation. Women are also more spiritual, more romantic, better with children. Women say that men are generally taken by surprise by their feelings, by love in particular, and that men are uninterested in emotions. Women, on the other hand, see themselves as being much more in touch with their own emotional needs.

The result of this division of knowledge is that marriage means more than a promise of companionship and loyalty between two compatible people. First, an unattached adult man or woman is incomplete, almost asocial. Second, the sort of expertise prerequisite to marriage manifests itself before marriage; it forms part of a person's identity and attraction for a future spouse. The teenagers who say they want a "strong man" or an "understanding wife" consider strength and understanding to be natural attributes, not

[57]

skills acquired situationally or in relation to another individual. Thus marriage is not a question of finding an appropriate partner as much as it is of being eligible oneself, by cultivating marriageable qualities. In this sense, marriage is very much an index of adulthood by which people can measure their own or others' personal maturity. Third, the perceived complementarity between men and women creates patterns of dependence that severely restrict an individual's mobility. In Martha Jean's case, narrated earlier, the fear of living alone with her children was an obstacle to her divorce, although she nevertheless considered divorce. But dependence can take other forms, as when one woman, in a discussion of the latest development in the Watergate scandal (then current news), said, "I really don't know what to think; my husband is in Nashville." An absent man postpones a woman's relationship to the world. Without a wife, a man suffers a different sort of confusion. Men need women to tame their wildness: "He needs a woman to make him settle down." Wildness is the result of men's disjointed and narrow emotions; it is as if people acknowledge that these things are not enough to live on when they say that a man ought to find himself a wife.

Finally, although a married couple may reach a point where each can "read" the other well, men and women do not seem to expect to reach agreements by the same route. People say that men follow their heads and women follow their hearts; ideally, heads and hearts lead in the same direction. That people presume this ideal implies a popular theory of natural law. In fact, disagreements between spouses are troubling because they are taken to mean that one or the other is out of touch with the natural order; there can be no agreements to disagree. All disputes are issues of right and wrong. Conciliation is of only limited use in such cases; the first two family cases described in this chapter suggest the limits of conciliation. Although this view of relationships would tend to sharpen serious disagreements, it also has the effect of harmonizing marriages. Most marriages within the community, in fact, seemed to be harmonious and cooperative. The expectation of differences perhaps has the effect of neutralizing them when they occur according to type. There were no divorces in the community about which I had any knowledge during my research.

An important point in any discussion of family is that it is the marriage bond that is considered the core of the family. It is that bond that "civilizes" the family, since a successful family life—and, by extension, a successful society—depends on the capacity of husband and wife to complement each other's natures effectively. Several people suggested to me that a physical relationship between spouses allowed them to enjoy the differences that are essential to their union. Thus sexuality seems to represent (at least on one level) these other sorts of differences and their potentially positive and balanced relationship.

Marriage creates the expectation of children. A childless couple is presumed unable to conceive. In the local view, children allow a couple to fulfill their natural inclinations, that is, for the husband to assume the role of authority over the family and for the wife to nurture an infant. From the child's perspective, his father is a remote figure, especially in early childhood. Women say that men want little to do with children until they are old enough to express themselves or do not need constant attention. On the other hand, men take pride in their children who imitate them; this notion of replication is encouraged by the frequent practice of naming sons for their fathers (never daughters for their mothers). A "Jim, junior" might be known as "little Jim" or "Jim-bo" in his family and among his parents' friends as long as his father lives.

The relative absence of even devoted fathers during the early childhood of offspring means that the family structure undergoes a dramatic transformation as the child begins to establish a relationship with his or her father. This is often a playful relationship, in which a father and especially his sons spend recreation time together, returning the child to the mother for caretaking such as bathing and feeding. As children become more independent, they may seek out the company of the more remote parent—usually the father. This transitional period may be a source of conflict, or at least of distress, for the parents. One such situation was explained to me at length by a woman whose children were approaching their teens: she missed the closeness she had had with them when they were more dependent on her and were more home centered. Now she thought they ignored her completely and criticized her unfairly. But their father could do no wrong. "I'm proud that they love him," she said, "and he knows that that means he has to be better than perfect for them, but I feel like I deserve some of that too. I brought it up at dinner one night when we were all together. I just said, 'Listen, Mother has a problem,' and told them exactly how I was feeling. Now my husband has started to help me by guiding the children." Areas of improvement were equal sharing of the children's displays of affection and a reduction in their criticism of their mother.

Children remain children long after they are adults, have left home, and have had families of their own. Since people in Hopewell marry young—often in their teens—four-generation families are not at all uncommon. This situation adds some further dimensions to family life.

Parents and grown children sometimes live together in the same house but more often on adjoining properties. In most cases, a single land lot is subdivided among children to provide them with a place to live. This was particularly feasible when the county was newly settled and when people retained the 202.5-acre land lots that their ancestors had drawn in the land lottery after the 1821 cessions by the Creeks. It is still a frequent practice. Distribution is not deferred until the parents' death but is initiated at marriage. The transfer of property is not always by gift. For example, one family's entire record of property sales and purchases for the one hundred years after the establishment of the county (1859–1959) is confined to transactions within the family, both vertically to sons and daughters and laterally to siblings and cousins. Now that the county is more densely settled, this practice is not so feasible as it once was; however, neighbors are very often kin. As parents die, heirs move into the parental house, and the remaining property is redistributed accordingly.

Corresponding to the authority that accrues to the father within the nuclear family, the anterior generations are endowed with their own special authority. Although they may or may not intervene in the affairs of their children's households, they are generally accorded "the last word" in matters that are brought to their attention or of which they are aware. Children—even young children—are capable of and trained to have formal relations with their parents; for example, they frequently address their parents as "ma'am" and "sir." Older relatives command more than the standard politeness in deference to and veneration of age.

The authority of older generations is explained by their descendants in several ways. First, the younger generation acknowledges a debt to them for a successful and loving upbringing. Second, through their parents and grandparents, people value their identification with the past; in some families, this represents a value placed on being southern in particular (see Chapter 4). Third, older generations maintain some economic power over younger relatives through their control of property. Gifts to adult children range from small cash presents and loans to major purchases, such as a house or furniture or a college education for their grandchildren.

Relations between parents and children of any age appear to be somewhat formal. The people to whom one owes one's existence are not to be treated as friends, even close friends. Parents are generally regarded with respect and affection, but they are less generally their children's confidantes. Especially, once a child becomes independently mobile with his own automobile or through a friend's, his joint activities with his parents and family become increasingly structured and bounded, for example, in household help, formal visits, and other family occasions. Typically, teenagers develop close friendships with one other adult, generally of the same sex, for counsel and conversation on subjects too sensitive to raise at home, such as dating and sex.

Sibling relations are also somewhat formal due to the same pressures that act on the relationships between parents and children. The most immediate factor in separating children within a family is age and the concomitant age-related distinctions that the local society draws. It is not at all unusual for a couple to bear children over a span of fifteen, twenty, or even thirty years, thus bringing the youngest child into a family where the child has two sets of adults over him or her. Often, older siblings are married and have children of their own before the youngest child is born. A result of this birth pattern is that individuals are often somewhat unclear on the details of their own siblings' childhoods and so establish independent relationships with their parents, rather than acting through the experiences of sisters and brothers.

Siblings, whether or not they are close in age, are separated by virtually all of their social activities: school, the church, and their peer-group associations. Schools age-grade children, and the church, as described in the next chapter, also divides its members into peer groups. Thus two brothers might share the same church and school, yet not have any experiences in common except the most formal—and they, generally, are the least interactive—group events.

Older siblings nevertheless exert some moral and social influence over their younger brothers and sisters, even if they are widely separated in age. Young people at the Baptist church often follow their elder siblings to the altar during the hymn of invitation, either the same day or some Sunday soon afterwards. Ellen's experience is an example: she told me that she joined the church at the age of eight because her sister did; she thought Christ was speaking to her as well. Later, at eighteen, she realized that she had been confused about her feelings then and that her "true" church membership in the sense of mature spiritual loyalty had just begun. In addition to exerting influence in religious matters, older siblings sometimes become more like trusted friends as the family grows older; girls, especially, go to their married sisters with problems and questions that they shy away from bringing to their parents.

In the social realm, the segregation of siblings tends to be complete. Occasionally, brothers date sisters' friends, often to the consternation of the sister, who risks becoming an intermediary or a mediator if problems arise. During my thirteen-month residence in town, I never met most of my friends' siblings, although we met in a wide variety of settings and on a wide variety of occasions. In some cases, I knew people for months before I knew that they had siblings at all. This reinforced my impression that siblings do not share many experiences once they are old and mobile enough to engage in activities independently. Siblings do not appear to provide especially strong role models for one another, although there are certainly exceptions to this generalization. Parents are the major unifying force between children.

The roles that constitute Hopewell's families preexist their actualization in family life. An adult develops into a husband or wife—these roles represent a threshold in the process of maturation—and then (or "and so") marry. What happens after that is not seen as a matter of interpersonal chemistry but as personal self-awareness. It is not surprising that marriage is often spoken of as a sacrifice but, ideally, a sacrifice that is amply rewarded in the material and emotional benefits of a good family life. Family members do not necessarily expect to understand one another, but they do demand one another's respect. When this is lacking, as in Martha Jean's case, the isolation is stultifying.

Martha Jean's case illustrates perhaps most clearly the widespread view that problems in relationships cannot be resolved by reforming the relationship itself but can be dealt with by enlarging the individual's capacity to cope with, or accept, feelings of conflict. My understanding is that Martha Jean did not attempt to renegotiate her marriage with Leonard before her decision to seek a divorce; her view was that the marriage relationship is unalterable. Her decision to join the church not only gave her a greater sense of allied resources but also gave her the feeling that she had found an ultimate remedy to her problems. Her efforts to change her relationship with her children were confined to their superficial behavior in her presence. Without the church, her situation simply might have frozen, since her view—which is widely shared—that people cannot be changed left her entirely without recourse.

Ted and Eileen's case was similar, except that they had the relative advantage of sharing a perception that their marriage was unsatisfactory. Their story, which was offered as personal testimony before the Baptist congregation, emphasized that by seeing each other through Jesus, that is, by realizing God's immanence in each other, they could appreciate each other in a new way. The ideology involved in this transformation is the subject of the following chapter; however, I include the case here to show how Jesus provides an idiom for reduplicating the self within family relationships. By seeing themselves and each other as a temple of God, Ted and Eileen enhanced their own self-awareness to the point of being "better" spouses. They did not refer to any attempt to reshape their relationship around new activities, new forms of communication, and so on, although these might have developed. Instead, they stressed that Jesus mediated between them. This mediation was symbolic and, in their view, active.

Ellen's increasing sense of distance and difference from her parents was distressing to her, and her initial impulse paralleled the previous two cases: she decided that God was directing her to move away from her parents should they fail to be saved. Her own ambivalence over what she believed would be abandoning her parents by leaving the country left her open to the suggestion that she fulfill her mission at home. Thus she was able to reconcile her sense of what a proper daughter's role should be with her sense of responsibility to the church. Even so, her ultimate decision should not be seen as an accommodation to her parents but rather a reassertion of her role as daughter. Her efforts to bring her parents to Jesus, if anything, polarized her relationship to them.

Lynn's situation is again similar to Ellen's except that the crisis atmosphere sharpened her need to redefine certain elements of relationship to her family. Her stated purpose in witnessing to her siblings was to regain some sense of family, of their being somehow alike. It was she who, years earlier, had left her family's church to become a Baptist; now she sought not so much a reconciliation as a synchronization with them. On one level, her appeals to Jesus express a complete rejection of her siblings and their way of life and also allow her to believe that they might eventually change their ways.

As in the other cases, Lynn's sense of isolation within her family is coupled with mutual intolerance. None of these family crises contains any relativities from the actors' point of view; the appeals to God only underscore the absolute values perceived to be at stake. Again, I must stress that nothing is negotiable in these relationships because individual's roles are seen as fixed in their personalities, which are unalterable except by God. Each of these people, in narrating their cases, said that Jesus had helped them accept the otherwise unacceptable. Jesus provides a definitive hedge against what would otherwise be the meaninglessness (and here I echo my informants' view) of living in a world that one is powerless to change. These ideas will be developed substantially in the next chapter on the Baptist church.

Warner argued that a relatively loose social organization of the sort described here is to be attributed to Protestantism itself, with its deep ambivalence concerning human authority (see Chapter 2). He saw the family thereby invested with social control (Warner 1961: 81). In Hopewell, the family is certainly a community of social control, although people there very much prefer to cast the matter in other terms. They prefer to see the family as a community of loyalty and responsibility; social control flows from God.

## Friendship

Although family life is conceptualized as essentially preordained, friendships are relatively unrehearsed, flexible, and private affairs. Friendships are emotional bonds, primarily between people of the same sex and age. Close friendships involve very frequent visits, telephone conversations, and joint activities. Although the principle of organization of family life is the ordered balancing of unequal attributes, the principle of friendship is equality. Friendship impressed me as the closest relationship most people enjoyed, although friendships are by no means free of tensions or costs. Still, friends offer one another perhaps the only uncharted social space in which expectations and roles can be invented and redesigned with relative freedom.

Not surprisingly, friendships are the most intense among young unmarried adults. Even if they are working and living with their parents, they can manage long visits daily with friends. Some of these visits are for helping friends or friends' parents with household chores—an afternoon shelling peas or remodeling a home. But more friendly time seems to be spent simply in companionable leisure: in front of the television, talking, "cruising," eating in restaurants, and so on. Friends share gossip and secrets; they are confidantes who know the most intimate details of each others' lives and feelings. They are the guardians of their friends' personal narratives. Within the Baptist church, Jesus is—significantly—spoken of as a friend ("Jesus is your friend," "Be a friend to Jesus"), not as a father or brother. The pattern for a sympathetic confessor already exists in many friendships.

One important aspect of friendship is that although it is multidimensional, it is private. "Best friends" are shared in a somewhat calculated way, perhaps because individuals invest so much of themselves in these others. People identify closely with their friends, taking on their hurts and angers, for example. People are also identified by the friends they keep perhaps even more strongly than they are by their family. The reasoning is that they cannot choose their family, but they do choose their friends to reflect something essential about themselves.

Apart from what friends reveal about oneself to the community, friendship itself is an important index of one's sociality.[3] A large circle of harmonious friends is a social asset; to be friendless is suspect. A large friendship network indicates not only popularity, which is valued in itself, but also a kind of spiritual maturity that is presumed to keep this group of people on good terms with one another. These are highly valued marriageable attributes among young people. Someone who is a loner is troubling to his or her peers. On several occasions, I saw concerted campaigns on the part of Hopewell's young people to attract another young man or woman into their sphere; generally, these campaigns were successful. The strategy was one of inclusion, of repeated invitations and tacit promises of acceptance. Relaxing the boundaries of tolerance for formerly marginal individuals had the effect of socializing them to the group. The attitude is, "Join us; you are already like us." Indeed, people advise newcomers to the community to "meet people halfway," which means to join in voluntary associations and to be like others. In this context, popularity is the most visible measure of social merit.

In a young person's life, as already mentioned, friendship has a special quality in that friends potentially link the individual's natal family to his family by marriage. Enhancing and displaying marriageable characteristics is one function of group gatherings among unmarried adults; indeed, finding a spouse is one important dimension of unmarried friendship. The major criteria of marriageability from a woman's point of view is that the man must be hardworking and ambitious and have status at least equal to that of her family. Status is an ambiguous concept in Hopewell, but it is very clearly in

3. For a full discussion of the cultural values that organize American friendship, see Varenne 1977. He posited that Americans look for themselves in friends and that popularity—acceptance—is a fundamental value. This image of friendship—one that my data support—contrasts interestingly with published characterizations of American patterns of neighboring. Perin (1977) portrayed the ideal of neighboring in affluent America as one of isolation (if simultaneously one of conspicuous solidarity). Useem, Useem, and Gibson (1974), on the other hand, saw middle-class neighboring in terms of relatively impersonal exchange relationships. Interestingly, they interpreted their finding of isolation of the nuclear family as being the result of geographic and occupational mobility among middle-class men. Fitchen's (1981) and especially Stack's (1974) studies show the importance of credit relationships among poor rural and urban families, respectively. I cannot comment on patterns of neighboring in Hopewell, about which I know very little, perhaps because so many friendships were defined by the church.

the background when people use phrases such as "honest and hard-working" (read: reputable blue collar) or "fine family" (pedigreed elite). However they define their terms, women are especially concerned not to marry beneath them, since they anticipate a lifetime of dependence on their spouse. A woman, from a man's perspective, should have good domestic skills, symbolized principally by her cooking, and should be interested in children. A woman is assumed to "take after" her mother: a young woman's mother is thus presumed to be the prophecy of appearance and domesticity for her daughters.

Young people marry young. A fifteen-year-old bride is by no means rare. I knew many women who had married after high school graduation or who had left college to support their husband's studies. Dating patterns of older teenagers are extremely stable and "monogamous." Several young couples I knew had dated only each other, having grown up together, and expected to marry at some appropriate time. When one of these relationships dissolved, the trauma was fully comparable to that of divorce. Once young people graduate from high school, marriageability seems to become a criterion for dating. Even if such romances do not end in marriage, they have the capacity to reshape an individual's life, as education and career plans are altered to accommodate the possibility of permanent attachment. All of the young people I knew expected and looked forward to marriage, although not without some apprehension. Marriage promises to them emotional and physical intimacy, as well as public acknowledgment of adulthood. For most young people in Hopewell, marriage offers them their first sexual experience and their first experience of living in a household independent of their parents.

Throughout a young couple's dating period and at least early marriage, each individual maintains close friendships within his or her same sex. Same-sex and cross-sex friendships are of very different natures and involve very different rules of performance. On many occasions, I observed young women who were outgoing and voluble when only other women were present become silent and passive when males entered the room. Mixed gatherings were, by default, dominated by males; their audience was their female peers. Conversational initiatives by young women in mixed company are suppressed by silence, even stares. Not only do young

[67]

women refrain from verbal initiatives toward males, they often do not talk to one another when males are present. When conversation between males and females occurs, it is highly stylized as teasing or joking. Male speech in female company can also be highly stylized in the same way, although males' stylizations exhibit somewhat wider variety.

Even when male–female interactions are formalized, the contexts in which they occur are not, although they are patterned. One frequent setting for gatherings was church fellowships, dozens of which I attended with the church's "young people's" group. The pattern of the fellowships—informal evenings for games and refreshments after a church service—is as follows: Before leaving the church grounds, a rough census is taken of who will be present. Invitations are not necessary—they are assumed. An individual's presence or absence, but especially absence, is taken as a significant index of his or her community participation. Beyond that, the person's participation, ability to give and take teasing, mood or expression, the length of a man's hair and the style of a woman's dress—all of these factors, too, are observed and mentally noted. Attendance did shift somewhat with changing friendships, romances, and involvement with the church. On the heels of a quarrel, presence or absence from group events was taken to be especially revealing. Presence implied conciliation; absence implied defiance.

The group met in some way at least three times a week; the information conveyed by the gathering of the young people could not be transmitted in other ways, even by the two older women in the group who served as go-betweens. The young people were adept at using these gatherings as channels of communication. The setting was always the same—the house of one of the teenagers' parents or, most often, the basement recreation room of the Sunday school teachers. The form of the events was also very similar from one evening to the next: a short period of conversation (teasing, joking, gossiping, storytelling), snacking (soft drinks, coffee, and cookies or sandwiches), followed by two or three hours of playing organized games. Card games were most popular because they were the most accessible and portable, but whatever games the hosts happened to own (for example, a Ping-Pong table or board games) were also used. The games were not interrupted by conversation, as such, but by joking one-line commentary on the "action." People continued to snack throughout the evening or as long as the supply lasted (everyone took turns bringing refreshments)—the women usually running upstairs to bring fresh ice or drinks down to the young men. These gatherings usually broke up by eleven or twelve o'clock at night, but most of these young people were undaunted by evenings that ran as late as two or three o'clock in the morning, even during the week. Each of these parties had a different implicit "topic" as the gossip and concerns of the group changed from week to week; each evening provided the fuel for long telephone conversations within the group until the next one took place.

Such gatherings provide people with a considerable amount of information about their standing in the group, particularly with regard to eligible members of the opposite sex. When a couple begins to date apart from these gatherings, their relationship is already taken to be serious, and many of its details are readily known by the group. In the year before I arrived in Hopewell, this same Sunday school group had produced thirteen marriages. While I was in town, there was only one marriage, although others followed. This situation reinforced my impression that identities within families (in this case, future spouses) are conceptualized as being complete before marriage, that is, not contingent on the relationship between spouses but, rather, vice versa. Compatibility is certainly an element in one's choice of a spouse, but that element is the least tested of all others that young men and women consider.

A wedding is a community affair. The Baptist weddings I attended were open to the entire congregation. A wedding service was followed by a coffee and cake reception (Baptists abjure alcohol, and at the time of the study, the county prohibited sale and consumption of alcohol). The bride, groom, and their families and attendants spent virtually all of the reception in line, greeting each guest. These occasions were well attended, both by several hundred persons. The bride takes her husband's name, and the wedding reception is the time when her new name is first used as a term of address, often in a joking way. After a short wedding trip, the couple returns to their new household and reconstructs a normal routine. Young women find it especially awkward to resume their friendships with their single female friends; single men and women treat the couple with a new deference. Their new sexual knowledge is slightly embarrassing; this and the demands of their new relationship tend to separate them from their old friends.

Marital status and age constitute major social distinctions in that people do not associate freely as friends with people from outside their own category. As already mentioned, a young unmarried person may develop a close counseling relationship with an older married person, particularly just before and after his or her own marriage, but these are exceptions that emphasize the rule. Young people who had divorced before moving to Hopewell were greeted with some ambivalence. They were single, yet had had experiences (particularly sexual experience) that, especially in the case of one man considered attractive by most of the young women, the same young women found threatening. "He's been married and knows everything," one young woman said to me. "He might be really fast." This man soon "settled down" with a divorced woman and her young son with the enthusiastic approval of their friends.

Dating generally features a meal at a restaurant or one cooked by the woman. After dinner, a couple might visit one of the shopping malls in Atlanta or one of the other suburbs (there is none in Hopewell) or, less likely, attend a movie. Hopewell has only one movie theater, and its offerings, for the most part, do not satisfy the popular taste for family movies with no violence or sex portrayed. Dating couples, especially, find such scenes embarrassing. Other popular activities include bowling or skating. Both roller skating and ice skating are available within about a half-hour's drive. If a young woman lives on her own, no one looks askance if her date visits her in her apartment. A mature young couple is presumed to behave appropriately, and nothing illicit is assumed.

## Ordering the Intimate Circle

The people of Hopewell whom the preceding pages attempt to portray are very much alone in their intimate lives. Their own definition of mature relationships stresses an individual's ability to cope by accepting the limitations of others. Emotional self-sufficiency is supposed to grow with age. If a couple are lucky enough to find mutual support in each other, as many are, their happiness echoes their sense of themselves. But if they are unlucky, as many are, their marriage depends on each individual's ability to develop internal resources, as each of the four principals in the cases described in this chapter has done. In default of that, their marriage depends on the promise that bound them in the first place. The distinction between status and role as the distinction between one's place in society and one's personal attributes is a recurrent theme in American sociology (Warner 1963: 158). In Hopewell, this distinction is played out in many ways: in the definitions of family and friends, work and home, God and humans, family and state. It is also evident in people's sense of their own shortcomings in their relationships and in the limits of the relationships themselves. In fact, it is this very disjunction—which is ultimately one separating one's self from one's life experience—that so deeply centers people's spiritual and social concerns. This point is crucial in the following chapters.

In social terms (the spiritual ones are the subject of Chapter 2), the fact of the promise, or vow, is a crucial aspect of all relationships. When people in Hopewell claim to have active relationships with others, they are referring to the social contract that binds them. Some vows are spoken: the pledge to marry, the marriage vow, the confession of faith that binds an individual to Jesus. Others are unspoken but felt in emergent patterns of reciprocity: a series of exchanged visits at home is a promise of friendship or at church is taken as a sign that someone is a prospect (see Chapter 2). In this sense, dating is supposed to lead directly to marriage—the fact that it often does not is a source of great distress. In any event, the spoken or unspoken vow socializes, civilizes. A person's capacity to live in fulfillment of the vow—indeed, to sacrifice even oneself to the vow—is a measure of his or her social maturity. This is true not only in family or friendship relationships but in other areas of civil life. In 1973, when several of the young men had recently returned from Vietnam, the question arose one evening as to how a Christian could kill, even in battle. One veteran, very much pained by the question, answered in terms of his obedience to the nation, fulfilling the obligation of citizenship (see Greenhouse 1986). Social interaction is a continual process of balancing, or assigning priorities to, the ties that constitute one's social life.

I proposed at the outset that family life provides a model for all other sociological forms as they are conceived by people from Hopewell. At the heart of that conception is the tacit agreement without which people feel society would collapse. In terms of family life, maintenance of family relations, or maintenance of individual roles, is the very substantiation of the marriage vow. Such a realization of family can take place without much speech or understanding. What makes up for communication is a full coming to terms with one's personal role; in default of being able to renegotiate a relationship, one renegotiates one's terms with oneself.

The women in the four cases who came to terms with their own negative feelings about their families by redefining their own roles live in a town whose social service agents talk of "taking care of our own" and where court clerks refer to "getting along." This kind of self-sufficiency, extended by public opinion to public institutions, sets early limits on acceptable forms and degrees of intervention. The place of such institutions in the private domain is—as we shall see—very limited.

The concept of role in relation to family and other groups orders those relationships in particular ways. When relationships are under stress, that is, when disputes threaten to become divisive or when conflict becomes intolerable, the importance of the concept of personal role becomes especially clear. In each of the four cases described in this chapter, the perceived isolation of the four principals effectively prevented them from even voicing their grievances. Such relationships are flexible within the limits of an individual's level of tolerance. What is essential for our understanding of this situation is recognizing that all conflict immediately becomes, above all, inner conflict. The only appropriate remedies to interpersonal problems are interior.

With the understanding that people hold of relationships, there is little to be gained by voicing complaints—in fact, there is more to lose than to gain, in most instances. Disputes are no measure of conflict, however. People deal with conflict by internalizing it and, in extreme cases, by avoiding the people with whom they cannot tolerate contact. As the next chapter illustrates, the church plays a tremendously important role in adding to people's inner resources and in giving them some semblance of public satisfaction when trouble arises. The church strengthens individuals' sense of themselves, in some ways isolating them even further from one another, but it does so in the name of a community, or communion, that they say makes them feel less alone. The principal effect of the church is in its symbolic reorganization of Hopewell's immediate social universe for its congregants.

# [2]

# Together in the Lord

The Baptist church is not the only church in town, but it is the oldest and the largest. For devout members, it dominates not only their leisure hours but their entire conception of their own participation in a temporal and social universe. As this chapter demonstrates, the fundamental tenets of the Baptist faith as it is practiced among these communicants reiterate and then transform the crucial principles of personal and family life, explained in Chapter 1. The relationship of the church and religious life to the domain of family and friends is supplementary. This chapter is devoted to the particular points of interface between private roles and public religious life and to sketching out the conception of order implicit and explicit in local Baptist belief. As elsewhere in this book, when I refer to "Baptist beliefs," I am referring only to those expressed to or observed by me during my fieldwork in Hopewell.[1] In fact, it is the very differences between Hopewell's experience and that described for Southern Baptists elsewhere that suggested some of the questions basic to this book.[2]

1. In effect, this limitation also excludes Hopewell's black Southern Baptists, whose church is one block away from that of the congregation whose ideas are the subject of this book. See Part II of Hall and Stack (1982) for ethnographic descriptions of black and white Baptist ritual and belief in other southern communities.

2. Studies of rural Baptists include those by Forrest (1982), Grindal (1982), Sutton (1982), Peacock (1975a and 1975b), Williams (1982), and Zaretsky (1974). Studies of southern communities with religious dimensions include Batteau (1979) and Bryant (1980). Studies that examine fundamentalist "pathologies" are LaBarre (1969) and Peacock (1971). The best general source is Samuel Hill (1966). The urban

In Hopewell, Baptists define three experiences as being crucial to their faith. The first is salvation, the recognition and acknowledgment of Jesus and acceptance of him into one's life (I am paraphrasing the idiom "Take Jesus into your life"). This experience is referred to in some contexts as "conversion," or as a "born-again" experience. One hears people say, "I was reborn in Jesus." All of these expressions refer to a single crucial moment in the personal spiritual life of an individual. The second experience follows from the first: daily, continual study of scripture, which is taken as the word of God, for guidance in daily life. Just as the Baptist faith relies on the individual conversion experience and adult baptism for inclusion, so it relies on personal interpretation of the word of God for its sustenance. Most Baptists I met knew the Old and New Testaments thoroughly and had dozens of verses memorized, verses that flavored their idiom in ordinary speech. Finally, the third experience is a lifelong commitment for Baptists: witnessing, or evangelizing, to non-Baptists so that they might be saved. Each of these three elements—salvation, study, and witnessing—is significant for the particular sorts of transformations that it is capable of producing in believers' social relationships.

## Salvation

*Salvation,* which is taken to mean the literal "saving" of an individual from death, is the purpose and consequence of becoming a Christian. Local Baptists use the term *Christians* to refer only to other Baptists. Other religious groups, even if they are nominally Christian, are unsaved. Salvation is technically salient only after death, when the saved rise to heaven, to eternal community with one another and with Jesus, and the unsaved descend to hell, where they are alienated from God. Hopewell's Baptists speak of heaven and hell only in these terms, eschewing the cultural cliches of "hellfire and brimstone." But salvation is also critical on Judgment Day, which might come at any moment. This is the day when Jesus returns to earth to claim his own—the saved—and to reject

conservatism and the historical development of Hopewell's Baptists introduces major differences between the present study and these other cases.

[75]

the unsaved. An evangelical film, shown one New Year's Eve at the church festivities, portrayed Judgment in a suburban neighborhood. Children at play, homeowners mowing their lawns, salesmen on their jobs, simply vanished, leaving their balls bouncing and their tasks untended. The purpose of the film was to show how lonely and frightened those who were left behind were, as their closest friends and family were taken into heaven. Salvation makes one's earthly community eternal, which is why people refer to the dead as having "passed," not as being "gone." The dead are gone only if they are unsaved. Fear of separation seems to be one element in conversion.

Salvation, or the conversion experience that produces salvation, might take only a moment, or it might be the climax of a long process of searching and contemplation. Local belief holds that the Holy Spirit, the communicating aspect of the Trinity, is "at work" on particular human souls. For an individual open to the work of the Holy Spirit, salvation is inevitable. An individual resisting the Holy Spirit is damned by this rejection of the Word. (Baptists cite scripture: "Those who are not for me are against me.") Signs that the Holy Spirit is at work are feelings of being troubled, confused, questioning, hopeful, or depressed. In the proper context, that is, in a community of believers, any psychic change in an unsaved person is taken to be the work of God. Once the Holy Spirit has spoken to an individual, he or she is considered to be a "prospect," that is, a prospect for conversion. If this is known to the individual's friends in the church, his or her state becomes a source of joy and concern, and the person becomes the focus of enormous moral support. Essentially, believers think that the final moment of acknowledgment of Jesus is unmistakable and undeniable; every conversion experience is equally authentic and compelling. People can be saved without willing it (as in the midst of crisis; see below), and they can also remain unsaved although willing it ("I keep waiting for the feeling," one prospect said to me). Believers urge prospects not to question their feelings too much and not to intellectualize (some of these statements were directed at me, since, as I asked questions about the church, I was considered a prospect for many months). One bit of Baptist doggerel is a verse about a man killed in a riding accident who accepted Jesus at the very last instant of life: "My life was saved 'twixt the saddle and the grave."

Once one accepts the logic of salvation, salvation itself becomes imperative. In other words, belief in salvation creates a problem to which salvation is the only solution. The logic is that time is linear and finite and that since Jesus may come "like a thief in the night" at any moment, or since death may come at any moment, salvation acquires some urgency. The life of a prospect, from the believers' perspective, is drenched in poignancy and potential irony. There are many stories of prospects for whom interest in the church came "too late" or for whom death came "too soon." A real tragedy that underscored these sentiments was the death of a young man who was much loved, and much witnessed to, by the Baptist community but who never acknowledged Jesus. When he died after a long illness during which he was the subject of intense prayer efforts, people wept not only for their loss but for his. Consolation took the form of a wish that in his last moments, he had realized Jesus in his life but had been too weak to say so. Belief in salvation pits life against death; or more accurately, salvation equates all life forces with Jesus and all death with the absence of Jesus.

The devil does not enter into local religious ideology. People in this church reject the notion of the devil as primitive manicheism. Their rationale is that Jesus is all-powerful and that there is no force or spirit or agent competing with him. The only competition to Jesus comes from human obstinacy or ignorance, but these things can hardly be called obstacles to God's work. Believers feel that God works through everyone, saved or not. If believers are capable of greater works, it is because realizing their relationship to Jesus energizes them by making them less selfish.

God not only accomplishes his work through every person, believer or not, but he is also the author of all events. This idea has some powerful implications, not least among them a disinterest in the possibility that history and culture might have some explanatory relevance in everyday life. Although the staff at the church were extremely helpful in my search for historical materials, for example, the relationship of the past to the present was not especially interesting to them. Every moment is created by God, and every situation in which individuals find themselves are created by God for each one personally. Thus belief in Jesus makes possible a personal universe in which the meaning of all things is insured, even if that meaning is beyond human comprehension. Devout Baptists say that people should not try to understand too much of life. Things that we might consider evil or tragic only appear that way to us because we do not understand God's plan. Perhaps the only evil is to deny someone access to the Word, or perhaps the only tragedy is the rejection of Jesus, but these ideas are my extrapolations, not examples drawn from conversation. Certainly, even extraordinary misfortunes are not beyond the power of Jesus to suffuse with spiritual possibility.

Some of the believers' responses to misfortune are accessible in a regular element of the Wednesday prayer service, the time of personal testimony. Each week, an individual or a couple go to the pulpit to explain how or why they believe that Jesus has "entered their hearts." Occasionally, the witness is a new convert or someone who has recently experienced some trouble; others are individuals whom the preacher or someone else in the congregation believes has the spiritual maturity to teach something to the congregation. One such testimony came from a woman whose response to her daughter's death was considered to be exemplary for all Christians:

Mr. and Mrs. S were not churchgoers, although they had both been brought up as Baptists. They had a beautiful four-year-old daughter, whom they were rearing without any particular attention to her religious training. The child expressed an interest in attending Sunday school, and they finally enrolled her after a long period of resisting. She loved the Sunday sessions and, her mother said, brightened the house with the hymns she learned. After a year or so, the child fell ill. During her long hospitalization, she maintained a patient and cheerful—angelic—disposition and continued to sing hymns for her amusement. One in particular seemed to be her favorite. When the girl died, her parents said that they were overwhelmed by bitterness at their loss. During this period, a neighbor invited them—really urged them—to go to church one Sunday. The hymn happened to be the one that their daughter had so loved to sing. Mrs. S felt a sharp pang of recognition, but she also felt that instead of increasing her agony, the hymn reconciled her with her daughter. She suddenly realized that Jesus had given the family an opportunity for eternal life in sending them their child. In other words, in cutting her daughter's life short, he had given them all the gift of the opportunity to be saved. She believes now that her daughter knew she had the power to save her parents by her death. Mr. and Mrs. S have been faithful churchgoers ever since and say that they have found complete comfort within their faith.

Mrs. S gave her testimony with composure, and the congregation responded with tears and awe. The moment was replete with the poignancy I have already mentioned, and part of the congregation's response was relief. An unsaved person is an unfulfilled possibility: the death without the rebirth of the parents would have been tragic, empty, literally meaningless, whereas the rebirth more than cancelled out the death—it transformed it. Mrs. S's narrative was moving in the extreme, and the themes she sounded are very much a part of the Baptist idiom. Time and again, death was the occasion to celebrate life, never to lament loss. People are expected to experience the loss of their loved ones with grief, particularly if the deceased was unsaved, but that grief is for things other than the impossibility of reunion. One young woman said during her testimony, "I can rejoice that my father is dead, because I know he is with Jesus." Salvation is the promise of reunion, the end of death.

Death is not the only sort of event whose meaning is transformed by an individual's relationship to Jesus. One incident that was covered in the local newspaper, and which received a good deal of public attention, was the kidnapping of a prominent local man's wife and daughter. The two women had been asleep in their unlocked home, and the intruders entered easily, abducted them, and held them for a ransom. The women escaped unharmed two days later. The kidnappers were arrested, and as the state prepared its prosecution, the family urged the court to dismiss or reduce the charges. This family was Methodist, but the Baptist minister preached a sermon extolling the family's exemplary act of charity, quoting Matthew 5:44 ("Pray for them which despitefully use you and persecute you") and Romans 13:21 ("Be not overcome of evil, but overcome evil with good"). The gist of the sermon was that by forgiving the kidnappers, the victims had offered a compelling witness for Christ. The salvation of the kidnappers was more important than their punishment.

Similar, if less dramatic, offenses are ideally met with similar equanimity. One woman lost several Bibles to a thief who took them from the front seat of her parked car. She had been planning to use them as gifts but concluded that the replacement costs would

[79]

be worth the price if the thief would open one of the Bibles and read a few verses. She said that perhaps Jesus had led the thief to her car and was using her as a witness. The same woman and her husband suffered extensive damage to their only automobile when another car ran a stop sign and hit them broadside. No one was hurt. The couple never sought compensation for the hundreds of dollars necessary for repair of the vehicle, nor did they ever have the repairs done. The woman said that she believed Jesus had caused the accident for some reason, perhaps to give her and her husband a chance to show their Christian charity to the family in the other car. In any case, she explained, Romans 13:19 exhorts Christians to "avenge not yourselves."

These misfortunes and other, petty annoyances are assumed to be part of a plan for the universe that, since it is God's plan, is for the best. Believers are assured by their faith that there *are* answers to all of their questions about the meaning of events, even if the answers remain inscrutable. Salvation permits a believer to participate in the answers in a positive way; the anticipation of entering the community of Jesus in heaven is an anticipation of full understanding.

Although it is true that believers feel assured of the meaning of death, it is not true that they therefore seek it or particularly welcome it. Life also has meaning for Baptists, and they express no hesitation about seeking medical care, prolonging life by all available means, or avoiding physical danger or discomfort. In fact, recent born-agains say that their lives and bodies are more precious to them now that they realize that God dwells within them (that is, in their hearts). A popular expression is that the body is a temple, and that it is an individual's responsibility to care for its health, strength, and chastity. Although the logic of death inherent in salvation would seem to justify asceticism, in fact, Baptists say that it is life that is rescued from meaninglessness by the transformation of death into "life everlasting." The lives of the unsaved are doomed to be conceits, believers say, because they end and end in oblivion. Salvation, in contrast, makes the end of time infinite, since God is eternity itself.

Salvation has many consequences in Baptists' lives, some of which, and some of whose implications, are explored later in this chapter and those that follow. As an experience, it is inextricable from the other two that are the present subject, Bible study and witnessing. Connecting all three are prayer. Born-agains describe conversion as a physical feeling. The descriptions suggest a sensation of ecstatic consummation, of physical tension followed by relief. Images such as an embrace, surrender, yielding, loss of consciousness (not literally; the implication is disorientation or lack of self-consciousness), lack of inhibition, and ecstasy are frequently offered in private and public testimony to portray the moment of accepting Jesus into one's life.

## Bible Study

The second fundamental element of what the Baptists consider their distinctive experience is their personal interpretation of the Bible in their daily study. Many people study the Bible routinely once or twice a day, reading successive chapters or parts of chapters at each session. Sunday school and training union (see below) both educate believers and prospects in reading the Bible, and discussion focuses on interpretive possibilities for each reading. Sermons also expand on scriptural verse. It is important to know that no one interprets the Bible for Baptists, however; independent interpretation is essential to their conception of spiritual maturation throughout a lifetime. They expect that a person's interpretive sensitivity increases with time. By the time a child reaches adulthood, he or she has read the scriptures many times, so that the average adult is adept at quoting scripture. Verses cited in ordinary conversation are generally emphatic, reiterating a proximate point or, in a sense, underscoring a point.

Actually, "interpretation" misrepresents what the Baptists claim they are doing when they read the Bible. They say that they are literal Bible readers, taking the scriptures as the actual word of God. Thus they might prefer a distinction between *interpretation* and *understanding*—one's "understanding" of scripture is said to change with one's spiritual growth. *Understanding* is the more suggestive word in that it implies that at the bottom of all possibility lies some absolute truth for one to know. This idea corresponds more closely to Baptist belief than the relativities implicit in a word like *interpret*. Baptists also consciously acknowledge a certain

[81]

amount of scriptural interpretation since they use *scripture* as a metaphor in many contexts: for emphasis, in arguments, in joking, in prayer, and so on. Each of these usages is discussed elsewhere in this and subsequent chapters.

Reading the Bible is said to be "easy" or "fast," meaning that one becomes readily involved and is compelled to read on, not that it lends itself to facile interpretation or understanding. In some households, the Bible, or each family member's Bible, is the only book owned by the family (although books owned is certainly not a reliable index of books read). A Bible is considered a gift of close friendship or love, and people show special care for their own copies not only because the Bible is a sacred book but because it holds sentimental value for them. Special covers, or special copies for home and away-from-home use, are common. A Bible is also a gift of kindness and support to a prospect. Gideon's, the same firm that presents hotels and motels with their copies of scripture, also publishes small pocket-sized copies for presentation to individuals. Like the hotel versions, each small copy is indexed by emotional need (for example, "Loss," "Anxiety," "Anger"), and the inside book cover includes a preprinted vow of acknowledgment or conversion, with spaces for the name of the new convert and the date of his or her rebirth.

Bible study is one of several components of a Christian life, and it is an important one. It provides two bonds, one that ties the individual to what is believed to be the authentic word of God and a second that ties believers to what becomes an epistemological community, their fellow Christians. The Bible provides a normative basis for the Baptist community without actually presenting believers with a set of rules. The Bible does not so much prescribe particular actions in particular contexts as it provides metaphors or parables for everyday situations. The scriptural episodes are taken as offering exemplars of Christianity, and many people express the wish that they could be "like" Martha, or Mary, or one of the other saints. Thus the Bible represents a certain social or spiritual order at work, and it is left to the individual believer to form the connection between that order and the one he or she actually lives in. Local Baptists express disdain for the Bible reading of the so-called Primitive Baptists, who read the Bible so literally that they acknowledge no permissible differences between the lives portrayed in scripture and their own. They are said to live with personal restrictions that Hopewell's suburban Baptists consider unreasonable: no cosmetics for women; no fashionable clothes; no card playing, dancing, or drinking of alcohol (although Hopewell's Baptists do not drink, either); and baptism by total immersion in a natural body of water, locally, in the old mill pond. Hopewell's Baptists consider such literal reading immature, arguing that the greater spiritual test would be to join the world without becoming tainted by it. The common motto in this church is, "We are in the world but not of it."

Of the multitude of verses in scripture, people are bound to have their favorites, ones that they believe especially speak for them. Several popular verses have to do with conflict: "Avenge not yourselves . . . Vengeance is mine; I will repay, saith the Lord" (Romans 12:19); "If a man sue thee for thy cloak, give him thy coat also" (Matthew 5:40). The crucial verse for the preacher seems to be John 3:16: "For God loved the world so much that he gave his only Son, so that everyone who believes in him may not die but have eternal life." This verse was taken to indicate the supreme sacrifice, of God relinquishing a piece of himself, his much-loved son. The effect, by comparison, was intended to make the sacrifices of daily life smaller. But the verse was also used in sermons and conversation as the essence of the Baptists' faith. The next verse reads: "For God did not send his Son in to the world to be its Judge, but to be its Savior" (John 3:17).

## Witnessing and Conversion

Inasmuch as the word of God is by definition compelling and persuasive, Bible reading is a major concern of evangelists who wish to extend the community of the saved. Witnessing, or evangelizing, is the third element of the Christian life that Hopewell's Baptists consider distinctive. They say that witnessing can take three forms and that all Christians are required by scripture to perform at least one. One is by direct education or what the local idiom calls "visiting" with a prospect. The second is dissemination of tracts, a method that is apparently the least used in Hopewell. The third is the one preferred by most people for its indirectness:

"the life of good witness." The phrase refers to a Christian life that is so exemplary that it seems to invite imitation, or acceptance, without any direct preaching. Virtually everyone I met in the Baptist community spoke at some time of aspiring to lead such a life. Doing so requires deliberate effort and seems to be considered a product of conscious choices. The naturalness of the Christian life, the ease with which such a life is accomplished, is no special index of an individual's merit, since Jesus enables people to struggle successfully with temptation.

Although every Baptist I knew seemed to acknowledge the obligation to witness, not everyone felt the call to do so. Some people are so deeply compelled by their salvation that they say that failure to witness, to spread the "good news" (of Jesus' "power to save"), would be a sin. This feeling of commitment is understood to be the work of the Holy Spirit; an example of such a feeling is found in the case of the young woman (narrated in Chapter 1) struggling with her vocation to join a foreign mission. People witness actively in many ways, for example, by invitations to join the church or by moments such as the following: on a visit with one local woman, I commented on how very attractive her young children were, to which she replied that her children were the Lord's work, that she and her husband had merely brought them into the world. Such a comment, or the stock phrase "Praise the Lord," is a polite deflection of compliments. In any case, these moments are arresting reminders of the place of Jesus in Baptists' sense of their everyday lives.

More formal witnessing takes place in the weekly visits that are a regular part of the church's nonworship calendar. Prospects are visited by a pair of church members, usually of the same sex and age, although the young unmarried adults sometimes visit across gender lines. Visits are generally brief and have three stages. First, the candidates are welcomed to the community, if they have just arrived, or there is ordinary social conversation if they already know the visitors. Next, the visiting couple describe the activities for their age and gender group and invite the prospects to attend church. The Hopewell church describes itself as a "fellowship of excitement," and the near-doubling of its membership during the past ten years is one testimony to its local appeal. Finally, the couple invite the candidates to join them in prayer, which is brief and spontaneous.

The selection of candidates for visits is a subject of considerable discussion among church members. The group that I knew best was the "college and career group," the group of young unmarried adults between the ages of eighteen and about twenty-five. Every newcomer to town, and every new acquaintance, was discussed as a possibility for inclusion. The major question was whether the person was likely to be interested, that is, whether the person was already a Christian in his or her heart. Some prospects are not Baptists, and others belong to Baptist churches in other communities. "Moving one's letter" from one church to another is often accompanied soon afterward by a born-again or conversion experience, as people reexperience their initiation into a spiritual community. The young people were generous with their invitations, which included people in whatever aspect of church activity they were supposed to be most comfortable with. Some young prospects at first went only to the informal gatherings after church and only later attended the Sunday or other services and finally Sunday school. The general pattern seemed to be full participation in the worship and nonworship activities of the church community, before membership and baptism or rebaptism.

Every worship service includes a "hymn of invitation," which accompanies a period of silent prayer while the minister invites the unsaved and other nonmembers to walk down the aisle to the altar.[3] A "profession of faith" must be made in public. This is an intense moment in the routine of the service, since the Holy Spirit is believed to have selected particular individuals for his efforts, and they are therefore locked in struggle with him, whether or not they know it. The congregation is asked to stand and to pray for their unsaved friends and family and—during this hymn only—to pray with eyes closed. The privacy of having everyone else's eyes closed is said to allow a prospect to feel alone with the Holy Spirit; it also minimizes the initial inhibitions in the first conspicuous steps that a prospect must make toward the altar. During those first steps, a prospect knows that everyone there is praying for his or her personal salvation. It is a powerful moment. As the hymn ends, people open their eyes to the one or more new members standing

3. For a description of testimony, invitation, and conversion in a North Carolina white suburban Southern Baptist church, see Peacock 1975a: 84–86.

with the preacher at the front of the church. There are smiles and sometimes tears of joy as the preacher embraces them, and at the end of the service, they together form a receiving line at the back of the church, where they are welcomed and embraced heartily by church members. It is a situation that calls for admiration, if not precisely congratulations, and the new members express a range of emotion—joy, relief, tears. A conversion experience is an event, and born-agains speak freely of their conversions. A new convert is believed to be a very effective witness.

Conversion or rebirth is followed days or weeks later by baptism. Baptists confer baptism by total immersion of the candidate in water. Methodists, who "sprinkle," are the subject of some mild joking, since sprinkling with water is taken to be somewhat half-hearted. In the Hopewell Baptist Church, the baptismal font is in a balcony above the altar. Ordinarily, curtains conceal it, but when baptisms are scheduled, it is lit in soft lavender lights. Candidates for baptism dress in white choir robes and proceed individually to the font, where the minister, also dressed in white, awaits them. After a brief prayer and reaffirmation of his or her decision, the prospect, held securely in the minister's arms, is submerged backward (face up) into the water, which is about hip deep. The minister holds a folded cloth over the candidate's mouth and nose while he is submerged. The immersion lasts only long enough to be complete—perhaps one second or two. After a blessing, the baptism is over. (For a description of a rural Southern Baptist baptism, see Weber 1946a.) The baptism is, among other things, said to be a test of the candidate's trust in God; indeed, no one whose baptism I witnessed seemed traumatized by the experience—moved, of course, but completely composed. People may be baptized as many times as they think that their religious experience requires recelebration.

## Prayer

The thread linking the three elements of the Baptist life—salvation, Bible study, and witnessing—with one another and with the rest of life is prayer. Prayer deserves special study as a form of speech or, more accurately, a collection of forms, but I did not collect prayers in a sufficiently systematic way to do so. On one level, prayer constitutes a person's communication with Jesus, but it has several forms and multiple functions. Baptist prayer is always spontaneous and unrehearsed. There are no prayer books or litany of prayer. Except for the Lord's Prayer,* there is no prayer in unison. (But hymns are sung in unison out of hymnals; they, too, are prayers.) Testimony and sermonizing are related to prayer in this sense; they are never written down to be read to a gathering, since the conviction is that God will provide the correct words if the speaker can open his heart and mind to Jesus.

Prayer is not an occasional thing or particularly ritualized. It is marked in everyday speech by a term of address, "Lord, . . ." People sometimes close their eyes in prayer to help them concentrate; prayer in public requires that a person not be inhibited by the audience. In the following pages, four contexts of prayer are considered: private prayer, prayer with a third party, collective prayer, and prayer narratives (people often narrate their prayers to others after the fact). Prayer can also be receptive, when an individual "calls on Jesus" for advice and believes that he or she receives it. *Prayer* is a broad category, and the word is used to refer to all of the times when an individual believes he or she has Jesus' attention in an especially personal way.

Private prayer is often routinized on first arising in the morning or at bedtime at night, when the believer kneels by the bed to offer thanks. Ideally, all prayers are prayers of thanks, although the number of sermons reminding the congregation of this and personal narratives of petitions to Jesus suggest that this is not always the case. The argument against making requests of Jesus is that his plan for the universe is already complete, and so to ask for something that he has not already provided is arrogant at worst and irrelevant at best. But a prayer for strength, understanding, or success in a particular trial is very common. People are less approving of contractual prayers, which also are the subject of sermons. In this form, an individual promises to perform some act or to reform in

* "Our father, who art in Heaven, hallowed be thy name. Thy kingdom come, thy will be done, on earth as it is in heaven. Give us this day our daily bread, and forgive us our trespasses, as we forgive those who trespass against us. Lead us not into temptation, but deliver us from evil. For thine is the kingdom and the power and the glory forever" (Matthew 6:9–13).

[87]

some particular way if Jesus will deliver a particular benefit or reprieve. These prayers are spoken of as conceits and are considered a sign that the individual making the plea is spiritually immature. These prayers lack faith, it is said. Apart from indirect evidence such as instruction in prayer during Sunday school, training union, and worship services and from personal narratives of prayer, I have no knowledge of (nor could any outsider know of) private prayer. People speak of feeling especially close to Jesus when they pray alone and often pray silently (but always verbally) during the day when they sense the need for such intimacy. A full prayer life is said to give people strength, the strength to resist undesirable social pressure and to meet misfortune without doubting Jesus' power and plan.

Private prayer is by definition inaccessible to third parties, but prayer is also very much a part of life in public. Friends often pray together, when one needs the added support of other voices. One person in the group may pray aloud, the others listening with eyes closed, or each may take a turn in a circle of prayer. An individual who is particularly troubled may invite friends home to pray for him or her, in which case the person participates silently. I also know of women who pray together over the telephone. Some people say that prayer in public has the certainty of being heard, since scripture reads: "Where two or three are gathered together in my name, there am I" (Matthew 18:20). On the other hand, no one seems to doubt that their private prayers are heard perfectly, so there are no relativities implied. Prayers such as these are sometimes for thanksgiving but more often are requests for help in specific crises. An individual who is troubled about a relationship may ask Jesus for patience and also work on the heart of the other person. Someone who is frightened may ask for reassurance and courage. A common prayer is for the strength to endure whatever may lie ahead and to renew one's commitment to Jesus in preparation for some personal ordeal. The possibilities are apparently infinite, and such prayerful gatherings also provide the focal individual with the support of close friends.

A prayer may be lengthy and contain considerable social information. One hesitates to write that people gossip through prayer, but in fact prayers either contain news or are themselves news in that they represent new developments in relationships. No one I knew of treated prayer as gossip in the sense of passing it on as such, but in a community where people hesitate to express negative feelings, prayer in public represents a crucial source of social knowledge. In Chapter 3, prayer is considered again from the perspective of social control.

Another regular context for prayer in public is at family meals or, with some families, at any meal, including one taken at a restaurant or at another's house. These prayers have the special name of "grace"; one "asks for grace" or "says grace." These are prayers of thanksgiving for sustenance, and if there are guests present, or if there has been some special occasion, thanks for these things are often included. Asking grace for the family is a privilege. Family members may take turns, the honor passing to the children in turn or to the parents. A guest may receive the honor of saying grace. Again, as with other Baptist prayers, there is a wide range of content and form in these prayers, although there are also stock patterns such as, "Lord, we thank you for the food we are about to eat and for the love at this table. Amen."

The most public form of prayer is prayer in church. The minister is not an intermediary between his congregation and God but is considered a learned, scholarly man with exemplary spiritual maturity. He leads by example in all areas of his life, and when he prays before the congregation, that, too, is an example rather than intercession. He does not pray *for* the congregation but *with* it. At Wednesday prayer meetings, the minister calls on members of the congregation to stand and pray aloud. Prayers at church are expressed in the same quiet, reverential tones as other more private prayers. In fact, these Baptists explicitly reject more enthusiastic or expressive prayer, such as speaking in tongues or "shouting"— raising the hands and moving to the cadence of the prayer. They reject tongues on the grounds that God's word should be accessible and intelligible to others: tongues do not constitute a good witness. They reject "shouting" on various grounds; in general, it is considered unsophisticated.

The fourth form of prayer is more precisely a usage of prayer as narrative. Narratives relate both what was said to Jesus and what Jesus was believed to have answered or just one side of the conversation. No one says, "And the Lord said to me. . . ," but one often hears phrases such as "I felt the Lord was telling me to . . ." or "So

[89]

I said to the Lord, 'Lord . . .'" with the narrative. Narratives are highly laden with social information in the same way that public prayer is. They are at the very least announcements that an individual has taken a matter to heart and is concerned, and the narratives permit the speaker a wider range of emotional expression than tends to be the case otherwise. Prayer narratives are very much a part of ordinary conversation among friends.

Thus prayer has several important forms and functions. It functions as social control, social communication, and emotional release at the very least. It marks the beginning of all public gatherings, including family meals, sporting events, meetings, and so on. It sometimes also concludes those events. "Calling on Jesus" or prayer about something are everyday activities, almost continual activities, for devout Baptists. For our purposes, the more interesting collection of prayers are those that are not structured into daily or organizational routine but are spontaneous outpourings to Jesus in private or in public. It is these forms in particular that suggest that a devout Baptist closely identifies with Jesus to the extent that all thought—and surely all certainty—comes directly from Jesus in response to prayer. Jesus' word thus glosses for private thought in general, for few people, in narrating difficult decisions, will be heard to say, "I thought about X and decided Y," but rather will say, "I prayed about X and felt that Jesus was telling me Y." In a relatively conformist society, the permission that Jesus is conceived to offer people to be individuals is apparently essential to their sense of well being. As one young woman said, explaining the effect of Jesus in her life, "Jesus lets me be me." Jesus supplants the self, or more accurately, the self is believed to exist to be fulfilled by Jesus. In the claim that Baptists make that individuals can lose themselves (cease to be self-interested) by joining Jesus, salvation simultaneously accomplishes the reiteration of individuality through the power of prayer. Prayer mobilizes and actualizes an individuality that would otherwise be ambivalent.

A second, more general impact of what Baptists consider to be the Christian life on the organization of their universe is that their faith entirely dissolves any possible distinctions between sacred and secular domains. Salvation reorients the individual as to time (life and death), Bible study guides the individual in everyday life, and witnessing further melds the strictly religious with the nonreligious. The Baptist community itself becomes sacred, and all else is profane, no matter how well intentioned. Doctrine supports this implicit classificatory scheme. Jesus' saving power comes from his power to "take away sin," to forgive. The saved spend eternity in heaven not because they are better people than the unsaved but because they have been forgiven their sins. Sin in a non-Christian is unforgivable because it is unforgiven by Jesus, because the non-Christian has not acknowledged the need for Jesus.

## Baptist Worship in Hopewell

The Sunday morning worship service crowns the weekly religious calendar at the Hopewell Baptist Church. It is the best attended—at peaks, close to a thousand people attend—and the most formal of the three worship services the church offers during the week. A worship service on Sunday nights and a prayer meeting on Wednesday evenings are also focal points of activity at the church. Worship-related activities are the religious training sessions offered on Sunday mornings and late Sunday afternoons, a community supper before the Wednesday meeting, and visiting on Thursday evenings. Fellowships—informal gatherings described in Chapter 1—follow the evening services. Apart from other church-sponsored activities, such as sports and service activities, a devout Baptist regularly spends from ten to twelve hours each week at church. It is a familiar and special place.

The Sunday morning service, which follows Sunday school, follows a routine structure whose details are distributed in printed programs at each service. The regular order is as follows: organ prelude, hymn by choir, hymn by congregation, pastoral prayer, hymn by choir, greetings, hymns by congregation, offertory and offertory hymn by choir, sermon, hymn of invitation by choir, benediction, and closing hymn. The service concludes in just over an hour, with hymns marking each segment. The routine of the Sunday evening and Wednesday services are similar, except that the hymns are sung by the congregation alone, and there is more participation from members in the form of prayer, prayer requests (for the sick, troubled, or unsaved), and personal testimony.

Sermons are based on verses from scripture, but are unscripted, unrehearsed comments by the pastor. Occasionally, a guest pastor is invited to preach, particularly during revivals. Revival weeks are periods of intense evangelizing, with nightly worship services. Such meetings are aimed at spreading the gospel and bringing Christians to new understanding of their spiritual commitments. They generally take place twice a year. Some examples of sermon topics drawn from church programs in 1973 and 1974 are: "God's Matchless Invitation" (Isaiah 1:18); "The King Is Coming" (John 14:3; Matthew 24:29–31); "How to Keep Up with the Joneses and Be Christian" (Luke 12:13–21); "The Light of the World" (John 8:12); "The Savior's Sacrifice" (I Corinthians 5:7–8); "Faith for Facing the Future" (Hebrews 11:8–19); "How to Get Rid of Your Enemies?" (I John 2:9–11); "The Need for Righteous Men" (Genesis 18:20–33); "How to Go to Bed with a Clear Conscience" (Hebrews 13:18). The same message echoed through all of these topics: trust in Jesus; call on Jesus; with Jesus no problem is too great. When a topic is the temptation of self-indulgent pleasure or materialism, the sermon encourages believers to remember that earthly things are conceits, since the Last Days (before Judgment Day) are almost here.

The church depends on weekly offerings by its members to meet its budget. This church is known locally for its success in funding drives; when a substantial addition to the church building was planned, the necessary funds were raised in under six weeks. Local Christians *tithe*, or donate 10 percent of their earnings to the church, and many donors have anecdotes about audits from incredulous inspectors from the Internal Revenue Service. Occasionally, personal testimony extolls the benefits of tithing: one couple lost nearly everything during the Great Depression but began to recover once they began to tithe. People say that tithing prevents waste, curtails materialism, and repays a spiritual debt to Jesus and the church or simply that they have an obligation to tithe. Young people and others without paying jobs are encouraged to donate 10 percent of their time to the church.

The church also publishes a weekly newsletter, generally no more than four to six small pages. The newsletter contains news about the worship service programs, the sick, obituaries, births, and the activity schedule for the week. The pastor contributes a short column, as does the youth minister, a college student who does some counseling and administration in the young people's "department," as it is called. A typical published schedule of weekly activities follows:

| | | |
|---|---|---|
| Sunday: | 9:45 | Bible Study |
| | 11:00 | Worship service |
| | 5:00 | Senior High Choir |
| | | Junior High Bible Study |
| | 6:30 | Church training |
| | 7:30 | Worship service |
| Wednesday: | 5:30 | Fellowship dinner |
| | 6:30 | Teachers-Officers meeting |
| | | Senior High Bible Study |
| | | Junior High, Junior Music Makers, Primary and Beginner Choirs |
| | 7:30 | Prayer meeting |
| | | Mission Friends |
| | | Teen activities |
| | 8:20 | Adult Choir rehearsal |
| Thursday: | 10 and 7 | Visitation |
| Saturday: | 10 to 12 | Youth visitation |
| | 10 to 11:30 | Junior choir rehearsal |

Again, this official schedule of activities does not include seasonal sports such as weekly basketball and baseball or the many hours spent around the church or in nonscheduled peer-group activities.

The newsletter also contains fillers, in the form of spiritual advertisements, with such slogans as: "Are YOU a Tither?" "Tithe to Tell"; "Just Suppose Everybody Tithed"; "Time Is Running Out; Christ Is the Answer for All the World"; "You Can't Outgive God"; and "Let's Make Wednesday Night a Church Night for the Whole Family." Fillers also contain more specific appeals for funds, choir members, or other forms of service. Appeals sometimes play on the theme of reciprocity, which is only marginally condoned in prayer. For example:

GOD HAS PLEDGED . . .

God has pledged to forgive our sins if we confess in humble repetance (Isaiah 1:18).

Our Lord has pledged to save all of those who come unto him (Matthew 11:28–30).

Our Lord has pledged never to leave us nor to forsake us (Matthew 28:20).

Our Lord has pledged to us the necessities of life if we put the Kingdom of God first in our lives (Matthew 6:23).

Our Lord has pledged to prepare a place where we can dwell with him throughout eternity (John 14:1–3).

Our Lord has pledged to reward us for our labors in his service (Revelation 22:12).

BECAUSE GOD HAS PLEDGED . . .

I WILL PLEDGE—FOR . . .

OUR CHURCH provides a place to worship God.

OUR CHURCH undergirds the family and home life.

OUR CHURCH sends missionaries into foreign lands.

OUR CHURCH stands firm for righteousness.

OUR CHURCH upholds the high standards of God.

OUR CHURCH preaches the message of eternal life.

OUR CHURCH holds forth hope to a discouraged world.

OUR CHURCH is ministering to the needs of the community.

OUR CHURCH is God's institution on earth.

GIVE GOD'S WAY . . .

PLEDGE TO TITHE.

The newsletter, which, by all accounts, is studied by the membership, is a place where members can find important spiritual themes expressed in ordinary and direct language. Appeals for service, good witness, and attendance at church are popular editorial concerns. The youth minister contributed the following paragraph at the time of the new year:

Young people, in just a few short days 1973 will be history. 365 days of your life here on the Planet Earth are soon to be over. Have these days been spent wisely or have they been used foolishly? Only you can answer this question honestly. From our Bible studies that we have had, both in Senior and Junior High, we know that our Lord and Saviour Jesus Christ is coming back soon. We read in God's Word that He will come when man least expects Him. You know with only a few days left, one realizes that He hasn't come yet. What will 1974 hold for us? It could very well be the year that Jesus returns to Earth to claim His people. Will you be ready to greet Him? Will He be happy with you when He returns[?] As the New Year begins, ask God to speak to your heart and seek God's will in your life. Be able to say *honestly*, "[I]f God came back tonight, I know I would go to be with Him."

This message reflects the young people's very real sense of urgency in their approach to salvation and the salvation of those close to them. Jesus' return is a very real event to them, and they in particular look to current events—even the weather, since Revelation predicts storms just before Judgment Day—for signs that Jesus is about to come. Older people express a similar sense of urgency in their witnessing, but their image is one of life cut short not by Judgment but by death. Several people told me that they feared for my death because I was unsaved and would be separated from them forever.

The pastor's messages also reflect the conceptions of faith, salvation, and the power of prayer discussed in this chapter. In the same new year's newsletter, the pastor wrote in part:

> Looking forward, we see 1974 as a year of exciting possibilities. We are not blind to the "discouraging signs of the times," but we believe that God works in human history and He will not forsake us now. This year can be epochal for [this church]. It can be the year of unprecedented growth—both numerically and spiritually. . . . Resolve, now, to do your best for God during this year. Be loyal and dependable Christians. Above all, love the Lord and one another.

Another message contained an appeal for prayer typical of those among friends: "Pray for the Pulpit Staff Committee. These people have been in prayerful conference recently and feel that they are very close to a recommendation for our much-needed Minister of Education. . . . We have not rushed this decision—we've sought the Lord's leadership—now we ask you to carefully pray that the right decision will be made."

Another focal theme of sermons and pastoral messages in print is that of Christian courage. Baptists often speak of their relations with non-Christians as if they (Baptists) were persecuted or mocked for their beliefs. Although I never witnessed such discrimination, it may exist. It is in a subject like this one that the power of prayer to strengthen the individual becomes especially clear (this passage is taken from a church newsletter):

> While all of us need encouragement, we shouldn't have to be prodded to exercise our Christian commitment. The stronger of two magnets will draw more iron filings, and if Christ is first in our lives our acts of devotion will flow toward Him and the things of this world will be less attractive.
>
> Don't you feel as I—we're living in an age when it is no longer popular to be a Christian? And if you're faithful to Christ and His church, it's not because everybody's doing it, for they're not. We've come to the point in human history when folks think Christians are strange people. But that's encouraging for Jesus said we would come to that.
>
> But I'm glad to be a Christian—O, so glad! And I'm glad you're my fellow Christians—and I'll see you at the meeting house Sunday.

This message is typical of an idiom that equates the capacity to be nonconformist with faith in Christ. In practice, Baptists use this style of self-defense in situations in which they feel they must resist accommodation. The equation of God's will with a "gut feeling" allows people to resist compromise when they think it necessary and also to tolerate considerable conflict where conflict itself can safely be acknowledged, that is, from outsiders.

### Ordering the Sacred Community

So far, the Baptist church has been described primarily in terms of the doctrinal elements that local Baptists claim as distinctively Baptist. These elements are salvation, Bible study, and witnessing; prayer is the element that links these three and integrates them into an individual's life. The conception of social order implicit in the beliefs expressed by Baptists constitutes an important reiteration and elaboration of the conceptions of intimate relationships described in Chapter 1. The conception of Jesus as a *friend,* and the meaning of that contrast between friendship and family, should now be clear. Sacred concepts appear to be understood very much in terms of daily life, although the Baptists claim that it is daily life that is transformed by sacred belief. The interweaving of these two spheres of experience (which, to a devout Christian, constitute a single sphere) is illustrated by the following tract on friendship distributed by a religious publishing house and popular among Hopewell's young people:

> Friendship is . . . the communication of a dog's wagging tail or the purr of a kitten, a child-pet relationship that promotes security in both, that protects each other from oncoming dangers, that allows one to be the other's toy, a young child holding a conversation with several of its favorite toys.
>
> Friendship is . . . a mother comforting her child who has been insulted or injured by a playmate, a mother listening to a teenage daughter who has been jilted by a boyfriend . . . a father and son sitting at a river bank fishing, talking about the son's interests. . . .
>
> Friendship is . . . often best communicated by mankind's universal language—a smile, always a sweet responsibility never a duty, the greatest love, the most open communication, the healthiest counsel, the greatest union of minds of which men and women are capable.
>
> Friendship is . . . not an automatic endowment installed by the Creator, something that needs constant and conscious development and practice . . . a way of life, developed through self-sacrifice. . . .
>
> Friendship is . . . a relationship with God, made possible through personal acquaintance with Jesus Christ, . . . relaxing in the presence of your Creator. . . .
>
> Friendship is . . . talking to Jesus Christ in the same type of language you use with other friends, because you know him personally, because he knows you personally, an eternal contact and closeness to God, because he loved mankind enough to send Jesus Christ to earth, to win back our allegiance, to forgive us of sins, to call Christ "the Friend of sinners". . . .
>
> Friendship is . . . God knowing even your hidden thoughts and still showering his love upon you and wanting you as a friend. . . .
>
> Friendship is . . . eternal in dimension when you are properly related to God through personal contact with Jesus; Jesus Christ can be your best friend! (Krutza and Krutza 1973)

This essay (actually printed in open-verse style) progresses from imaginary relationships, to unilateral relationships, to a relationship with God, all under the rubric of "the most open communication." The association of these images suggests what quality communication among friends is believed to have: it derives not so much from interaction, or relation, as from a commitment to identify with and accept another person. The need to renew that commitment continually is thus an important element, since it suggests that the commitment does not renew itself. The important point of the tract is the emphasis on total acceptance between friends, including between Jesus and sinners. The self has no private space ("God knowing even your hidden thoughts . . .") but no need for privacy. How different is the image of family roles in these passages: they convey—as do the people in the community—isolation, self-sacrifice, and a veiled self. The image of Jesus as friend thus provides commentary as much on conceptions of friendships as it does on conceptions of the family.

The antinomianism of the Baptist sect individuates believers; they enter the sect individually, their salvation is personal, their prayer and sense of God's word mirror their private thought. But unlike secular family life, their religion reduplicates the individual in Jesus: he is "in-dwelling," that is, lives in everyone, and he is the most powerful representation of the self. In fact, where family roles would threaten to engulf the individual, Jesus provides a bulwark by representing the equation of personal conviction and God's will. When I asked people how they could identify God's will, the usual reply was, "Well, I just *feel* it." In this scheme of things, certainty is authenticity and truth.

If certainty is truth, argumentation and persuasion have little place in social relationships. Similarly, as mentioned above, conciliation or willingness to compromise reflects a lack of certainty or conviction, which in turn reflects an ambivalence in one's spiritual life. Doubt in any matter—spiritual or secular (although I must again point out that the two are one from the believer's perspective)—necessarily means doubt in one's relationship to God, since God's will is experienced as certainty. At the same time, as we have seen, the equation of personal thought with God's word strengthens the individual to tolerate conflict, indeed, to expect it. The logic of belief then makes the individual the vehicle of conflict, yet denies a person the tools for resolving it: conciliation, accommodation, compromise, surrender. Instead, as we shall see (Chapter 3), conflict is carefully redistributed across the social map.

Importantly, although devotion in a believer may lead him or her to expect conflict in some quarters, it abolishes the believer's ability to acknowledge conflict within the church community. If all Baptists are equal in their salvation, all have an equal relationship to Jesus. At least, all relationships to Jesus are plausibly equal; since some Christians are more mature than others, the more accurate phrasing might be that Jesus is equally available to all. At any rate, if certainty derives from Jesus, and Christians believe themselves to be more sensitive to his authorship of events, conflict should be impossible. Jesus unifies; he *is* unity or the heart of unity. To put this another way, Jesus literally normalizes society. By creating society as a reflection of his will, he defines the normal and instills it in those who come to him and call on him. By this reasoning, Baptists distrust the unsaved as being somewhat asocial: they refer to someone's childishness, or self-indulgence, or preference for sin as signs of their lack of faith. Salvation represents the crucial transformation of the individual from an asocial to a fully social being.[4] Unless the unsaved person is a prospect, there are few close friendships between Christians and non-Christians.

The nature of the transformation produced by an individual's acceptance of Christ is a crucial element of the Baptist conception of order. The saved and unsaved persons are qualitatively different. The unsaved individual is childish, selfish, uncontrolled in the sense of being a sinner; furthermore, the unsaved person is believed to live in the shadow of a fundamental error of judgment. Sermons on this subject suggest that the error is in mistaking the nature of the person's private interests as residing in material things, specifically, in material success (see Warner 1963: 37 for a comment on Americans' ambivalence over the importance of money). Materialism and ambition are imagined to organize the lives of the unsaved, and Baptists speak of this error as pathetic, or ironic, since death effaces all wealth except spiritual wealth and since the unsaved are doomed to death. Baptists acquire wealth but claim not to give it much value in their lives. In effect, the unsaved individual is untamed and represents a kind of negative, untrammeled individualism, in Tocqueville's precise sense of the term (Tocqueville I, 1945: 104): exclusive identification with one's own family and per-

---

4. Personal transformation is part of the cultural logic of conversion and its instrumentalities in secular domains, such as business, discussed by Weber (1946a). Membership in a church was a prerequisite of credit in the southern community he visited (Weber 1946a: 305).

ception of society as an adversary, a competitor. Baptists are clearly deeply ambivalent about this form of individuality and reject it in their insistence on salvation.

In normalizing the individual, Jesus eliminates individualism and instead joins the individual to society in a concert of interests. Hopewell's Baptists claim that their Christianity obviates an individual's being concerned with his or her own interests at all, freeing the person to devote attention and energies to others. Jesus tames Christians by socializing them to a concept of the self that demands society for its fulfillment. For a Christian, "others" are not adversaries, or competitors, but constitute the very motive for spiritual maturity: one witnesses to others, one does good works among others, one realizes the power of Christ in oneself among others, and so on. This is a substantially different concept of the individual than the one that Christians identify among non-Christians; one cannot call it individualism.[5] Importantly, individualism presupposes scarce, limited resources (and hence competition); people in Hopewell say that the Christian conception of the relationship of the individual to society is based on an unlimited resource, God's love. They say that it is this replacing of material goods with an unlimited good that accomplishes the transformation of an unbeliever into a Christian. (See Chapter 3 for a discussion of how Hopewell's Christians perceive and deal with the contradictions capitalism imposes on them.) This is a centrally important point: Baptists see themselves as being *liberated* by Christ to actualize themselves, by which they mean to engage fully as individuals in society. The mechanism that accomplishes the liberation is a redefinition of central values away from capital toward Christ and a concommitant reformulation of the relationship of private interests to public interests. Salvation thus dramatically reorganizes an individual's assessment of personal priorities.

5. Nor can one call it "civil religion" (Rousseau 1952, Bellah 1968, Moseley 1981). Bellah and Moseley noted the importance of the Revolution in providing the discourse of public religion in the United States (equality and freedom) and the transformations in that discourse following the Civil War (rebirth and sacrifice). Although these themes are certainly invoked by Hopewell's Baptists, their refusal to see the public sphere as separate from the private (see Chapter 1) means that they distrust the capture of religious language by public officials or by private citizens in public settings.

It is in precisely this respect that Weber (1958: 144) distinguished Baptists (along with Mennonites and Quakers) from Calvinists. Weber associated the Baptists' repudiation of material things with their "radical devaluation of all sacraments." In their elimination of the idea of salvation through works or through a church, Weber concluded, the Baptists had "accomplished the religious rationalization of the world in its most extreme form" (1958: 148). The local Baptists' rejection of the central place they believe non-Christian society gives to capital does not extend to any expressed ambivalence over capitalism itself. Although business and the marketplace were not by any means major subjects of conversation among the people I knew, I never heard anyone question either the efficacy or the freedom of the marketplace or of the national economic system in general. In fact, capitalism and its associations of personal freedom appear to be positively valued, and success in the marketplace is interpreted by local Baptists as an individual's ability to actualize his or her own potential (by accepting Christ) in the public domain. This is entirely consistent with Weber's (1958: 180–181) analysis of the association between the concept of duty and the concept of renunciation among the middle class. Wallace's (1978) study of early nineteenth-century capitalists shows them embracing evangelical Protestantism with none of the ambivalence Hopewell's Baptists express. In Wallace's Rockdale, the notion of "stewardship" was enough to ensure the industrialists of the sacredness of their success at the mills.

Local Baptists do not seem to shy away from business or careers in business, nor do they eschew conspicuous consumption. Rather, they claim to give different weight to these activities and possessions than non-Christians would; their own sense of freedom of choice seems to permit them to accumulate things or not. Their liberation from what they see as the tyranny of materialism seems to be expressed almost completely in their refusal to measure their fellows by their material wealth rather than in forms of asceticism.

Local Baptists are able to redefine some of the basic concepts of the marketplace to express religious values. Competition creates an arena in which Jesus can play a part in their lives; a financially successful Christian can be (by his very success) a good witness. Success and failure are, simultaneously, leveled by the expressed preference for spiritual over material success. Ambition is not personal ambition but ambition for Christ; profits or a comfortable income permit an individual or family to increase their material support of the church and charities. In fact, success in the economic world follows the same logic as the forbearance from alcohol and gambling: the money spent on these things would be better spent on others. It is the financial self-indulgence of alcohol that Baptists reject, although alcohol has acquired some additional meaning as being symbolically polluting. At any rate, just as preserving one's personal and material resources for the church is valued in the case of alcohol, acquiring resources for the church is valued too.

One consequence of the devaluation of material goods in the congregation is an egalitarianism that members say distinguishes them from outsiders. The absence of an explicit or expressed system of social ranking based on wealth constitutes a major difference between the people I knew in Hopewell and Americans reported elsewhere (Warner 1952: 1). Warner (1949: 22–34 and 77–100) is unambiguous in his characterization of the "all-pervasive rating system" that no one in Jonesville can escape (Warner 1949: 22). In both Jonesville and Yankee City (Warner 1949: 161 and 1963: 190), Baptists tend to be lower class or relatively poor. This is not the case in Hopewell, although it may once have been true (see Chapter 5). In the contemporary church, the absence of a materially based status vocabulary is striking. Indeed, wealth, education, occupation, one's home—these things make virtually no difference that I could detect in the way a person is treated by others. Some markers of wealth are eliminated, at least in public, for example, no one "dresses up"—people tend to wear ordinary business clothes or street clothes to worship services. Manners among relative strangers are cordial but not deferent; the presumption of brotherhood and of the potentiality of an egalitarian relationship are strongly present. New visitors to the church, for example, are enthusiastically welcomed, given a small ribbon to wear to mark them as visitors, and are later sent a card encouraging them to attend often. At the church, no one is anonymous, no one is neglected, and no one is special except the pastor, who is deferred to because of his experience and his burdens. Baptists perceive non-Baptist society to be one riddled with false pride and pomposity.

A second consequence of the concept of social order among Baptists is the theoretical impossibility of authority. "Human instrumentality" has been problematic for fundamentalists and a major theme of their discourse since the early nineteenth century (Loveland 1980: 69). (See Chapter 5 for an extended discussion of this point.) Although some individuals are acknowledged to be especially skilled in some area, they do not express such skills in terms of authority. Power in the sense of control of others is an extremely difficult issue in the logic of the faith we are discussing, since to acknowledge human power would be to compromise the equation of private certainty with God's word. Thus in the group decision mentioned in the pastor's message (quoted above), the idiom of decision making was group prayer. A decision comes when all involved open their minds to God, definitively *not* when one person persuades others to compromise or change their minds. In fact, Christianity leaves individuals only a truncated vocabulary for expressing and analyzing their decisions: one hears the phrase "I realized" more often than one hears "I decided," since realization comes from God.[6] A political idiom that would cover behaviors such as debate, persuasion, compliance, compromise, strategy, leverage, and so on must be entirely absent from a Christian's acknowledged domain of social thought.

Third, the Baptist concept of order admits conflict in limited ways but does not admit disputing at all. Disputes must disappear with the political rhetoric just mentioned (above). Decisions are not made by adversarial debate over their merits but by opening one's communication with Jesus. Decisions are in any case not supposed to be self-interested, that is, there is no social structure of adversarial, dyadic disputing. Conflict, as I have suggested, and as I explore in the next chapter, is essentially mapped by the division between the saved and unsaved. Thus it is not only the scriptural encomiums against disputing that prevent its expression in the Baptist community but also concepts of individuality, society, and reason that preclude it.

Now we are in a position to broach the primary issue of this book. It is for these three reasons that the one important indicator Baptists have of their level of spiritual maturity is the way in which they

---

6. Indeed, the merging of thought and feeling effectively obviates authority since all questions of authoritative control are (theoretically) moot. Rosaldo (1984) made this point in the context of Ilongot ethnography.

respond personally to feelings of conflict. Their ability to live at peace, to refrain from disputes when they disagree with others, and to *feel* no disputes are important measures of an individual's ability to live up to a promise to Christ. As we shall see, the only appropriate responses to conflict are prayer and/or witnessing. No self-interested response is appropriate, since one's interest is fully protected by Jesus and since there is no Christian vocabulary for expressing those interests. An important exception to all of this is competition in business, which I believe Baptists control in their own lives by compartmentalizing their work lives from their other activities and by minimizing the importance of their work in their sense of their own lives. It is Baptists' private lives that are the subject of this book, and in that domain, the absence of conflict is a crucial test of one's spiritual strength. Conflict is a very frequent subject of prayer since any conflict with others becomes inner conflict for a Christian. Every adversary pits a Christian's sense of self-interest against his or her own faith in Jesus. Baptists find it just as difficult as anyone else to turn the other cheek, as the gospel enjoins them to do, and the stakes in that contest with oneself are very high.

In this chapter, we have seen that a Baptist's faith defines and redefines some crucial aspects of his or her existence, from the end points of the individual's autobiography to the meaning of transactions in family, friendship, and business. In the domain of family and friendship, the religious experience of Baptists in Hopewell reiterates and elaborates the principles of personal order that were described in Chapter 1. The isolation of the individual is almost a premise of everything that follows; here, the salience of Jesus as friend is the contrast that friendship provides to both family life and life among strangers. But in elaborating an individual's sense that he or she alone must cope with problems in personal relationships, the Baptists believe that, in accepting Jesus, they acquire some powerful tools: the mind, eyes, and hands of a powerful and divine ally. Prayer, and particularly the equation of personal conviction with God's word, appears to be an effective resource in individuals' struggles to define or—as they would say—yield to their own existences. Salvation means that the community of the saved endures forever. Baptists in this community do not speak of looking forward to their reward in heaven but instead say that the promise of eternal life makes relevant many personal efforts that otherwise would not be in a world of material things. Thus Baptists speak of peace of mind.

Importantly, Baptists speak primarily of two other sorts of things when they talk about how they experience their Christianity. One is the transformation in their relationship to capital or, more accurately, in the place they give to capital in their lives, which we have just discussed. The second is their relationship to other people, expressed in conflict and potential conflict. An ability to get along, to preserve harmony, to *create* harmony, is, as mentioned above, a sure and ready test of an individual's spiritual maturity. In the next chapter, this crucial element of the Baptists' experience with Jesus is the subject of discussion. My hypothesis is that in focusing on conflict as the testing ground of their concept of order, Baptists are making a statement not only about their own relationship to Jesus but also to one another, the community around them, and the state. As we shall see, it is their understanding of conflict that links them, unbeknownst to them, to their region's past and future.

The local Baptists' interpretation of their religion's doctrine increases their tolerance for conflict in some quarters, that is, from the unsaved, but it eliminates their tolerance for conflict in their own community. The logic of their faith denies them any means for engaging in disputes or other sorts of confrontations that would create winners and losers or—more generally—authorities and constituents. Instead, they define their community as being harmonious a priori by virtue of having accepted Jesus. Individual differences in interpreting scripture can be accommodated under the concept of differential spiritual maturity, within limits, and collective acceptance of Jesus substitutes for any overt need for normative consensus. A dispute thus represents a spiritual contradiction on many levels. What follows is a description of the way in which Hopewell Baptists address this contradiction in what is an elaborate scheme for avoiding personal confrontations.

# [3]

# Ourselves amongst Others

So far, we have been exploring the two domains of an individual's experience from the point of view of Baptists in Hopewell: the intimate circle of family and friends and, intimately tied to that, the interpretive community of the Baptist church. The first two chapters described the personal roles and social relationships that Baptists say comprise those two domains. In both of these areas and, in fact, in all areas of a Baptist's life, one's status as a "good Christian" is measured in terms of how one responds to conflict, both inner and interpersonal. Conflict is thus an important indicator of one's spirituality or lack of it, and as we shall see in this chapter, conflict is the major axis along which Baptists conceptually organize the social universe in which they live. At the same time, we have seen that the interpretation of Baptist doctrine in Hopewell precludes any obvious vocabulary for expressing, resolving, or even acknowledging conflict *except* as inner conflict. Essentially, people conceptualize their relationships with others not as relationships, subject to negotiation and accommodation, but as roles to be perfected as an individual matures. The need for perfection is experienced as a need for salvation.

In this chapter, data on Baptists' concepts of conflict derive from conversations with individuals and observation of public worship during the better part of a year. One set of issues derives from the importance that Baptists place on resisting confrontation. There is the pragmatic problem of living in a community without any legitimate means of expressing one's self-interest. This discussion leads to the Baptists' theory of conflict, which, importantly, locates all conflict and disorder among the unsaved. Thus the view of society I have been presenting not only stresses conflict as a key sign but uses that sign in constituting a social map. The second set of issues charts the way in which the Baptists' theory of order distributes value across social space. Subsequent chapters suggest how it was that that distribution came to be and its significance.

## The Social Relations of Conflict

The local concept of the "community of Christ" has meaning in three time frames: past (the historical community), present (the living congregation), and future (the community rejoined in heaven). Baptists see their own lives as a relatively brief transition between two spiritual states, each symbolized and celebrated by physical immersions: baptism (in water) and burial (in the earth).

As temporal and spiritual markers in an individual biography, the acceptance of Christ (celebrated at baptism) and reunion with Christ (celebrated at burial) constitute an explicit imagery of liminality. At baptism, an individual is said to have left the ordinary world; at burial, an individual joins the eternal community of the saved. Baptists in Hopewell see baptism and burial in terms of the same elements of rites of separation and incorporation with which anthropologists have long been concerned (van Gennep 1960, Turner 1969).[1]

The notion that earthly life is merely a transitory and transitional state between birth (or spiritual birth) and death has two important dimensions. First, as we have seen, baptism marks a convert's transition from one group to another. The group of origin is de-

---

1. Turner defined Gennep's terms further: "The first phase (of separation) comprises symbolic behavior signifying the detachment of the individual . . . from an earlier fixed point in the social structure. . . . During the intervening 'liminal' period, the characteristics of the ritual subject . . . are ambiguous; he passes through a cultural realm that has few or none of the attributes of the past or coming state. In the third phase (reaggregation or reincorporation), the passage is consummated" (1969: 80). Williams (1982: 69) discussed the Baptist conversion ritual itself in terms of Turner's three stages.

picted as non-Baptist society, the society of the unsaved. Baptism ostensibly (but never actually) replaces these social relationships and also restructures relationships around new values. A private conversion experience must be validated by a public declaration of faith during regular church services. In practice, this means that a new convert walks down the aisle of the church to the altar to announce his or her "decision." One's spiritual state is a matter of public concern. At the other end of a Christian's life, heaven awaits, with its promise of a pure Christian community. Thus for the living Christian, the oft-repeated phrase "in the world but not of it" signifies the individual's transition between two fixed points: the impure (unsaved) and pure (heavenly) worlds.

The second dimension implied in the Baptists' conception of their immortality is their egalitarianism.[2] Baptists believe that Christ's saving power is available to all people, regardless of their previous sins or lack of faith, their wealth, or their race—although in this town, blacks and whites do not worship together. Segregation is explained as a distinction between levels of spiritual maturity; the whites accept blacks as authentic Christians but not as Christians capable of a deep understanding of faith. (The corollary of this belief is the fatalistic egalitarianism that posits that all people, regardless of good intentions or earthly acts, are doomed to hell unless they accept Jesus once they have heard the "Word.") With these universalities as paramount, other social considerations from the secular world recede in importance: rank, opulence of dress, affluence, concerns with social status, personal or political ambition, forms of secular elitism. All of these things are considered the conceits of godless people, sandcastles at the edge of a rising tide of mortality. The Baptist world is one where friends are called by sibling terms; all of God's children are equal as spiritual siblings. But no relationship is more important than an individual's

2. Turner stressed the egalitarianism of ritual communities in a set of contrasts between liminality and status systems. Some of the properties of liminality are homogeneity, equality, anonymity, absence of poverty, reduction of all to the same status level, sexual continence, abolition of rank, humility, disregard for personal appearance, unselfishness, total obedience to the prophet or leader, sacred instruction, the maximization of religious, as opposed to secular, attitudes and behavior, simplicity of speech and manners, acceptance of pain and suffering (1969: 92–93). This list of traits describes the Baptists' collective sense of themselves rather well.

relationship to Jesus. Salvation can separate spouses from each other, parents from children, and siblings from one another. Baptists see the purpose of their lives as twofold: to "grow in Christ," that is, to practice perfect subjugation of personal will to the will of God; and to live a life of perfect "witness" so that non-Baptists may be brought into the congregation and the "family of Christ."

The Baptists' egalitarianism distinguishes it, in Baptists' eyes, from the community around it. The Baptists see egalitarianism, in practice, as the result of a symbolic negation of status markers. Acceptance of Christ effaces the salience of other distinctions among people. Wealth, education, occupational status, and so on are not undesirable or unacceptable in themselves, but they have no relevance in the church community. Thus egalitarianism does not eliminate differences in material wealth or prestige among church members; it transforms their meaning. Egalitarianism is also conceptualized in terms of power: no believer should judge another, since Jesus is the sole author of judgments. Baptist egalitarianism, then, equalizes all believers beneath Jesus and strips self-interest of any positive and legitimate meaning. These two features constrain individuals severely when they are confronted with adverse relationships, that is, potential dispute situations, since they add up to a proscription of adversarial remedial action of any kind (see Greenhouse 1982b).

A consequence of egalitarianism is that conflict cannot be overtly expressed for several reasons. First, because Jesus is presumed to have everyone's interest in mind in his plan, untoward events should not be questioned but should be taken as objects of reflection and thresholds of spiritual development. Second, since Jesus has everyone in mind, pressing one's own interests in the form of a claim or expression of anger is superfluous. These two reasons constitute important checks on individuals' much-felt impulses to express themselves in conflict situations, and the verse from Romans, "Avenge not yourselves . . . I will repay, saith the Lord (13:19)," is perhaps quoted more often than any other. It is important to note that Hopewell's Baptists have not eradicated their feelings of anger or overt conflict but that a fundamental aspect of their experience with their faith in Jesus is to refuse to act on those feelings. To accept Jesus is to accept the logic of the ideology that makes conflict among humans unnecessary in an absolute sense.

It is important to note that this concept of conflict precludes disputing in any forum, private or public. The result of this logic does not distinguish Hopewell Baptists from other Americans. In fact, most Americans do not or prefer not to litigate their differences (Baumgartner 1980, Curran and Spalding 1974, Merry 1982, Tomasic and Feeley 1982). Even more strikingly, Americans seem to prefer very strongly that *others* refrain from court use. Indeed, litigiousness is widely interpreted by Americans as a negatively valued sign of personal or group identity (Engel 1984). Importantly, local Baptists are not *proscribed* from using the courts any more than are Americans elsewhere. That they do not use them does not, in itself, warrant explanation. What does distinguish this community is the cultural logic with which the members account for their preferences—a cultural logic that links Jesus, the futility of disputing, and the inevitability of ultimate redress. The Baptists do indeed have a conception of conflict; it is not oriented around remedies but around a person's spiritual state. As we saw in the first narrative in Chapter 1, questions of remedy are resorbed into questions of salvation. The woman in that case was considering divorce: if her husband had been Baptist, the divorce would have been only temporary, since all Christians are to be reunited forever in heaven. Since he was not a Baptist, divorce was premature, because he would spend eternity in hell, in this woman's view.

## Resolving Conflict without Disputes

Baptists do find themselves in overt conflict situations and with inner feelings of conflict, and they draw on a number of effective (or at least satisfactory) responses. Baptists' remedies are verbal: narratives and gossip, joking, dueling with scripture, and prayer.

The efficacy of narratives as conflict resolution hinges on a number of premises about the teller, the listener, and their shared social context. First, narratives are predicated on gossip, which is in turn based on observation: this gives the episode of conflict or tension a collective base beyond whatever personal animosity exists. Knowledge of an offense implies one or more absent witnesses. Second, the listener is assumed to be receptive and sensitive to the message of the narrative; for prospects, one's ability to learn the rules through such subtle measures is almost a test of spiritual

maturity. Third, narratives usually have one of two contexts: verbal
or other offenses (by direct statement, by neglect, by a favor denied, and so on) or postures of participation (for example, inadequate church service attendance). Generally, sins of commission
are presented as individual failings; sins of omission are phrased in
terms of having failed the group as a whole. Among church members, narratives may be loosely but comfortably included under the
general meaning of witnessing, and their instrumentalities as remedies are vague enough to be inconspicuous.

I was often the target of narratives during my thirteen months'
residence in the town, both because I was considered a prospect
(see Introduction) and because of my unusual status as an anthropologist. That status was unusual but not unprecedented, since
my visit had been coincidentally preceded by that of an archaeologist whose failure to complete his report disappointed the local
historical society. Thus in addition to hearing many tales of salvation, damnation, and the dangers of social isolation, I heard many
accounts of the scholar whose failure (in the eyes of some) had cost
him local cooperation. I learned to register appropriate responses
that were equally indirect, in omitting any first-person reference.

Narratives are always in the first or the third person: "Something
happened to me once" or "I know someone who . . ." There is only
the most oblique connection for the listener to draw to his or her
own situation; the teller does not make it for the listener in the
context of the narrative. Second, narratives stress the theme of
relationships to the group. Third, narratives are not emphasized in
conversation. No one says, "Let me tell you a story you may be
interested in"; the narrative is simply blended into the course of
everyday speech. Scripture is also used in this way: verses are
recited not only *in* conversation but *as* conversation.

Such narratives have three functions that are related to conflict
and conflict resolution. First, the teller gives the listener an opportunity to hear how other people are talked about or, at least, to hear
the opinions of the teller and the teller's group about a specific type
or behavior (or about a person, if behavior toward that person is
crucial to the group's dynamics). Conversely, the narratives give
the listener a chance to respond to an abstract situation instead of
having to react to a concrete one that might be more threatening.
In other words, it is a way of "testing the waters": if the listener's

response to a tale of someone else's faults is: "Well, and what was wrong with that?" he or she risks marginalization (more below). On the other hand, an appropriate response is an indication that the listener is receptive and sensitive and has the correct orientation to the group. The third function has to do more particularly with the grievance at the heart of the tale. Without directly confronting the listener, the teller affords the person an opportunity to recognize and even atone for his or her failing. This creates the appearance of the offender's having recognized his or her faults and of taking the initiative in correcting them, thus reiterating the person's identification with the group. Both teller and listener can achieve the results of a more direct confrontation without the costs: an ordinary conversation among equals potentially adjusts their relationship (by adjusting the offender's performance of his or her role) without any obvious application of authority or direct references to norms. In such situations there can be no demands or expressions of apology or compensation.

Extensive recourse to narratives gives ordinary conversation, and particularly gossip, a potent ambiguity. Since any bit of social information might be allegory, for the listener to apply personally, the overall impact of interaction with others can amount to considerable social pressure. Apparently, some people are much more often narrators, and others are much more often listeners. One such listener was a teenager, Mack, who was considered a maverick by his peers, although he was also well liked. He was friendly and fun loving and therefore popular, but his being a relative newcomer to the church and his "different" background—he was a factory worker's son—made his mildly rough language and his good-humored pranks subjects of gossip and some negative speculation. Although Mack generally bore this with overt equanimity, his easy manner belied what he acknowledged to be great tension and insecurity both around his peers and adults. He said that he thought he was judged more harshly than other young men and finally said to me with some bitterness, "These people call themselves Christians, but I'm more Christian than they are, because at least I don't talk down people's backs all the time saying bad things about them. Well, I guess we'll find out in the end who's Christian and who isn't." "Talking down people's backs" was his phrase for the narratives that made his life so miserable occasionally; indeed, for a

[112]

sensitive person, every conversation can be filled with warnings and censure, even if no disapproving word is ever uttered directly. Ervin-Tripp (1976: 138–140) suggested that such "hints" are effective because they refer to a normative system shared by listener and teller. Even though their normative reference is implicit, their indirectness is substantially directive. One element in Mack's conversion as a born-again may have been the desire to escape from the judgment of his peers and to replace it—or at least to challenge it—with the egalitarian ethic of the church, but at the time I knew him, he was still uncertain about whether the church could offer him the social acceptance he felt he deserved. Later, his friends told me that he had "improved" and had become more "mature"; apparently, he was more a part of the group than he had been earlier.

Mack resented the narratives by which he felt so constrained, but he apparently learned to respond to them appropriately. Other people simply cannot. One elderly and childless widower, involved in a protracted dispute with his family over an inheritance matter, drew the line at litigating but nevertheless attended law school at night so that he could operate more effectively on his own. He said that he knew that active pursuit of his own interests was wrong but felt that he had no choice. He said that he is "God fearing," as his grandparents had taught him to be, but that "if you turn the other cheek, you only let yourself be exploited by people with dollar signs in their eyes." In the same context, he said that he knew he was a subject of gossip: "I would like to be a gentleman, and I try to be a gentleman, but I'm not going to be a gentleman if it means giving up what's mine."

Joking and dueling with scripture are less formal but more patterned than the narratives I have just described. The implicit idiom of gossip and narratives is the group, but joking defines a smaller social field, usually the two participants. Joking means trading mild insults and challenges and occurs exclusively among insiders: relationships between prospects and believers are too fragile to be subjected to the vigorous buffeting a joking session can become. I saw joking primarily between teenagers but also between adults, in a milder, less personal, and more abbreviated form. Dueling with scripture is a form of joking in that passages from both Testaments are applied to everyday situations, almost hyperbolically to an outsider's ear. The following brief example started in a good-natured

[113]

argument between two people over whether one of them had acted properly in speaking to a third about not attending Sunday school more regularly: One was told: "Judge not lest you yourself be judged." He replied: "If I see my brother wander from the way and I do not help him, am I truly a Christian?"

This kind of dueling has several interesting features. First, in arguments over spiritual matters, it allows for adversarial debate without abandoning the sacred and sacrilizing mode of speech— scriptural reference. Second, since the Bible is usually quoted only in the context of prayer, arguing with passages from the scriptures minimizes the conflictual content of the debate. Third, both sides can claim to be right since no part of the Bible is wrong, and neither side has to face the embarrassment of winning or losing the question under discussion. Fourth, there is no possibility of escalation, since going from the biblical mode to a more secular mode of speech would appear sacriligious. Fifth, since the Bible, and not an individual's opinion, is being asserted, both sides save face; as with narratives, here, too, the speakers avoid the appearance of directly and personally criticizing each other, and it is important that they do so. Quoting passages from the Koran cloaks reprimands in a similar way among Arabic speakers (Nader 1968: 280).

Both narratives and dueling with scripture share some important features that relate to the fundamental nature of the church community. First, they obviate the need for open expression of conflict; yet to a listener who is sensitive and receptive, they are unambiguous enough to be effective. Second, they occur only within the boundaries of the group, not across them. Third, they are self-contained; they contain no mechanism for escalation or extension of conflicts beyond the church community. They can operate *only* in the inclusive social setting of the church.[3] (Narratives and gossip as social control do occur outside the church community in this town, although along different themes.) Finally, they are remedies that are consistent with the structural consequences of their egalitarianism, which, as we have seen, sets early limits on personal initiatives and self-expressions in conflict situations.

3. Hill said of southerners in general: "One adaptive mechanism of Southern culture is indirectiveness. Southerners generally avoid direct confrontations" (1977: 313). Hopewell Baptists give a particular meaning to this preference.

People measure their own inner strength and their spiritual maturity by their ability to transcend conflict. They succeed to varying degrees. Although I found no names that I could recognize as Baptist on the court dockets for the past ten years, that evidence is too ambiguous to be taken alone as proof that Baptist ideology precludes litigation. In fact, it probably does not preclude disputes but offers believers the strong suggestion that such disputes are merely conceits and that the only truly important issue is the conflict between the Holy Spirit and an unsaved person. Later, I argue that the Baptist concept of conflict is not adversarial in the same sense that disputes are: ideally, a Baptist construes offenses by others not as interpersonal conflict but as a sign of that person's spiritual defects. If one feels anger at those offenses, it is not an anger that calls for action but rather calls for prayer for oneself and others to be spared becoming victims to the offender's lack of grace and for the offender to find renewed salvation.

What happens to conflict *across* the boundary between the sacred community and the secular community that surrounds it? The verbal strategies current among insiders have the potential to reduce conflict and for anticipating conflict that would not apply across the boundary between Baptists and nonbelievers, since nonbelievers do not share the same ideological concerns. Narratives, or dueling with passages from the scripture, are ineffective between parties who do not share the same understanding of their capacity to transmit messages.

On the other hand, although Baptists can control the appearance of anger, they cannot control external events, such as when they feel cheated in a transaction, or when other drivers damage their cars, or when they are otherwise put in the position of being victims. Even in justiciable cases, conflict across this line simply dissolves. Auto accidents, incidents of violence, and debt are explained as simply being an example of "God's will." The rationalizations of nonaction are also explained by Baptists in terms of the wider ideological reference point of the group. By refusing to engage in open dispute, church members reaffirm the power of their own faith and simultaneously believe they are witnessing to the potential defendant.

Along with the effect of keeping some cases out of court that might otherwise end up there, and maintaining the social boundary *around* the church group, this pattern of behavior has the effect of reiterating the Baptists' conception of the social order within their ideological community and outside it, simultaneously. The ability of the local Baptists to define conflict out of their existence—as, in their own terms, they must—permits them to live (again, in their phrase) "in the world but not of it." More generally, the church community provides both the demand and the rationale for a substitution of meanings that makes ordinary secular life possible for this group of believers, even while they claim to reject its premises.

Like many other people, this group of Baptists places high value on harmonious relationships and, like other groups, develops strategies for resolving conflicts that are effective in certain sociocultural contexts and within the particular limitations of their beliefs. The manipulation of verbal exchanges allows local Baptists to obviate what would be a fundamental contradiction to their perception of the secular and religious order in which they participate. The crucial element is adversarial conflict. The temptation to pursue one's own ends is continual—indeed, a premise—in modern society. If Baptists preclude disputes, it is not because they cannot conceive of self-interested remedial action but because they *can*, all too well. The effort of refraining from adversarial conflict forms the reservoir that feeds the transformation of meaning so crucial to their social relationships. In other terms, their refusal to dispute makes Christianity both important and possible for believers.[4]

Informal resolution of conflict has received a great deal of attention in the anthropological literature (for synoptic reviews, see Collier 1975, Moore 1970a, Nader 1965, and Snyder 1981). In general, anthropologists have found that although the availability and significance of specific dispute resolution procedures vary cross-culturally, there is a positive relationship between disputants' efforts to preserve their relationships with each other and their attempts to minimize the confrontative aspects of their interaction (for one formulation of this idea, see Black 1976: 40–48). Koch, Altorki, Arno, and Hickson (1977) suggested that where these social incentives are

---

4. Yngvesson's (1979) report of "nonaction" among Atlantic coastal villagers offers an interesting parallel case. Villagers have different normative standards for insiders and outsiders; an offense potentially leads to an individual's reclassification. The difference between the two cases is that for the villagers, nonaction is a stage of a dispute; for Baptists, disputes are not a part of conflict resolution.

particularly high, disputes are obviated by formal systems of apology. Although it may truncate a dispute, an apology stands out as a tacit acknowledgment of the adversarial relationship behind the dispute; thus among Baptists, apology is not a primary mode of dealing with conflict. The absence of apology underscores the refusal to concede any adversarial element in relationships. Furthermore, the strong social incentives to minimize conflict compel the further step of redefining conflict as some other sort of relationship—counseling, witnessing, joking, friendship—in order to eliminate the adversarial element. This situation suggests that where neither avoidance nor confrontation is feasible, a structural alternative to disputing is brotherhood. Brotherhood, as it is defined in the strictly antiauthoritarian, egalitarian terms the Baptists express, permits a level of interest and a kind of intervention in others' affairs: the qualification is that the referents of censure be extremely implicit and collective. Such censure is patterned in such a way that it can be recognizable by the church community as attempts to "help" another individual improve his or her spiritual life. Such efforts are never classified as sanctions, except occasionally by their targets—Mack and the widower mentioned above, for example, but rather as counseling, help, or support.

It is not only conflict resolution that is redefined by Hopewell's Baptists; conflict itself is redefined and relocated. The very possibility of conflict within the church community is moot in its own terms, since the order of the church reflects God's plan and so contains no contradictions. Even among the saved, then, offensive behavior is presumed to derive from a spiritual defect and is tolerated only within limits, for example, if the offender is responsive to narratives and seems anxious to remain close to the group. Others are selectively avoided, although I did not know any cases of avoidance personally. All conflict is said to flow from the self-interest of non-Baptists; thus the two important experiences associated with belief—absence of conflict and resistance to materialism—become linked. Since all conflict is said to come from non-Baptists, conflict is also equated with non-Baptists, and non-Baptists are said to be avoided partly because one can expect trouble from them. Furthermore, it is known that non-Baptists have none of the spiritual faith that would prevent them from going to great lengths in their own interest. Because non-Baptists do not belong to the community of

God, Baptists believe them to be dangerous and corrupting (see Greenhouse 1982a: 63).

### Resolving Conflict without Rules

The consequences of this system of belief is that Baptists do not conceptualize or discuss conflict in terms of cases or rules but in terms of salvation. Cases and the adversary model of conflict are entirely extraneous to this idea. The difference between harmony and conflict is not one between the sanctity and violation of rules and their lapse, or even the Bible's exhortations, but simply the difference between salvation and damnation.[5] Any mode of processing a dispute that involved a remedy—and none of the techniques discussed above does—would be beside the point. The only valid remedy, in the Baptists' eyes, is salvation; the only valid sanction, damnation (Greenhouse 1982a: 63).

The fact that Baptists claim to be literal Bible readers and take their daily direction from Jesus does not contradict this last point that their concept of conflict does not entail a concept of rules. Although it is true that Baptists consider it crucial to be in touch with God, it is not to take his orders but rather to cultivate in themselves a sensitivity and openness to his design for the world. This design is in no sense a legal code but rather a system of knowledge. The logic goes something like this: I am in the world, and God created and continues to create in the world; if I am to act properly, I can do so only to the extent that I understand the world, that is, God's design for the world. Since I cannot fully understand God's plan, I must accept it on faith. Correct behavior, then, is not correct in reference to rules but correct in reference to a system of facts and reasons, which my faith makes available to me. Morality therefore exists in reference to knowledge and faith, not to some presumed code of conduct.

5. Hopewell's Baptists are by no means unique in their use of conflict as an element in the semiotics of their social identity. Engel (1984) pointed to a similar construction in a locale he called Sander County. There, the issue is not cast as one of religious doctrine but of "insiders'" concerns about newcomers. Insiders present newcomers' alleged (and misperceived) litigiousness as the source and proof of their marginal status in the community. For a somewhat parallel case, see Todd (1978) on "litigious marginals" in Bavaria. For a general discussion of American concerns with litigiousness, see Galanter (1983).

I have elaborated this point because it is important to understand that the Baptists' rejection of the ways of life they call "unchristian" is not over the assumption that these others live by different rules; it is not a legalist prejudice. Rather, they assume that the others do not accept God's plan and, therefore, make innumerable mistakes of judgment. Importantly, it is not that non-Baptists cannot *understand* the divine plan but that they *choose* not to be open to it (after all, the Holy Spirit works on everyone, and God works through everyone). Baptists consider themselves an elect, but they add that they elect themselves; although salvation is a privilege, they do not reach the point of salvation by means of any privilege. It is on their own initiative that they open themselves to God, and this equality of access is an important element in witnessing their faith. All people are perfectly eligible to be saved, if only they would choose to be saved. More would choose Jesus, Baptists say, if only they were less selfish. This is the inverse of the reasoning behind the comments that Baptists sometimes make in reference to a non-Baptist whose conversion they especially seek: "He's practically a Christian already," or "He's already a Christian; he just doesn't know it yet." Such people are deemed ripe prospects, who lack only the name for their understanding, Christianity, and an encounter with its source, Jesus.

In part, the Baptists' lack of concern with rules for behavior helps explain their lack of concern with establishing accountability when things go wrong or, perhaps, vice versa. Their only accountability, they would say, is to Jesus, and he expects them only to do their best. Jesus is said to know every person's potential. Thus all individuals must decide what their relationship to their faith will be and must choose their own measure of spiritual maturity (see next section for a discussion of these two problems). This is an important element in the Baptists' belief that Jesus accepts them as they are (the popular hymn of invitation is "Come as you are"). It is also an important piece of their philosophical framework that allows them to tolerate diversity while claiming that the world rests on absolutes. Their epistemology demands that complete knowledge of the universe be denied them, and this theme is sounded again and again in sermons, conversation, counseling, and personal reflection. The salience of conflict within the Baptist community disappears in the knowledge that all human knowledge is incomplete.

The relocation of conflict to an equation with the unsaved gives Baptists their understanding of the social organization of their community beyond the church. Simply put, the system of knowledge that belongs to Jesus and that obviates conflict defines Baptists. Its absence defines the other, non-Baptist "world." The boundary that divides Baptists from others, then, is defined by the presence of conflict. Just as Hopewell Baptists experience their salvation in part by transcending conflict, they experience the secular world as conflict that they must transcend. The unsaved are presumed to live in perpetual conflict and inner unrest.

The Baptist theory of conflict entails a few further distinctions beyond the crucial one that identifies the domain of conflict as coterminous with the domain of the unsaved. First, all conflict is believed to result from self-interest; the ethnographic discussion above already suggests this point. In Chapter 2, we saw that Baptists are ambivalent about capital, although not capitalism. Importantly, material things are not devalued in themselves but as markers of personal status. Indeed, in the earliest days of the Baptist order in Hopewell County, materialism was a concern only to the extent that young people might wish to display their fashions inappropriately or to the extent that money that might be used for good works was squandered self-indulgently. But the records do not show the negative sentiment regarding the seductions of money and material things to be nearly the collective preoccupation that it is today. Since Baptists today are certainly active participants in the capitalist economy, they are continually faced with contradictions between their daily lives and their antimaterialist ethic. They represent these contradictions as "temptations" and resolve them with prayer. In the case of unsaved, Baptists are skeptical that anyone can resist temptation without Jesus' help and so mark materialism as their major sin.

Second, the phenomenon that Baptists seem to have in mind when they refer to conflict is best imagined as a clash of absolute values. Conflict is not a matter of perspective, *chacun à son goût.* Instead, it is as if conflict simply emanates from some people. These poisonous characters are continually scheming to achieve their own ends and to cause gratuitous trouble (and temptation) for others. Such people should be avoided, since Baptists consider themselves innocents in comparison to those whose lives are continual rehearsals in subtlety and guile. Conflict thus becomes an attribute of a person and only indirectly an aspect of a relationship. Conflict and harmony reflect a person's essential self in that one's nature is one or the other. To all intents and purposes, the two categories are mutually exclusive.

These characterizations of conflict emerge not only as extensions of the logic that locates conflict among the unsaved but, more concretely, in people's discussions of temperament, character, and personal development. Although I did not encounter the sorts of family reputations that Batteau (1982a) did, individuals do have strong reputations that sometimes color the way a family is represented in the community. One family is known as "good, honest people"; their small business has served the community for several generations. Others are known as "eccentrics" or "rebels." Individuals' experience of their own salvation is sometimes expressed in terms of the change it represents in their character: "Jesus really turned me around" and "I only had a mind for sin until I took Jesus into my life" are two such comments. Although a person cannot be thoroughly "bad"—for the premise is that Jesus dwells in everyone—people are nevertheless sometimes characterized that way. "He turned out good" or "bad" is a frequent reference.

Socialization is credited with molding a person's character only very indirectly and, even then, in a way that is largely formulaic. Stern or strict parents are said to benefit a child, and I observed that at least some parents find truth in the saying "Spare the rod and spoil the child." Children are more often punished for misconduct by direct verbal censure or some other sanction (especially confinement to their bedrooms for a specific time, usually an hour or two or an afternoon). These corrective measures are believed to benefit the child, primarily instilling a sense of respect for parental authority. But respect for authority, although it might contribute to order in the home, does not in itself make a child "good." This is more a matter of having a "sweet" or "angelic" nature or of general "friendliness." That good character is conceptualized primarily in terms of social disposition suggests yet another way in which Baptists believe their community to be held together without rules or applications of human authority beyond the family. A successful community is comprised of people with a natural affinity for one another and for good. Where affinity and good are lacking, the deficit is temporary if the individual can accept Jesus. These things come with salvation.

Thus the Baptist theory of conflict appears to consist of three elements: an interpretation of conflict that endows it with sacred meaning, specifically, the rejection of God; a mapping of conflict onto the local social organization, which is then understood in those terms; and a characterization of conflict as deriving from a person's immanent qualities. At no point in the local theory are rules, disputes, sanctions, adversarial relations, or third parties at all emergent. As we have seen, Baptists resolve whatever feelings of conflict they have by means of prayer or through minor social adjustments accomplished verbally. Furthermore, focusing for the moment on the Baptists' refusal to enter into disputes, this preference should not be understood first or only as an affirmative function of their close social ties, that is, in terms of relational distance, but should be understood in terms of the consequences of their theoretical rejection of all forms of human authority.

## Conflict, Value, and Meaning

The Baptists' theory of conflict has been examined as a dual problem; as posing particular difficulties in accomplishing even minor social adjustments and as a central image in their understanding of the local society beyond their church. Conflict emerges not only as the major idiom in terms of which (by negation) Baptists claim to experience the effects of salvation in their lives; it is also their major marker of social classification in their community. Thus by understanding conflict from the Baptists' perspective, one learns simultaneously—and the simultaneity is key—of their cosmology and their sociology.

In the process by which that sociology acquires particular meanings, the Baptists draw lines around themselves (and, as we have seen, that line is the border of a landscape of conflict) not for the sake of some principle of exclusion; rather, their view of conflict makes clear the schema by which they distribute positive value across their immediate society. Here, we examine the terms in which that valuation is expressed and set in motion across social space; that is, we explore the semiotics of social identity in Hopewell. It is in this context that the heart of the ethnographic problem emerges, and that is the significance of the Baptists' avoidance of conflict and the cultural logic that makes that avoidance not only possible but necessary. This problem leads us to Hopewell's past, but first, why are the actors *these* actors, and what is the significance of their differences?

## The Value of Being Holy

Hopewell's Baptists have a double theory of elites, which is reciprocated in part by other groups in community. Hopewell's Baptists are very clear about what they believe constitutes elite status in the church community, and they are equally clear about what they think their unsaved neighbors value. On one level, these conceptualizations of elite status are extensions of the imagery already discussed: Baptists value spiritual maturity and assume that the unsaved value wealth. But the elaboration of that imagery is particularly interesting, partly because it appears to be acknowledged by non-Baptists and partly because the images themselves include significant incongruities. The next question becomes that of why Baptists and others' conceptions of social value should coincide in the particular way that they do. That is the subject of the next two chapters.

The effect of the Baptists' view of their own lives as both sacred and subject to Judgment Day is twofold. First, ordinary concerns such as wealth, prestige and disputing—all of which the Baptists see as obsessions in the non-Baptist world—are, theoretically, irrelevant because they are earthly concerns, of no permanent importance. Second, because material wealth and other "worldly" concerns are irrelevant, the Baptist community is structured on other principles. As we have seen, scriptural ideas of sacrifice and asceticism reinforce the ethos of antimaterialism in the congregation. Local Baptist egalitarianism is based on the premise that the Word and salvation are available to all and avoid all forms of interaction that suggest secular hierarchy. This idea is resumed shortly.

In Baptists' thinking, the corollary of their own sacred community is a reciprocal conceptualization of the world of the unsaved. Interestingly, Hopewell's Baptists use the word *world* as a euphemism for hell in expletive speech contexts, and indeed, in the local

[123]

terms, the world outside the church is one sort of hell, although there the absence of God is due to rejection by nonbelievers, but in actual hell, God's absence is inherent. The Baptist image of society of the unsaved is reciprocal on several levels, although this is not to imply that the others concur entirely in their self-image. First, Baptists lump all "non-Baptists" together as an undifferentiated community, which they certainly are not by anyone else's standard. Baptists differentiate among Christians and non-Christians and among Christian (non-Baptist) sects only in a limited way for purposes of discussion, for example, of strategies for conversion. For the sake of convenience, I temporarily adopt this usage to describe the Baptists' sense of the social dynamics of Hopewell.

Baptists see non-Baptists as being obsessed with material things—with conspicuous consumption, with status symbols (in the colloquial sense), and with aggression, contention, and self-interest. These characterizations apply less to known individuals than to strangers and to the general category of non-Baptists. Furthermore, non-Baptists are said to be greatly concerned with hierarchy. Baptists perceive secular power in the hands of the unsaved both as an end itself—gratification—and as an instrument of hierarchical machinations. Finally, Baptists see non-Baptists as living lives of pathetic self-delusion, since the pleasures of the flesh and purse are temporary, confined as they are to the earthly, mortal realm. To the Baptists, the only true pleasures are the pleasures of prayer and Christian community, including family life, which is thought to be less satisfying among non-Baptists.

When Baptists refer to the "group" they stylize as non-Baptist, they use a number of other labels that are meant to be synonymous. Primary among them is the reference to "city people," as if urbanity itself were ungodly. Other references are to people who are materially successful, as if Baptists were not. In general, Baptists are presented as insiders, autochthonous, and non-Baptists are sometimes referred to as if they were all outsiders. This is not accurate, since although the Baptist church was the first founded in the county (in 1824), the Methodists founded a church in 1849, well before Hopewell County was officially organized. In any event, the Baptists' imagery of salvation and damnation is strikingly local.

In effect, the Baptist image of the non-Baptist world can be reduced to a paradigm of images that show "the world" to be at once a contingent and independent reality:

> Baptist:non-Baptist
> :: sacred:profane
> :: saved:damned
> :: heaven:hell
> :: spiritualistic:materialistic
> :: rural:urban
> :: egalitarian:elitist
> :: poor:rich
> :: insiders:outsiders

Some of these categories appear to refer to the community's past when it was indeed rural and poor, but it would be a mistake to interpret the images as attempts at historical or sociological description. The paradigm suggests that Baptists see themselves as products of the authentic, that is, rural southern, or local, society; that their society is exclusive and implies special knowledge; that they see themselves as relatively poor or inured to poverty; that their true riches are spiritual; that they are unconcerned with earthly (temporary) status markers; and, as already explained, that they are the community of the saved, destined for eternal life in heaven and a sacred community on earth. The non-Baptists are seen as the opposite category in each case, sometimes erroneously. For example, Hopewell's Baptists no longer live only in the rural areas, nor are they poor—or even relatively poor in comparison to local Methodists and Presbyterians. Furthermore, the paradigm ignores the fact that many of the congregation's members (but not the deacons, who manage the church's secular affairs) are newcomers to Hopewell. The fact that these categories do not match demographic or ethnographic reality very well increases the significance of their durability.

These categories do organize people's social choices to some degree. In their private lives, devout Baptists appear not to seek close relationships with non-Baptists, except under the controlled circumstances of witnessing. The workplace, school, and the myriad settings of daily life (for example, the supermarket) are unavoidable contexts of interaction, but Baptists urge prospects and one another to avoid the temptations of leisure time in Atlanta, as well as inappropriate social forms, such as disputing. These are examples of avoidable contexts of interaction. Baptists are concerned not to give even the *appearance* of worldliness in speech, dress, or life-style. They dress fashionably but not distinctively. Their homes are modern but not "fancy." Decisions are justified in terms of the church, sacred values, a verse of scripture, and so on. Even family relationships are not consistently valued more highly than the Christian community; many members attend church without their families. Even adolescents have spiritual lives independent of their parents; the anxiety among these young people that their parents will be damned and eternally separated from them after death is not uncommon. The Baptists' ideal is that the church be the center and crucible of family life, not that families be divided. In general, though, the Baptists' concept of the non-Baptist world divides them from it, both conceptually and, to a lesser extent, behaviorally, even when the non-Baptist world begins at home.

The conceptual structure of the Baptist community can now be examined more specifically in relation to the community's organization. The church is organized by two egalitarian principles. One is the age-grade. All church activities—training union and Sunday school—except worship are roughly organized into peer groups. The college-age group is the transitional category, since members remain there until they marry. It is also the group for the few divorced members (but, significantly, not widows or widowers).[6] The groups are not segregated by sex, although there are separate activities for the Sisterhood (married women) and Brotherhood (married men) of the church, which are not age-graded. As we have seen, age tends to structure friendships outside the church as well.

Older church members use sibling terms (plus surnames) as terms of address: all men are "brother"; all women are "sister" except for mothers and mothers-in-law. "Father" is reserved for

6. An indication of the ideal relationship between biological and spiritual age is the differential spiritual status accorded persons who have divorced and persons who are widowed. Divorced people are "demoted" to the singles group; widows and widowers remain with the adults. Divorce, being an act of will, reflects a loss of spiritual maturity because of its active remedial aspect (all vengeance belongs to God, according to scripture). Widowhood, being an act of God, potentially increases spiritual maturity.

God; the preacher is called "brother." Younger church members do not follow this traditional usage, but the use of kin terms reiterates the widely shared idea that church members are children of God and equal in their sibling status.

The other principle that structures the church is the concept of spiritual maturity, for which age-grading provides the vocabulary but not the substance. The new convert to Baptist Christianity, or the Baptist who has renewed his conversion, is referred to as a "born-again Christian." The allusion is felicitous, since the new Christian's faith is believed to be fragile and vulnerable to destruction, as is the life of a new-born infant, but—like a baby's birth—full of potential. As a new Christian experiences his or her faith through the communal life of the church, the individual's commitment is presumed to strengthen. Spiritual strength enables individuals to resist the temptations of the world: quarreling, lying, materialism, promiscuity, and so on. Baptists do not drink alcohol, which is seen as a particularly strong temptation to young people. True spiritual maturity is not a function of age but of spiritual age, that is, experience in faith, experience in turning away from "the world" as it is described in the paradigm above and in the next section. A young person may be more spiritually mature than his or her parents. This theme is sounded when a young person has died. Ideally, perhaps, the structural principle of spiritual maturity parallels the organizational principle of age, but in fact they cross-cut. Importantly, spiritual maturity does not depend on ritual knowledge, either, since the Baptist church in Hopewell involves minimal ritual of an esoteric sort.

In their own terms, the Hopewell Baptists' concept of elite status stems directly from the two principles of age and spirituality, by combining them. Believers are conscious of their own growing maturity, or of their struggle for maturity, and they are also interested in the spiritual struggles of others. Spirituality is a subject of prayer and conversation. Most criteria of spirituality are in-dwelling; a perfect life of good witness, a practiced serenity derived from devotion, perfection in moral and material charity, and persuasiveness of counsel. Each of these characteristics assumes and subsumes a thorough knowledge of scripture and insightful, creative interpretation. In the affairs of the world, the church's elite are not so much withdrawn as untroubled, untempted. Because of this last criterion, the concept of elite status also implies advanced or advancing age: only an older person can have experienced all of the temptations of the world and all of its trials.

That the Baptist concept of elites should entail the dual aspects of spiritual experience *and* worldly experience is particularly significant. It implies that it is not the world itself that is dangerous or polluting but only the relationship between the world and a spiritually unformed Christian. In symbolic terms, the Baptist faith purifies the world's pollution by purifying *individuals,* by rendering individuals so spiritually strong that they cannot be stained. The triumph of maturity is the conquest of pollution through pure spirituality, but importantly, the conquest is by perfect spiritual resistance on the part of the Christian. Thus the Baptists' quest to purify the world in advance of Judgment Day is through individual, inner struggle, *not* through any attempts to control or reform the secular society. To my knowledge, Baptists in Hopewell never speak in terms of "taking over" the instruments of the material world and converting them to spiritual uses. This group vehemently rejects the secular political activity of Christian groups on these grounds. Their rejection of participation in public institutions is paradigmatic, not substantive.

In the Baptist view, as long as the world exists, a Baptist elite will exist in relation to it within the church community. When the world ceases to exist after Judgment, so will the elite. The concept of elite status has no relevance beyond the world: the elite person is not "more saved" than the rest of the congregation. Salvation cannot be qualified. Heaven is not compartmentalized according to access to Jesus. The elite have no special reward beyond the benefits that all Christians are said to derive from their faith; the elite simply appreciate them more fully. To put this another way, elite status is contingent on the possibility of sin.

Because the Baptist concept of elite status is entirely in abstract terms, there exists no coherent group that corresponds to it. There is no action-set or quasi group that corresponds to the criteria discussed above. Baptists might not even agree on the question of which individuals are the most mature in their spirituality, but then again, the group as a whole is never relevant simultaneously. The question is relevant as a practical matter only under very narrow circumstances, for example, seeking advice. Then, the elite are

[128]

visible singly and in relative terms: they are always older and most often women. (Men who work are continually engaged with the world and have a more difficult time shedding it inwardly.) In general, however, the Baptists' elite does not have sociological functions as a group.

They do not manage the church's secular affairs, as I have said: that business is in the hands of the deacons. They do not administer the church's sacred affairs; that is the preacher's role. They are heavily involved in the church's "extracurricular" activities—teaching Sunday school, coordinating age-group events in the evenings when services are not held, arranging sporting events for young men, and conducting the daily nursery school—but service to the church is not reserved for the spiritually mature. Such service is itself considered redeeming and maturing.

The function of the elite is conceptual and is particularly important in the continual dialectics of the quest for a sacred life in a secular world. Hopewell's Baptists are very much in the world, and the sacred life is one of resistance, not withdrawal. They are indistinguishable from non-Baptists on every visible dimension: they include no disproportion of poor, unemployed, or disadvantaged. Their ranch houses and split levels are as well kept and well furnished as the non-Baptists', and their jobs are just as high paying. Baptist men participate in exactly the same business world as the non-Baptist men, and their economic constraints are identical. The difference is in the way in which Baptists understand and value their material situation.

In this suburb whose population is largely upwardly mobile financially, the pull of material benefits and of advancement poses Baptists with a contradiction. In the contest between their spirituality and their materialism, Baptists tend to deny any great importance to material aspect of their success. Promotion, for example, is discussed not so much in terms of reward for merit as a God-given opportunity for greater service through personal responsibility. Education is seen in terms of training for service, not for personal satisfaction or for the instrumentalities of a higher degree in the job market. Wealth is seen as an opportunity for tithing and charity, not as an end in itself. Baptists in Hopewell are successful in the secular world, and although they see success in Christian terms, they also see the temptations to take credit for success in personal terms. Thus the invitation of Christ through the gospel and through the community of the church is continually relevant even to devout Christians, and it must be continually renewed because the world persistently beckons with its rival order.

In this context, the Baptists' concept of the spiritually mature elite is at one end of a symbolic spectrum that is in contrast, at the other end, to the material world in which they are involved daily. The spiritually mature are presumed able to resolve the inner conflict that derives from the conjunction of the sacred and the profane and to live lives of perfect witness in a world of stress and distraction. It is not important that there is no one identifiable group of people to match the description of the mature Christian, because the local concept of Baptist Christianity is not one that inheres in the institutional or sociological order. It has nothing to accomplish there. Instead, it inheres in the Baptists' understanding of their own faith. The idea of mature spirituality is a standard by which Baptists can measure the effect of their participation in the secular world on their own spirituality and assess their own spirituality in relation to that of others.

Their concept of elite status further allows Hopewell's Baptists to compartmentalize the secular world from their sacred Christian community. Although the settings of the workplace and the city produce ideological contradictions, the concept of the elite facilitates their dissociation from life within the church. The church offers believers a total identity, and the terms from the paradigm described above are the images with which Baptists conceptualize their contingent identity (contingent in relation to their own elite and the secular world). Their image of themselves as rural, for example, is important because it symbolically opposes urban life. Its origin may have been Hopewell's agrarian past, but now it encodes "not city." Thus although Baptists work in the same settings as non-Baptists, their rural self-image permits them to dissociate their own identities from the urban workplace. They think of themselves not so much as farmers as of being inwardly uninvolved with the city and its corruptions. Importantly, the rural image is not a literal but a sacred image.

Compartmentalization has two principal effects in addition to, or as a consequence of, the Baptists' symbolic dissociation from worldly images: First, as we have seen, Baptists expect conflict from nonbelievers, partly because their image of non-Baptists is of amoral, quasi-socialized beings but also because they realize that non-Baptists have different priorities and therefore make different choices. When conflict does occur, Baptists respond only by reaffirming their negative image of the secular world. Conflict does not provoke substantive response. Compartmentalization thus enables Baptists to tolerate high levels of conflict in the outside world.

The second effect of compartmentalization is in the Baptists' response to change. Although the Baptists see themselves as oases in the urban desert, the city imposes itself on Hopewell residents, Baptists or not, in many ways. Except for a few square blocks in the center of town that were recently designated a national historical district, the town is vastly changed from even a few years ago. Its population has increased many times since 1960. In the early 1960s children could walk barefoot on a dirt road alongside grazing cows, under a canopy of pecan trees, on what is now a six-lane neon strip feeding into the national highway system. The changes have also brought in thousands of newcomers and, simultaneously, acres of new subdivisions and miles of new streets, dividing the old Hopewell neighborhoods and consuming former farmlands. The Baptists, too, live in the new subdivisions, and their community can tolerate dispersal because their community is not territorial. The church has grown as newcomers join, but the new arrivals and converts do not soften the boundary between Baptists and non-Baptists by challenging its imagery. City people who join the church simply move from one side of the paradigm to the other. The transformation of the physical face of Hopewell has not placed any external stress on Baptists particularly. The social nexus in which Baptists live and find meaning has not been altered by the process of urbanization because it does not depend on a specific sociological or institutional arrangement. Baptists perceive and regret the changes to their town, but these regrets are largely aesthetic. Because the Baptists compartmentalize the secular world from their sacred community, the symbolic level on which that community exists is not threatened by these rapid changes at the sociological level. This is one of the points on which non-Baptists can be distinguished most easily from Baptists. As the prime example of these other groups, I take the network of businessmen and professionals from downtown Hopewell. For the sake of convenience, I call both of them "the businessmen."

## The Value of Being Local

The group of people who run the retail establishments along Hopewell's Main Street, who provide services (for example, doctors and lawyers), and who administer the public institutions (for example, judges and clerks) are Hopewell's central business and professional network. There are many other businessmen in Hopewell and in Hopewell County, but they are outside of the network I describe here. Unlike the church members just described, this group is a network, not a community. Their association involves only a partial identity. Their roles as storekeepers or bankers do not constitute a "way of life" but a shared set of partial interests and constraints. They are not Baptists.

The businessmen were once a more tightly knit group than they are today. As late as the 1920s they were all related either by marriage or by sibling and first-cousin relationships. That situation has changed—has *had* to change—owing to the expansion of the Atlanta business sector into the surrounding suburbs. The businessmen had to be able to absorb newcomers or, more accurately, had to be able to accommodate the influx of greater wealth and larger-scale commercial activity by urban newcomers. The local businessmen now include many newcomers. Here is a further differentiating feature between Baptists and the businessmen: while the Baptists' symbolic community has protected them from exogenous changes in their pattern of social relations, the businessmen have responded to change by altering and expanding their patterns of local interaction to include the metropolis and newcomers to Hopewell. This fact has bearing on the local businessmen's concept of elite status.

Since the influx of newcomers, the business network is only partially autochthonous, giving rise to a double "constituency." Janus-like, the businessmen must look both to the city and to Hopewell: to the city for the associations that will expand their credit, furnish their supplies, and tie them into the southern regional markets; and to Hopewell and Hopewell County for their clients and customers, as well as for their social relationships. They consider themselves mediators between the city and Hopewell economically, politically, and socially, and in a very real sense, they are. For the Baptists, liminality is a symbolic concept that imposes particular contradictions on believers that, as we have seen, they resolve by means of their abstract concept of elite status. For the businessmen, their mediational status poses particular problems in the sociological realm, which they resolve with a sociological concept of elite status. These two concepts of elite status are counterparts and form one conceptual whole (see discussion below).

The principal sociological dilemma that the businessmen face is how to resolve their cross-cutting identifications. First, the businessmen must maintain effective business relationships within Hopewell, because of their shared interests. The business sector is too small to risk overt conflict, for example. My research did not include an investigation of the economic ties among businesses, but I know that they do cooperate in noncommercial ventures, for example, in an active Chamber of Commerce dedicated to the expansion of Hopewell County business opportunity, in tourism, in zoning, and in the delivery of social services to the county. These cooperative ties cross-cut the groups of natives and newcomers in the business network who must also be concerned with their wider constituency. The natives, for example, are concerned to cultivate effective ties in Atlanta's business community, for the reasons I have explained. The newcomers, who are predominantly Atlantan, or who move to Hopewell from Atlanta, are concerned to maintain their legitimacy and foster their assimilation in Hopewell. Thus their separate interests foster mutually dependent interrelationships in the wider social sphere beyond their businesses.

There appear to be at least two settings where the integration of the two segments (native and newcomer) is nurtured: the Country Club and the Historical Society. There may be more than two, but in any case, the Methodist and Presbyterian churches do not appear to be as important nexi of interaction as the Baptist church is to Baptists. At the Country Club, facilities include a restaurant, meeting rooms, large banquet facilities, a golf course, and tennis courts. The Country Club enjoys special privileges with the county police, since liquor is served and consumed there in violation of the local law. It is a popular place for private entertaining, business lunches, and family dinners, since until a motel was built in 1975, it was the only local restaurant with what might be called a comfortable atmosphere (the town's other restaurants include fast food and "country food" establishments, which provide service too quick for conversation). The club is a modest and unpretentious place, but its image among some of the town's Baptists is one of a sinful, degrading place (because of the alcohol and dancing), where businessmen "make deals" and women flaunt their finery.

The Historical Society was founded shortly after the first influx of new commercial development and the completion of the interstate that cuts across the county. The Historical Society's general purpose is to discover and preserve the oral, written, and architectural history of the town, and its numerous projects have included the renovation of the train station as a museum, the restoration of an old house as a museum, and the compilation of a book of local genealogies. Each of these tasks required the mobilization of considerable personnel, funds, and services from both Hopewell and Atlanta. Its most active members were the women in the business network: wives of businessmen and the very few women who also held positions on Main Street. Men's functions were primarily to serve as brokers in arranging assistance for the society's projects. Active members were fairly continuously involved, sometimes on a daily basis. Their involvement was intellectual but also deeply emotional; disputes—largely over budgetary priorities—were deeply felt and loyalties intensely expressed.

The Historical Society serves a double function: one is its manifest function of historical preservation and documentation, and the other is its role as a locus for satisfying the cross-cutting and potentially contradictory needs of both the newcomers and the natives. I believe that this second function is at least as important as the first and, furthermore, that this is why both natives and nonnatives are equally enthusiastic and why the group's activities are so vested with emotion. Finally, the fact that the devout Baptists do not participate in the Historical Society's activities, even though their pedigree in Hopewell is just as well established, reflects their awareness of the society's business-related functions, as well as the fact that their voluntary associations do not generally include non-Baptists. In other words, history has the capacity of neutralizing the differences between natives and newcomers but not the differences between the spiritual Baptists and what they see as the materialistic world.

History, through the Historical Society, has a neutralizing effect because both groups desire and allow that it be so. By working for the Historical Society, newcomers show their willingness to participate in and value Hopewell's past and, implicitly, show that they do not desire to transform Hopewell's society or to condescend to it, only to be engaged in it. For their part, the natives welcome the Historical Society for the opportunity it gives them to establish social ties to the urban business and political networks. In broader terms, involvement in the Historical Society gives the newcomers legitimacy in Hopewell and gives the natives access to the city. In other contexts, history separates newcomers from natives, and newcomers never lose their stranger status completely. For example, one of the county judges is considered a newcomer, although his parents moved to Hopewell in 1914.

The businessmen's concept of elite status stems directly from their sociological position as mediators and from the structure of the dilemma (cross-cutting identifications) in which their position places them. Newcomers and natives share the same elite concept, although they relate to it differently. For the newcomers, it is an emblem of contemporary identification with Hopewell; for the natives, it asserts their authenticity and historical precedence. For both groups, the concept of elite status reflects their consciousness of the city as a separate place and of the relativities resulting from that separation. The businessmen's concept of elite status also produces a collection of contrastive symbolic images:

> Hopewell:Atlanta
> :: traditional:nontraditional
> :: conservative:progressive
> :: safe:dangerous
> :: poorer:richer
> :: egalitarian:elitist
> :: rural:urban
> :: insiders:outsiders

The terms of this paradigm reflect the businessmen's shared valuations of their relatively rural situation; for them, too, Hopewell is "rural" *only* in the contingent sense of "not city." Their claim to tradition along with their invocation of their collective, quasi-mythicized, rural past suggests a claim to authentic social structure, as opposed to Atlanta's, which is newer. Businessmen also express the view that the local social structure would have been different had they not developed the county differently. One farming family was generally cited as being "feel-funny" at the reversal in their status, now that farming was no longer important. The businessmen seek and accommodate readily to social change. In some contexts, "authenticity" implies a valuation of southernness over northernness, since Atlanta is known as being a "Yankee city built with Yankee money," in the words of one businessman's wife in Hopewell. Hopewell is not a poor community, although there are fewer opportunities for and signs of conspicuous consumption than in Atlanta. Egalitarianism refers to the local businessmen's mutual assimilation of newcomers and natives or, in other terms, city and country folk. Atlanta society is seen as elitist because it is closed to rural styles and images. Hopewell businessmen portray themselves as conservatives in many domains, from historical to political. Safety and danger refer to physical safety in Hopewell, and although crime, particularly juvenile crime, is not unknown in Hopewell County, it is a physically safe place compared to Atlanta, whose dangers are perhaps exaggerated. Finally, Hopewell's businessmen see themselves as belonging, which, newcomers or natives, they *do* when compared to outsiders. The newcomers "belong" in Hopewell only in this contingent sense, which encodes "not Atlanta." By sharing the paradigm and its implied shared relationship to Atlanta, newcomers and natives achieve the appearance of the unity they seek. Thus the paradigm is not meant to describe empirical reality but, as in the Baptist case, to establish positive, contingent signs of sociological categories that have meaning in the social context of the town. That context, once again, is their mediational position and their reciprocal need to submerge their cross-cutting identifications in convergent interests and shared symbolic associations.

Unlike the Baptists, for whom the concept of elite status did not describe a particular set of people, the businessman's concept necessarily relates to a particular subgroup with a correspondingly significant social role. These are two, and possibly three, families that are powerful in terms of their central positions in very wide friendship and instrumental networks. They are, incidentally, wealthy, but they are not the only wealthy families in town or the wealthiest. Wealth may be a function of elite status; it is not a criterion. Importantly, it is not their wealth that makes them elite but their ability to mobilize urban and local resources very quickly for the sake of the community. Two of the families participate intensively—more than any others—in the Historical Society through their female members. One of these families moved to Hopewell recently from Atlanta: the other was native to Hopewell and neighboring counties. Other families are elite in corresponding degrees, and through them and their associations, the businessmen are able to continue to resolve their structural conflict, both on the sociological level of actual interaction and on the symbolic level in terms of the paradigm above. Hopewell's businessmen are able to respond to their own increasing urbanization and rapid social change without sacrificing their carefully constructed symbolic identity. This identity helps preclude disruptive conflict from dividing newcomers from natives.

## The Value of Being Southern

The question of why the Baptists' and businessmen's concepts of elite status are interrelated is crucial. The Baptists' view of "the world," epitomized by the businessmen, is not reciprocated by them as such, that is, the businessmen do not see themselves as profane and the Baptists as holy. Instead, the businessmen and Baptists seem to see themselves as occupying the same side of the paradigm; they are in a sense competing for the paradigm. How and why should this be true?

We have already seen that concepts of elite status are contingent ones: the Baptists' concept is contingent on the symbolic distinction between the spirituality of the church community and the perceived materialism of the non-Baptists. The businessmen's concept is contingent on their perception of differences between themselves and the Atlantans. In both cases, the position of the symbolizing group is mediational: the Baptists perceive themselves as living in a liminal state, and the businessmen perceive themselves as mediating between the city and Hopewell. Furthermore, these mediational positions pose members of both groups with a specific

[137]

structural conflict that gives rise in the case of the Baptists to ideological contradictions ("Be in the world but not of it") and among businessmen to sociological contradictions (the need to maintain support both in the city and Hopewell). The concept of elite status in both cases resolves the contradictions. Among the Baptists, the elite is defined in spiritual terms, and among businessmen, the elite is defined in sociological terms. Correspondingly, the Baptist concept of elite status does not match a subset of specific individuals, but among the businessmen, it does and must in order to resolve the sociological dilemma in which the businessmen currently find themselves.[7]

It is significant that neither concept of elite status is expressed in especially specific or exclusive terms. For example, the Baptist concept does not entail any arcane ritual knowledge of any kind or a particular type of conversion experience. Similarly, the business concept does not require any particular type of occupation or a particular level of wealth. For Baptists, it is not important that the elite concept be realized sociologically at all in an absolute sense. In the businessmen's case, although it is true that blue-collar workers and poor people are not considered elite, this fact is a product of other factors (for example, network effectiveness), not the result of some absolute criterion. In fact, a comparison of the two paradigms shows them to be essentially the same, except that the Baptists seek the ultimate end of salvation in a sacred community, and businessmen seek the ultimate reward of bilateral community support. Otherwise, the terms of the paradigmatic relationships and the valuations that both groups place on them (the left-hand column) are the same. The reason for the parallels is that the source of the paradigms is neither Baptist theology nor business but something more general associated with other aspects of their shared experience as townspeople.

The Baptists and the businessmen have Hopewell in common, although they relate to the idea of Hopewell differently. They share its history and its changes, although they have had different roles in Hopewell County's urbanization. The valuation of the image of

7. For an elaboration of the idea of concepts of elite status as constituted in the symbolic resolution of social conflict, see Greenhouse 1983.

rural poor, cultural authenticity, and democratic virtue has historical relevance for both groups. The two groups certainly make different use of these images, but both invoke their local past and, in
wider terms, their identity as southerners in their symbolifications
of themselves as Baptists or businessmen. This observation is pur-
sued in the next two chapters.

The social categories that comprise the metaphors of each group
are occasionally and temporarily incorporated by the other. For
Baptists, for example, the conversion of a well-educated, urban
non-Baptist is an especially joyous occasion. Secular elite status
enhances the intensity of the conversion for the individual. It is an
intensity that flashes and quickly fades, as the moment of transition
from the damned to the saved is itself ephemeral. The Baptists
already believe that their faith is inherently compelling, but a conversion from the heart of the "other side" strengthens the conviction of the faithful exactly because it appears to reaffirm that one
can be successful in the world and yet not be ruled by earthly
passions. Similarly, the businessmen seem particularly to value
participation by devoutly religious individuals (not only Baptists).
Importantly, religious fervor is not a criterion for elite status, but it
enhances the value of that individual's association, at least at the
outset, since it suggests a low level of self-interest. The high value
placed on these symbolic crossovers has at least two explanations:
First, since each group is aware of the image that the other holds of
it, crossover is known to have direct meaning (vindication) in the
reciprocal group. A businessmen's conversion "shows the world"
that the Baptist faith is meaningful "even" in the secular world. A
devout person in the Historical Society, for example, shows the
Baptists that not all secular affairs are profane. Second, crossover
implies some sacrifice, which is valued in itself. A businessman is
believed to sacrifice material wealth and personal advancement by
joining the Baptist church (although, as we have seen, he does not
necessarily compromise his success). A devout person involved in
secular affairs risks sacrificing his salvation or at least his serenity.
Such performances receive interested local audiences. Each group's
consciousness of the other "system," so to speak, defines the scope
of their conceptual complementarity.

Each group identifies itself in terms of the symbolic negation *of*

[139]

*the other,* but as the foregoing discussion shows, the negation is a form of inclusion. The two sets of symbols that until now have been discussed separately are more properly merged:[8]

| Baptist:non-Baptist | Hopewell:Atlanta |
|---|---|
| :: sacred:profane | :: traditional:nontraditional |
| :: heaven:hell | :: conservative:progressive |
| :: saved:damned | :: safe:dangerous |
| :: spiritualistic:materialistic | |

:: poor:rich
:: egalitarian:elitist
:: rural:urban
:: insiders:outsiders

This two-headed paradigm shows the way in which both Baptists and businessmen measure their relationship to both their own group and the other simultaneously and in terms of related images. The ultimate functions of the paradigmatic concept of elite status are, from Hopewell's perspective, first, to create a social boundary and, second, to indicate degrees of mutual participation across that boundary. Both groups have an interest in measuring their mutual involvement. The bottom half consists of the symbols that argue the nature of local identity. Baptists and businessmen do not argue with each other's characterization of Hopewell, but they propose two routes to that identity: one through the Baptists' theory of salvation, the other through the businessmen's theory of history. The two concepts of elite status are not two that just happen to coexist in contemporary Hopewell but two that constitute each other out of a single framework. That framework consists of a meaningful imagery that is distinctly southern. In its humility, it is a post–Civil War imagery but one deeply touched with longing for the original South. Local identity is forged with the elements of sectional solidarity.

In examining how social classifications are constituted in Hope-

8. I have not merged the paradigms fully in order to retain the fundamental opposition of the two concepts within a single framework. For example, to head a single column with "Baptist:Business . . ." would suggest that each group's paradigm is internally reciprocal, which, as I have explained above, it is not. The two constitute reciprocals *as whole paradigms.*

well, we see that the new dimension to this analysis is that the specific terms with which Baptists express the value of particular social categories is fundamentally derived from wider issues of historical and regional consciousness. This is the significance of the parallels and divergences between Baptists' symbolic social valuations and that of other groups in town. Thus we are faced with the question of how it is that Baptists and others come to share the very symbols that both groups insist divide them. It should now be apparent that the way in which Baptists conceptualize doctrine is at least in part a function of how they conceptualize their identity vis-à-vis other social groups in the local context: these were the elements of the paradigm that they must compete for against others. For Baptists, the stakes of the competition are continued assurance of salvation; for others, there are other goals, some of which I have suggested in this chapter. The limits to the competition for signs is in the wider semiotics of the South, as it is locally understood. In the next two chapters, we explore the development of the social structure both in the town (Chapter 4) and in the church (Chapter 5), a social structure that people from Hopewell—Baptist or not— today identify as theirs. In both chapters, the theme of conflict remains important, although the meaning of conflict is shown to have undergone some important transformations and revisions during the past century and a half.

# [4]

# Others amongst Ourselves

As the previous chapter shows, the idiom of social ordering in Hopewell is not only religious in character, it is also distinctly local. In this chapter, Hopewell in general—Baptists and others—is the focus and, particularly, the semiotics of local identity that emerged in Chapter 3. The questions this chapter addresses are: what historical experiences provided the images of conflict (for example, between urban and rural) in terms of which Hopewell defines itself? What is the connection between the past and the present in the cultural conception of order evident there? My argument is that where interpersonal avoidance on a small scale allows (and requires) a relationship to transcend its differences, the result is a silenced history. In Hopewell, the past is largely reduced to a few narratives that accomplish their business by providing contexts for sharply contrasting signs. But the reverse is also true: where the past has been silenced, social conflict loses a major set of referents and so is reduced to contrasting signs of personal genres of identity rather than conflicting positions or politics. I approach this double problem by exploring the ways in which contemporary residents of Hopewell discuss the past. My ability to reconstruct the past around these narratives is limited. The purpose of the following discussion is largely ethnographic, specifically, to clarify the meaning of the images in terms of which people in Hopewell portray themselves.

## Consciousness of the Past in Hopewell

People in Hopewell honor the past in two major ways: through historical reenactments and in the collection of personal histories, including genealogies and memorabilia. What people know about the past is another question, one that requires more subtlety. It is not fair to say that people know little or nothing about the origins and development of Hopewell, but they know it in a particular way. For example, they might know in considerable detail what one ancestor experienced during the years of the Civil War but little or nothing about the personal pasts of friends or neighbors. Some people can recount verbatim conversations that occurred on the eve of the Battle of Hopewell, a major campaign late in the war, but draw a complete blank on the tumultuous contests between the Populists and the Democrats at the turn of this century. Any cultural memory is likely to be selective, and in this chapter I am interested in exploring Hopewell's principle of selection, its expressions and silences concerning the past. Ultimately, the data suggest that the greatest silence surrounds the periods of most intense strife.[1] These dangerous zones of the past are fenced off with a well-defined set of symbols, which themselves can be understood in historical terms.

Historical reenactments in Hopewell involve the Civil War and the period immediately preceding it. *Reenactment* is not entirely accurate here, not only because many of the celebrants' families were not yet resident in the county at the time of the Civil War but also because the enactments are of a style of life that was not the

1. The selectivity of Americans' historical consciousness has been noted in other communities. Perhaps the most sweeping assessment is that of Gorer, who noted the way in which "the South" "remembers" the Civil War: "The memory of the traumatic period . . . is not altogether suppressed, but it receives remarkably little attention in conversation or fiction. Memory instead lingers happily over a beautiful version of the preceding period" (1948: 200). This is certainly true in Hopewell, where stories of ancestral sacrifice in the period of settlement culminating in the Civil War play a role akin to that which Warner described as Lincoln's in Americans' sense of unity in the light of his "martyrdom" (see Warner 1949: 14–17 and 1962: 23). For further commentary, see Singer (1977) on the bicentennial and Fitzgerald (1979) on the revisions of America's past in history textbooks. Warner (1961: 101–226) described Yankee City's revisions of the past in local commemorative ritual.

norm locally—aristocratic plantation agriculture. The local historical society, which was founded in 1973, formed around the purpose of preserving the past through programs of restoration and reconstruction, as well as through a genealogy project that is not yet complete. The restoration and reconstruction projects are extensive, including registration of the main street of the old downtown as a national historic district, contracting with a historical archaeologist to document the late Creek settlements and early white settlements in the central part of the county, relocation and restoration of one of the few "big houses" that stood at the outskirts of town, renovation of the old train depot that marks the center of town, and an annual round of festivities that take place at the depot and the historic sites near it. These efforts, which have involved large sums of money and human energy, are now largely complete. For the most part, they predate the development of tourism in the area, that is, they were originally for local consumption.

Tourism has added another dimension to the local conception of the past, a dimension that amplifies, or exaggerates, the local view. Importantly, the focus of tourism is not the town's past but a representation of the past. Local people say—with degrees of conviction ranging from assumption to conclusive proof—that a novel about the Civil War was set in their town.[2] Indeed, the author's grandparents owned property in the county. People in Hopewell take some evident satisfaction in the fact that the author's meticulous research allowed him to "disguise" not only the setting but the characters of his novel. The supposed site of the novel's local scenes was a modest two-story, clapboard house, decrepit from years of neglect, its sagging porches covered with kudzu, a fast-growing vine that flourishes in the South. It is possible that the disappointment of tourists who drove the hour from Atlanta to see an antebellum plantation inspired the destruction (rather than restoration) of this critical site. Now the lot stands empty, but tourists are still directed there.

It was not only the fact that the property belonged to the author's family that convinces local people that the book is about their town.

2. This is not the place to name or to analyze the novel itself, although that would be a rewarding enterprise. See Postel-Coster (1977: 140–144) for a general discussion of the relevance of novels to anthropological analysis.

Other details of the local landscape tend to confirm their view. Genealogy, religion, and other elements of the town's social history provide additional evidence in the local debate over the book's authenticity. There is also considerable local debate over exactly who the characters were modeled after and over many other details of the book, but no one doubts that it is "about" Hopewell. One popular idea is that the entire novel came from the author's grandmother's diary. A motorists' guide to Georgia a generation ago restricted its reference to Hopewell to a dismissal of the novel's legend: "[Hopewell] . . . is often identified as a source of scenes for [the novel], . . . but [the author] always insisted that . . . [the setting] was entirely a figure of the imagination." Be that as it may, it is the novel and not the town's history that preoccupies most people's overt interest in their town's past.

A local bus tour visits sites from the Civil War and from the novel without distinguishing between them. The tour guides are local women, each independently knowledgeable of the sites and costumed in antebellum-style dresses. The "settings" from the novel include the jail, the courthouse, several plantations, and several antebellum and postwar homes still privately owned by local people. In only one case is the house in question occupied by descendants of the original family. Importantly, the blend of the actual and fictional versions of the war allowed the guide I heard to make several graceful references to the war in a way that minimized the conflict itself. For example, she noted that although Sherman's army was a terrible scourge in the area, the local people benefited from "many individual acts of kindness" on the part of Union soldiers. (More on this prevalent theme below.) Later, she pointed out that Memorial Day is celebrated locally on April 26, "not because we couldn't agree [with the North] on a date, but because we have more flowers in bloom then." She also included a reference to sectarian rivalry. Her story was that when the old courthouse was abandoned for a newer building after the Civil War, it was sold to the Presbyterians and the Masons. The Presbyterians paid six hundred dollars for a 60 percent share, and the Masons paid four hundred dollars for a 40 percent share. When the roof leaked, the Masons asked the Presbyterians to contribute to repairs, but the Presbyterians declined, pointing out that their part didn't leak. Eventually, the Masons acquired the full building, and it still stands. The story—whether or not it is apocryphal—seems to have more to do with the Presbyterians' local reputation as political eccentrics than it does with the history of the building's title. Another story, almost definitely apocryphal, is about the builder of one of the town's oldest homes. He is said to have been a school-teacher from Connecticut who built the roof at a steep angle so that the snow would slide off.

In short, the tour brings visitors to more than just Hopewell. For the people of the town, the novel brings the community a well-deserved celebrity; the novel, in what is seen as its complete authenticity, in effect *reveals* the town. In the local view, the novelist wrote about Hopewell because it was an important place. Thus the contextualization of the private homes, dating from before and after the war, in the settings believed to be those of the novel, accurately reflects the local people's appreciation of their own place. The guide's gentle weaving and reweaving of the once-divided elements of her town and region are an assertion of the town's contemporaneity. The seams of the modern social fabric are woven with humor, allegory, and resignation.

The public activity that is committed to restoration and recreating the face of the past is matched privately by widespread interest in personal genealogy. Baptists participate more in this private search. Some personal efforts in genealogy are extensive, dating from not only the time of the first white settlers of the county but beyond their crossing the Georgia frontier. The typical pattern of migration took settlers into Virginia in the early to mideighteenth century and then west and south, through the western Carolinas or eastern Tennessee and into northern Georgia in the 1820s and 1830s. Census records are excellent, so that it is possible to identify individuals as they moved south, generally one county farther every ten years. People in Hopewell make good use of the state archives in Atlanta and are adept at locating new resources.

Although many people collect genealogies and memorabilia associated with their own families' pasts, to my knowledge, only those whose families were resident in Hopewell at the time of the Civil War do so. To collect genealogies, perhaps, is to be concerned with the Civil War, although certainly, the people themselves do not express their interest in these terms. In fact, they do not offer explanations of their interest but dismiss it as a personal quirk. People could—when pressed—refer me to others who compiled such records, but they do not talk about each other's families' pasts. To do so would risk impoliteness, since (they say) anyone might have some family secret he or she would prefer to conceal. There is, in fact, an actively covert aspect to genealogical research in that "discoveries" can divide families. On two occasions, I was asked (and I agreed) not to cite privately held manuscripts so as not to advertise to other family members their existence and possession. Yet even though these individuals treasured their records as personal possessions, they registered amazement that I might find them interesting and useful in my study of the town's life. No one was reluctant to share the materials with me; rather, their surprise was that the materials had to do with anyone other than themselves. The personalized past in this way isolates people from one another and from the events that produced the modern town. To the people whose histories they are, the genealogical records serve to differentiate individuals, not to tie them together.

A minor activity that is concerned with the past is a small but continuous trickle of historical research and publication in Hopewell. The town's centennial was held on the anniversary of the county's formation in 1858, and since then, individuals have sought wider audiences for their personal memories. So far, Hopewell is the subject of three small books and countless articles in the local newspaper. One of the books was written by an outsider, whose volume was dismissed in some quarters as an attempt to capitalize on the town's rich past. The most serious of the three is the bicentennial volume (published in 1976), offering a few pages on each of the centuries of settlement in the area. Much of the volume consists of lists of names, for example, of local veterans, a fact that perhaps has contributed to its popularity. The third volume is a collection of personal reminiscences by an elderly resident; several people referred to it as "goody-goody," although its genial tone is, to me, indistinguishable from other local historical writing. The unofficial historian of the town is a young businessman whose family was among the early settlers and who still maintains a home in the county. His knowledge of local style and family histories is vast, and although he is a young man, older residents defer to his expertise.

He seems to have acquired the mantle from an older woman, now approaching her nineties, who is the surviving daughter of one of the original white families. She is widely known as someone who knows local history, and she has a keen memory for the long-ago changed face of the county, and a life-style and manner that she now considers gone forever.

For most people, knowledge of the past converges not on events but on characterizations of the human strengths or weaknesses that shaped particular moments. This is a fundamental point. People who talk about the past identify strongly with their own sense of the past. It is a personal vision. For example, the book by the elderly resident is carefully constructed around his own long experience and perspective. It begins with "a cordial invitation" to "walk down the memory lane of the past." The first chapter is written from the vantage of the front porch of the author's childhood home. His book is also an example of the delicacy with which people present the past, a delicacy inspired by the etiquette that forbids raising difficult subjects in conversation. In fact, his narrative is presented as being not quite his but as a mechanical replay of a video tape or sound tape (the imagery is mixed): "DO NOT ADJUST YOUR SET! . . . but kindly overlook our memory faults and typographical and other mistakes; and please accept these as being just a part of an initial venture and a purely home town production" (emphasis in original). The last chapter of the book is about the relationship of contemporary individuals to the past. The theme is a lesson in a selection process:

> Once enlived, these memories are yours to do with as you see fit. You may forget them, ignore, or cherish them, but there is one thing for sure, you can not change them, at least not without cheating.
>
> Our suggestion is that you forget or ignore the sad or bad ones because you can not back up and change them, retaining only such parts of them as may be sacred to you or which may be balanced off as valued experience.

The community's historical memory is selective in just this way. What follows is an examination of what is "remembered" and what is "forgotten" of crucial periods in the town's history.

## Talking about the Past

People do talk about the past, albeit in ways that are highly stylized. Although people are generally blank when asked about the town's past, others can refer to the days when Hopewell was a larger social and commercial center than Marthasville, now called Atlanta. Some people can identify historical sites and their sequence of owners. Especially since the town's rapid suburbanization, with the development of the interstate highway, some people are fond of surprising visitors with descriptions of this or that neon- or mall-covered place prior to the new construction.

Some people—locally known as experts—do talk about "the old days." They tell stories and, in my conversations with people reputed to "know a lot about history," I heard these few stories again and again. I did not understand them when I heard them, and I did not understand why they were the stories to tell; they seemed so fragmental, or beside the point. But when I heard the same stories, almost word for word, with minimal contextualization, no explanation, almost always followed by a bemused chuckle, on both of my visits (the first in the early 1970s and the second in 1980), and when I found them printed and reprinted in newspapers and in the historical books written by local people, they began to seem more important. The stories are reprinted below. There is a way to tell these stories, which is to present them as fact, without any marker. They are presented as personal, not public, knowledge, although they clearly are public knowledge; they are simply woven into the narrator's discussion and punctuated with a gentle smile or a chuckle. There is a way to listen to these stories, too, and a way to acknowledge them, which I learned from a local woman who accompanied me on my first historical interview. She shook her head, sharing the bemusement, and said, "This town really used to have some characters," or "It's hard to believe all of that could go on in a place like this, isn't it?" Then the subject of conversation shifted. Indeed, the concluding paragraph of the elderly resident's book reflects this response: "For those of the younger group, our narrative, we hope, may enable them to compare the transpirations of the beginning of the century with those of its ending. The results will no doubt be astonishing almost to misbelief."

The supply of these stories is limited: three in particular appear to be most often retold. The source of each version is indicated below. They follow in full, in chronological order. They might have been taken from many other sources; there is very little variation among the multiple versions. They are about actual people, and naming them is an important aspect of the narration, although I do not name them here.

1

The Baptist Church used to be a bit farther north than it is now. The day that the first train came through town on the new railroad [in 1843] was a Sunday, and the minister was preaching his sermon. The train blew its whistle, and the whole congregation ran out of the church to see the train go by, leaving the minister there alone. (Field notes)

2

The house [of a locally prominent family] was the Union headquarters at the Battle of [a nearby town in Hopewell County]. A resident of today's Hopewell reported her great-grandmother as having said that "the officers were perfect gentlemen." The soldiers spared the house but burned the [cotton] gin, the grain storage house and the equipment. The family and a slave cared for a Union soldier who died on their grounds, and built a tomb for him when he died. (From published accounts)

3

During the [1892] campaign [X] was an earnest and faithful Democratic worker from beginning to end, and much good did he render to the party. It was he who assisted in the organization of many of the Democratic Clubs throughout the county and it was he who was ever ready to make a speech in defence [*sic*] of the honored principles of Democracy. On one occasion it is said that he attended a Third Party "rally" and requested the orator of the occasion to divide time with him. The gentleman objected but agreed for [X] to speak and he would follow. [X] took the floor and held it firmly until the sun had sunk behind the western hills and the audience began to retire. It was a good one on the boys for a long time afterwards. (County *Annual*)

In conversation, these narratives are presented as they are presented here—without contextualization or explanation. In the following sections, I attempt to explain the referents of each one and conclude with a discussion of why these are the important things to say about Hopewell's past. Their relevance to the ethnographic problem central to this study is in their providing narrative contexts for confrontation between competing identities. These symbolic, or emblematic, contrasts are references to major social divisions that once cleaved Hopewell into deep factions. Today, they are taken, I think, as references to human nature and its enduring idiosyncracies. It is its transformation from social division to differences of human nature that makes these narratives important. The equation between a kind of position and a kind of person—an interpretation of conflict as a sign of personal identity—collapses all history into the study of human nature or, in the Baptists' case, the word of God. That is the shape of this chapter.

## The Baptists and the Train

This story is undoubtedly apocryphal, since the Baptist minister featured in the story migrated west in 1842, and the first train did not come through town until 1843. The nature of the narrative, though, is suggested in one of its variants, in which the minister's name is changed slightly, perhaps a misspelling arising from local pronunciation and/or the pun that is its result. The error in the dates and other details suggests that the narrative was composed sometime later, about the tumultuous years between the county's settlement and the Civil War. I do not know when the account was first told, but it is widely retold today. What is striking about the retelling is its consistency on the details: it is always the Baptists, the minister's name is always given, and the occasion is always the first train. The narrative is told as a humorous story; it is as if it were a joke on the Baptists (the Baptist church's anniversary booklet recounting its own history mentions the first train but not in the context of this tale). In the telling, the Baptists are presented as hypocrites, as revealed by their fascination—attraction—to the emblem of worldly change, the train. Why should the Baptists have been singled out in this way? What is this narrative about?

The first whites settled in the Hopewell County area even before the Creeks were driven from the area in the late 1820s and early

1830s. The earliest description of the area comes from Hawkins (1848), who traveled in the region in 1798 and 1799 while it was still occupied by Creeks:

> [The Ocmulgee and Flint rivers] have their sources near each other, on the left side Chattohoche [Chattahoochee], in open, flat, land, the soil stiff, the trees post and black oak, all small. The land is generally rich, well watered, and lies well, as a waving country, for cultivation. The growth of timber is oak, hickory, and the short leaf pine; pea-vine on the hill sides and in the bottom, and a tall, broad leaf, rich grass, on the richest land. The whole is a very desirable country. (1848)

Adiel Sherwood's (1837) guide does not mention Hopewell, although the records show a town on the site by the early 1840s. In 1849 George White listed Hopewell as a post office and added:

> Hopewell, on the . . . Railroads, 10 miles N.E. of . . . , has been settled about six years, and has a population of 200. It contains one church of the Methodist denomination, three schools, besides stores and shops. The population is improving. . . . The citizens are spirited, industrious and temperate. Great changes have been produced through the instrumentality of religion and temperance. . . . The climate is generally healthy. The most common diseases are fevers of the remittent and unremittent character, pleurisies, &c. (1849)

A few years later, White wrote that Hopewell "is a thriving place" (1855). It was the railroad that attracted that famous traveler General Sherman to Hopewell. In the troop movements preceeding the seige of Atlanta, Sherman's army moved through the area and fed themselves and their animals on the local corn harvest. The medical inspector for the U.S. Army reported scurvy among the troops, but "the symptoms were much abated and modified by the abundant supply of blackberries and green corn which the men obtained on their march" (United States War Department 1891: 117). A few days later, the fall of Hopewell guaranteed Sherman a crucial battle in his Georgia campaign; his letters give a vivid image of the town by their account of its destruction.

White settlement in the attractive region around Hopewell began in 1794, when Elijah Clarke—later to be prominent as the leader of

Georgia's Clarke party—illegally built forts and a settlement on unceded Creek lands. The governor and eventually the federal government succeeded in arresting Clarke after a lengthy confrontation, but the incident marked the beginning of a generation-long battle between frontiersmen and their governments over the issue of honoring treaties and tribal rights (Phillips 1968: 47–48). Elijah Clarke's antipathy to the Creeks and Cherokees stemmed from the fact that the Cherokees had fought on the side of the British during the American Revolution: Clarke, a veteran of the Revolution, sought revenge. Local political factionalism focused on the tribal rights of the Creeks and the Cherokees. A series of hotly contested cessions proceeded in spite of their doubtful legality, until they were complete in 1826. The territory that became Hopewell County was ceded in the Indian Springs treaty of January 21, 1821 (Phillips 1968: 53–66).

In a dispute with the Cherokees ten years later, Andrew Jackson, who had successfully campaigned for the presidency in 1828, took a radical antitribe stance. Although John Marshall, chief justice of the Supreme Court, upheld the prohibition against white settlements on tribal lands without a license, Jackson publicly advocated flouting the law. A Georgia judge—for whom Hopewell County is named—was horrified at the removal of white settlers from tribal territory by federal troops and made it known that "he would disregard any interference of the United States Supreme Court in cases which might arise before him from the Act of Georgia. 'I only require the aid of public opinion and the arm of executive authority,' he concluded, 'and no court on earth besides our own shall ever be troubled with this question'" (Phillips 1968: 74).

The local political configuration of Jacksonians who opposed the tribes was led by Elijah Clarke and, through him, the Clarke party. Elijah Clarke was a veteran not only of the war for independence but also of the War of 1812, in which he had fought under General Andrew Jackson. There is some indirect evidence of the extent to which the local people felt the impact of the controversy between the Jacksonians and the pro-Cherokee faction in a pattern of naming that lasted into this century. Two related families whose genealogical records I copied named children after Andrew Jackson during this period; another related family named a child for John Marshall. This pattern suggests that families—or at least this family—were

[153]

divided over the issue. In fact, I would suggest that they were strongly divided, since I found no other indication in these or other families of naming for national public figures. (A possible exception is a child named for subsequent state's rights issues: her first two names were Carolina Missouri, and she was born the year of the Missouri compromise, 1849.) The name Andrew Jackson eventually became "Jack" in the 1880s, and John Marshall became "Jim." I asked the descendant of the original John Marshall about the origins of his grandfather's and cousins' names. He said that Andrew Jackson was named for the Civil War general "Stonewall" Jackson and that the John Marshalls were named for the Supreme Court justice. "Stonewall" Jackson's given names were Thomas Jonathan; the slippage of both the form and content of historical memory is significant.

The frontiersmen in and around Hopewell were not uniformly for the pro-Jackson Clarke party. In the early 1820s, the period when Hopewell County itself was first settled by whites, the Clarke forces and their opponents (who favored Governor Troup) were fairly evenly matched in the state. Jesse Mercer, a prominent Baptist minister, was a strong supporter of the Troup faction. Phillips's description of Georgia politics credits Mercer with the political leadership of the Georgia Baptist order:

> [Mercer] mixed politics with his gospel to such an extent that he never failed to carry his county overwhelmingly for Crawford or Troup or the candidates of their party. Governor Lumpkin lays at his door many of the votes that were cast against him in his numerous campaigns, saying that although the Baptist Church was not a unit in politics, yet Mercer always carried the bulk of its members for the Troup candidates. (Phillips 1968: 102–103)

The extent to which Hopewell Baptists followed Mercer's leadership is difficult to know; at least one prominent Baptist family experienced his ministry in the town. Mercer's position is the first suggestion in the historical record that associates Georgia Baptists with the statewide political faction that represented aristocratic interests. Troup's primary support came from the older parts of the state toward the Atlantic Coast, where aristocratic Virginians and other planters were well established (Phillips 1968: 96, 104–105). Yet Hopewell County was on the frontier in the 1820s, when the contest between Troup and Clarke reached its peak. The frontier counties, with few exceptions (and the exceptions did not include Hopewell County), supported Clarke. If Hopewell Baptists followed Mercer's lead to support Troup, they were at odds with their neighbors.

The intensity of the regional conflict over the status of the tribes gave considerable heat to sectarian debate over missions. An important local issue was the question of whether or not to missionize among the tribes. The establishment of missions was widely taken as an assimilation, pro-Cherokee position; locally, it was a minority view. The local association of Baptist churches was deeply divided on the question of missions. The minister of the Hopewell Baptist church during the years 1837–1840, when this conflict was most intense, was the same minister who figures in the narrative about the Baptists and the train. This man was widely known for two things during his ten-year ministry from 1832 to 1842. First, he was a committed and effective evangelist. He regularized the church services to once a month and later to twice a month; he established the first Sunday school in Hopewell and also was a ready guest at other churches' pulpits. He was active in the local Baptist church association's attempt to reunify the antimission and promission factions, but the secession of the antimission group was institutionalized in the Primitive Baptist church by 1840. He was a popular man and was difficult to replace when he moved west. According to the Baptist church's records, the congregation had no pastor during the year following his departure; there was no regular minister at the local church when the first train went through town. The second source of this minister's renown was his position in favor of missions for the Cherokee. The Cherokee still inhabited Hopewell County during his ministry, until 1839, when their removal was complete. His importance to the community of his day is perhaps suggested by—once again—the name given to a child. The same parents who named one of their older sons for John Marshall named a younger son for this pro-Cherokee preacher.

The political factions that organized the state in the 1820s over the status of the tribes were continuous until the time of the Civil War (Phillips 1968: 169). Although the Troup and Clarke parties changed their names (to States Rights and Union, respectively), the parties themselves remained stable over shifting political causes.

These causes were benevolent associations, slavery, states' rights, and secession.

The controversy that began over Cherokee missions expanded to become a question of "benevolent associations" in general. Benevolent associations became a general label for a specific concern, and that was abolitionist associations. The Cherokee question quickly melded with the slavery question; the Baptists in the South divided over the "benevolent association" issue (yielding the Primitive Baptists, who opposed the associations). This debate was intensely argued locally (see Chapter 5). The Hopewell Baptist church supported benevolent associations but lost a number of members over the issue. Hopewell County appears to have been relatively indifferent on the slavery question, except to the extent that it roused vigorous local support for states' rights.[3] The Baptists in the southern states seceded from the organization of American Baptists to form the Southern Baptist Convention in 1845 (Mead 1975: 41); the local Baptist church association supported the secession with a statement in the minutes at its subsequent meeting. As the national conflict preceding the Civil War increased its pitch, the local Baptist church association again drafted a resolution supporting the formation of the Confederacy, but this time, there was division. Contrary to the assumption of everyone with whom I spoke about the Civil War, Hopewell County's delegates did not vote unanimously for secession at the Georgia convention of 1861. The source of this division can be traced to the founding of the county.

3. Regionally, Southern Baptists were avidly proslavery (Eighmy 1972: 3–20); this was not the case in Hopewell. For the most part, the farmers of Hopewell County were too poor to make slaveholding profitable. The migrations that populated the uplands were small farmers from Virginia and North Carolina who did not own slaves, and as the discussion of cotton production shows, cotton agriculture was not on a sufficiently large scale to warrant the heavy expense that slaveholding demanded. The plantation agriculture that is part of the South's mythology rose and fell south of Hopewell County. It was there that the cotton gin so greatly simplified the processing of cotton that production exploded in the early years of the nineteenth century; by 1830 the soil that supported the first cotton boom was already depleted (Flanders 1933: 61, 68). The first half of the nineteenth century was a period of clearing, planting, and exhausting soils and then moving westward to find virgin lands. With the advent of fertilizers, renovation of land became cheaper than migration, and westward migration finally slowed during the 1840s (Flanders 1933: 92). Hopewell County developed during the second half of this period of migrations; the development of Hopewell in particular was in large part due to the presence of the railroad that increased the profitability of agriculture in the area.

Hopewell became the seat of Hopewell County when the county was created out of two adjoining counties—"Lynette" and "Harold" counties—by the state legislature in 1858. The town had been founded in 1823 under another name, chosen to honor "a prominent citizen" (Krakow 1975). Hopewell was the second town in Lynette County, after Lynetteville, that had been organized two years before. Adiel Sherwood's *Gazeteer* (1837) does not mention Hopewell in his list of "principal places" (pp. 103–105), perhaps because, without a major road connecting Hopewell to other towns, he did not find it in his journey around Georgia.

Although "Lynette" County and "Lynetteville" can claim the major role in parenting Hopewell County (see discussion below), Harold County was, at the time, the more thriving place. In population, it was nearly twice the size of Lynette County (10,566 versus 5,504 in 1837, according to Sherwood [1837], and its farms were more productive. Harold County held more slaves, more aristocrats, more businesses, and was a cultural center of sorts.

Adiel Sherwood, whose work is a standard reference on early Georgia, found three main attributes to admire in McDougall, Harold's county seat. First, he shows some fervor for the temperance movement in what was apparently an evangelical stronghold. Sherwood was a Baptist preacher who, in 1827, preached a sermon at the "Great Revival" at Ramah Church (the Baptist church in McDougall) that produced four thousand converts. The local historians of that church credited Sherwood's sermon with fifteen years of conversions; they reported sixteen thousand by 1829. These figures may be somewhat overenthusiastic, since, as noted above, the entire population of the county was under eleven thousand; perhaps they referred to a regional movement.

A second reference that may be significant is Sherwood's observation that residents from the coastal areas spent the summers in McDougall. There is no record of who these people were, but their presence indicates one source of aristocratic influence in Harold County. During these early years of Georgia's history, Savannah was the political and cultural center of the state. Harold was relatively more aristocratic than its frontier neighbors; its geography made it possible to become an uplands outpost of the coastal aristocratic elite.

A third reference of importance is to the existence of a "small paper." This newspaper was one of twenty in Georgia at that time (Sherwood 1837: 318). It supported the Clarke party, the pro-Jackson, anti-Cherokee, antiaristocratic coalition. One index of the shifting political situation in this area is that by 1849, and probably earlier, its editor had moved to Lynetteville, where he edited a Lynetteville newspaper (White 1849). (He is mentioned in White's *Statistics* not because of his political influence but because he had reached the age of ninety.)

In microcosm, McDougall displays some of the dynamics that were then developing in the region at large. The first was the rise of churches with various secular associations; second, a growing tension between proslavery aristocrats and pro–states' rights small farmers; and, third, the rising importance of Cherokee removal as an issue that crystalized party formation and had a major impact on the development of the state as a whole.

Each of these issues was important in the establishment of Hopewell County, which was, in effect, gerrymandered to increase the strength of the Populists (formerly the Clarke party) in the legislature. Although the debate is not recorded for either the senate or the house of representatives, the pattern of ayes and nays is highly suggestive. The bill to establish the county was introduced by Senator "Smithson" of Lynette; once it had passed, he successfully proposed amending the county line to include in Hopewell County four of his political allies. Harold County already had two representatives in the legislature; now Lynette would, in effect, have two as well—one of its own and that of its new political clone, Hopewell. In the senate, where each county was uniformly represented, Lynette's power would be doubled. The senator from Harold is not recorded as having voted on Smithson's bill, but the thirty-seven negative votes (against the formation of Hopewell County) came from a diagonal swath across the central part of the state that included Harold but not Lynette. These were the plantation counties, where cotton and slaveholding were the most firmly established. In the house vote, these lines emerged even more clearly: there, negative votes also came from the aristocratic "Virginian" counties along the coast and the eastern end of the border with South Carolina. In the house, Harold County voted against establishing the new county. The strongest support for the bills in both houses came from the anti-Cherokee, pro-Clarke counties: the

[158]

mountain counties (from which most of the residents of Lynette County and the new Hopewell County came) and the newly settled tribal cessions to the north and west. The naming of the new county for the defiant judge who refused to implement John Marshall's order to halt white incursions into Cherokee lands in 1826 was a fitting gesture toward the county's genesis.

Thus Hopewell County was created by the Clarke party—by then the Union party—for its own uses. Smithson went to the state senate as a Hopewell County delegate (Georgia *Official and Statistical Register,* 1975–1976). Much of Hopewell County's local power elite came from Lynette. The major exception was the handful of men who formed the Baptist leadership. According to local published history, they emigrated to Hopewell from McDougall, in Harold County, to settle in the new town by the railroad.

In sum, in the early years of the new county, the three major political issues were relationships with the tribes, slavery, and secession. In each case, Hopewell's Baptists appear to have been associated with minority positions, in local terms. Specifically, the data suggest that the leadership of the Baptist order in Georgia had sympathies that responded more to the interests of aristocrats and planters than to the common folk who lived on the frontier. The pressures on the local churches by the local Baptist church association were in the direction of eliminating dissent, by "withdrawing" from dissidents, if all else failed (this is the subject of Chapter 5).

At the time, the major questions that put Baptists at odds with the local community in Hopewell were seen as questions of expansion. First, the occupation of Cherokee lands and, second, local issues related to states' rights were advocated by farmers whose goal was to push the frontier westward. That would be progress. Thus in returning to the narrative that has the Baptists running away from the preacher at the pulpit to see the train, we find a well-focused challenge to the local Baptists' perceived conservatism. It is aimed at the Baptist leadership in a way that suggests sectarian, rather than personal, referents. Railroads were not only a local concern; evangelicals all over the South used the image of railroads operating on Sunday as an example of "wholesale . . . shocking immoralities" by the society of the unsaved (Loveland 1980: 176).

The Baptists tell a story that is also about a train in the early days of its route through Hopewell. It is more in line with the evangelical position on the railroads. The following version is taken from the church's published history: "This story is told about Reverend . . . [a much beloved minister of the church from 1859 to 1885]. A yearling of his was killed on the railroad and the claim agent came to make a settlement with him. The agent offered him twenty dollars which Reverend . . . said would not be satisfactory. He said, 'Just give me ten dollars because that's all it was worth.'" In contrast to the popular narrative about the minister and the train, this one uses the train to show the Baptists' security in their sacred values. Furthermore, the reference to the minister in the popular tale is a reference to the era of most intense local political turmoil, as evidenced by fissions in the churches in and around Hopewell County. The reference to the minister in the Baptist narrative is to the Civil War and the era of the community's solidarity in war and afterward (this minister served two terms in the state legislature). It is altogether a different tale with a different message: the popular narrative is about conflict and "the world"; the Baptists' narrative is about unity and "the Word."

The conservatism of Hopewell's Baptist church was widely shared by evangelicals across the South. Loveland noted the extent to which these churches were "alienated from the society in which they lived, and how far they were from accepting the dominant ideology of self-reliance, democracy, and progress. . . . Evangelicals were concerned that Christians—indeed all Americans—placed too much faith in human institutions and efforts (government, political parties, banks, material improvements, mechanical contrivances) as the means of securing peace, order and prosperity" (1980: 125).

Today, the tensions between politics and evangelicalism are not a dimension to the *telling* of these tales. Contemporary narrators focus on the train itself and the contrast between the past—when people ran outdoors to see trains—and the present—when they are commonplace. Yet the world of man and the world of God remain distinct in people's accounts of their own experience, and as the discussion in previous chapters also shows (see Chapter 3), today's Baptists are somewhat obliquely viewed by outsiders as being "worldly" behind the walls of the church. The narrative thus has contemporary resonance. In the retelling of the narrative, people invoke the epoch of the past that established the Baptists as a "special" group, a reference group whose modernity and authenticity were continually called into question. The telling of the tale allows this dynamic to persist; its obliqueness and its fragmentary quality allow the critical questions themselves to recede. Some of the contrasting signs for which groups in Hopewell compete are to be found here: conservative/progressive, sacred/profane, spiritual/materialistic, rural/urban. The narrative preserves the salience of these contrasts and their meanings.

## The Kindness of Soldiers

The narrative about the Hopewell family and their Union guests refers to the time just following the Battle of Hopewell, which was among the last crucial campaigns in the Battle of Atlanta, close to the end of the Civil War. Importantly, the narrative is not about the battle itself, nor does it dwell on the devastation that it entailed. Instead, like the guide on the local bus tour, the narrative focuses on the underlying sympathy uniting groups that were in appearance divided. The Battle of Hopewell is an important element of local people's presentation of the past. Visitors are shown the cemetery, the antebellum houses, bullet holes in walls, and even the bullets themselves—called "miniballs," they were lead balls the size of a small marble. The road between Atlanta and Hopewell is dotted with roadsigns, historical markers that point out major stages of the battle. The local geography, too, bears names that refer to the calamitous days of fighting. The battle and its significance are summarized in the town's bicentennial booklet.

> The Civil War came to Hopewell . . . as the last phase of the Atlanta Campaign. Federal forces had not been able to take Atlanta by direct attack; so the strategy to starve it of supplies was undertaken. . . .
> The result of the Battle of Hopewell was exactly what the Federals desired. With all railroads and supply lines cut off, the defenders and inhabitants of Atlanta were forced to give up, and the city was surrendered in a day or so. After unbelievable destruction there, Sherman began his infamous March to the Sea in November, 1864.

This "official" account does not begin to convey the scale of the battle and bloodshed that swept over the town or the acrimony that

[161]

defeat engendered on the Confederate side. As the local account suggests, the federal troops were not interested in occupying Hopewell but in destroying the railroad there. On the morning of the battle, General Sherman concluded a message to one of his generals in the field near Hopewell with a reminder of the urgency of the campaign: "I will be near Hopewell tomorrow, prepared to act promptly, according to the signs, but again beg to impress on you and all the great importance of destroying that railroad absolutely beyond hope of repair" (United States War Department 1891).

The next day, the federal troops had the advantage of information supplied by a local citizen. As Sherman's army prepared for battle, they knew from this person where the Confederate forces were gathered and where they were weak. The Confederate general in command, Hardee, held Hopewell on the first night of the battle. The next day, Sherman wrote to his commander that Hopewell "is of no value to us, but we are now trying to cripple and destroy the army now there" (United States War Department 1891). In sending orders to a second division in the field, he gave detailed orders for evading the confederates where possible and fighting if necessary: "[If] fighting occurs, or you have a chance to attack, the orders are always to attack. We don't care about Hopewell, but we want to destroy the enemy" (United States War Department 1891). Indeed, the fighting in and around town was extensive; on the afternoon of the second day (September 1), Sherman reported that Hardee had lost one-fifth of his army there—four thousand men disabled. Sherman's report of Union losses placed the figure at under twelve hundred (United States War Department 1891). During the fighting, the armies converged on Hopewell and its vicinity. Although, as Sherman's correspondence indicates, the town itself was not the Union's objective, the devastation of battle and its aftermath must have been extraordinary. In spite of this narrative and others' implications that individual soldiers treated local families kindly, a letter from a field commander to one of his colonels suggests that there was considerable illegal looting by Union troops:

> In riding through the camps this morning I was very much grieved to find . . . lying shamelessly exposed to the whole command, a lot

of male and female clothing and wearing apparel, shirts, bed-quilts, &c., evidently recently pillaged from some of the neighboring helpless citizens. . . . [I] order you to ascertain [the name of the officer in command of the company] and prefer charges against him for conduct prejudicial to good order and military discipline, in permitting the thing to be done under his eyes and not taking steps to punish his men.[4] (United States War Department 1891)

The destruction under orders to Confederate soldiers was summed up by Sherman:

We have as the result of this quick and, as I think, well-executed movement 27 guns, over 3,000 prisoners; have buried over 400 rebel dead, and left as many wounded that could not be moved. The rebels had lost, besides the important city of Atlanta, immense stores, at least 500 dead, 2,500 wounded, and 3,000 prisoners, whereas our aggregate [loss] will not foot up 1,500. If that is not success, I don't know what is. (United States War Department 1891)

The end of the battle was not the end of the community's trials. In the evacuation of citizens that immediately followed the occupation of Atlanta by Union troops, Sherman sent Confederate sympathizers southward to the front and Union sympathizers northward to the rear. Hopewell became a way station for refugees. He prohibited all manufacture and commerce in order to free the roads for troop supplies and burned or confiscated all of the cotton, which was then ripening in the fields—"All cotton is tainted with treason," Sherman wrote to one of his commanders (United States War Department 1891).

The hardships of war—*hardship* is too mild a word, as even a

---

4. Even the loss of a quilt or some clothes represented substantial deprivation to families who, by this time, had very little. According to the county ordinary (judge of probate), few people in the 1860s had enough property to warrant a will; however, examples from the probate records of 1865 show the following household inventories from Hopewell: The estate of one man included, in toto, 2 books, 3 razor strops, 2 pitchforks, 1 looking glass, 1 pair of steelgores, 1 grindstone, 1 clamp and jack, 1 box, 1 mule, 1 buggy, 1 scythe and cradle, 1 running gin, 1 gin, 1 thrasher, for a total value of $328.00. Another estate left the widow with 700 pounds of meat at 30¢ a pound, 80 bushels of corn at $1.50 a bushel, 4 [illegible] $30, and $90.00 in money. She also had a bedstead and some furniture. The largest estate in 1865 was assessed at $7,563.85, including two slaves valued at $2,400.00.

casual reading of the record of military correspondence shows—fell on a population already seriously disrupted by the previous four years. As early as November 1861, the presentments of the county's grand jury, which assessed the county's administrative needs along with recording court cases, reported the presence of "sharpers and speculators who seek to enrich themselves by taking advantage of the present unhappy state of our country" (County Superior Court Minutes, November term, 1861). In the May term, 1862, the jury reported the bad condition of the county's roads and recommended that a local tax be levied to support the destitute families of soldiers. The October 1862 session was adjourned early because of the presence of smallpox in the "immediate vicinity"; the epidemic swept through the army and many of the neighboring communities around Hopewell. In May 1863 most of the court's cases were debt suits against one man, James F. "Smithson" (a pseudonym); he figures prominently in the records of the court and in Hopewell's history (however, he is not the Smithson who served in the senate at the time of the county's establishment). The presentments for the May term include praise for the county treasurer, who had undercharged for his services: "At this time of speculation and extortion when each seems to be after what he can get the jury take special pleasure in calling attention to an officer who does not exact fully even what the law allows and what we would cheerfully see him have." The jury also recommended discharging the county debt, given the "unsettled state of our currency." The minutes conclude: "In the present Struggle which calls for all our energies means and courage we are contending only to establish according to our own notions of right, law and order. Under these circumstances we deeply regret the prevalence of crime and the seeming disregard of those laws which are the only safeguards of our property, our Liberties and our Lives" (County Superior Court Minutes, May term, 1863). The minutes for November 1863 and May 1864 are written in too pale an ink to be legible; perhaps the jury, in an effort to be frugal, diluted its ink with water. In May 1864, the docket shows a new kind of crime, crime involving slaves, who were by then technically free. In one case, two slaves from a town north of Atlanta were charged with armed robbery during the night, in which they allegedly cleared the household of all of its goods, consisting of utensils and china, and a quantity of bread, meat, and butter, assessed together at ninety dollars. In the second case, a local man was charged with "associating in the nightime in the town of Hopewell with his negro slave woman." This was a capital offense, and the defendant fled the town.

The outcome of the battle of Hopewell was thus the ultimate blow against a community that had been struggling since the very early months of the war. Questions immediately arose about whether defeat could have been avoided. The bicentennial booklet mentions General Hardee's "mistake" at Hopewell in commanding General Cleburne to withdraw his support from the Second Confederate Division in battle (thus opening the front to the Union troops). Hardee himself became the focus of debate over the defeat, both officially within the Confederate military and among the people. In response to charges of incompetence from his commander, General Hood, Hardee defended his conduct of the battle in a letter to John Breckenridge, the Confederacy's secretary of war (United States War Department 1891). Hardee's own description of the Battle of Hopewell and the confusion that clouded the Confederate effort in the crucial early hours offer clear illustration of why the local people might have felt betrayed and yet uncertain about who had betrayed them (United States War Department 1891). Hardee concludes:

> The fate of Atlanta was sealed from the moment when General Hood allowed an enemy superior in numbers to pass unmolested around his flank and plant himself firmly upon his only line of railroad. If, after the enemy reached Hopewell, General Hood had attacked him with his whole army instead of with a part of it, he could not reasonably have expected to drive from that position an army before which his own had been for four months retiring in the open field. (United States War Department 1891)

What is important about Hardee's account of the battle and its significance is not only the multiple ambiguities that made the situation so tortuous but also the contrast it offers to the local version of the same events. The bicentennial booklet's assessment of Hopewell's importance in the battle is that its loss, under Hardee, ensured the loss of Atlanta and the South. Hardee's account— admittedly in defense of his own conduct—rejects this interpretation and lays responsibility for Atlanta's loss higher up in his own

[165]

command. The booklet's account represents the popular understanding of Hopewell's role in the Civil War, and it is a role explained today with some pride: Hopewell, though now a small place, say the local people, was the keystone of the southern cause. In identifying the importance of the local battle in this way, the people of Hopewell, then and now, decide against Hardee in the question of why the war was lost. If he betrayed Hopewell by his own error, Hopewell's celebrity as the last bulwark of the South is assured.

The sense of betrayal by their own army perhaps accounts for one dimension of the narrative that is the subject of this section: the emphasis on the first moments of recovery and reconciliation rather than on the battle itself, which, in spite of the gallantry so often commended by the troops' officers in their letters, could scarcely have been other than an agonizing, embittered (embittering) epoch. Indeed, in the retelling of the battle for tourists and other visitors, local people describe the route of the armies and the sites of their confrontations, but they do not talk about Hardee or his alleged errors. They do not name Hardee, but they indict him in effect when they explain Atlanta's fall as the result of his defeat. This is not a conscious revision; the local tradition is that the battle has this meaning.

But there is another dimension to the narrative, and others like it, that focus on the kindness of the Union soldiers or, if not kindness, the exemptions they made for particular individuals (one published source reported that wives and children of Masons were saved from ruin at the hands of Union soldiers if they showed the Masonic insignia). The reference to kindness undoubtedly has multiple significances: for example, it is retold in a reunified nation, and in some respects, it is a metaphor of reunification. It is also possibly a reference to the local situation before the battle or the war began—and such a reference would sharpen the sense of betrayal and futility in the battle almost beyond endurance. The fact is that only one of the two delegates from Hopewell County voted for the secession resolution in the state convention in January 1861. Letters among residents at the time suggest that the delegation's lack of unanimity was a source of bitterness; however, both men returned to the county to resume active and successful political lives. Of the convention, Phillips wrote: "In every county the foremost citizens stood as candidates for the convention, and among the candidates those who were held in greatest esteem for strength of judgment were, as a rule, elected. . . . It was without doubt the most distinguished body of men which ever assembled in Georgia" (1968: 201–202). The delegates apparently voted their consciences; party lines were "destroyed" (1968: 201). The convention as a body fell into two groups—supporters of immediate secession and supporters of the possibility of secession. The latter group divided at the convention into two groups—those who proposed eventual secession and those who opposed secession. Hopewell's two delegates were J. F. Smithson, who favored secession, and another man, who voted against it. In the balloting, Hopewell reflected its political parentage: Lynette County, where Smithson was from, voted for secession; Harold County cast two votes against and one for secession. The final ballot was 209 ayes to 89 nays (Milledgeville *Federal Union,* January 15, 1861).

Thus not only was the battle fought and lost, but the war itself was something over which the local people had divided. Hopewell apparently supported the war effort fully, contributing men, money, and prayers. In the next chapter, we shall see that at the moment that the war began, Christianity and harmony were fused into a single symbol of southern identity. The vitality of southern identity required that the ambivalence and ambiguity surrounding both the fact of the war and the fate of the war be set aside. The people of Hopewell cannot forget the war; indeed, several adults told me that I was the first "Yankee" with whom they had held a conversation. As the discussion at the beginning of the chapter suggests, the war is the emblem of Hopewell's importance to many of its residents. Yet just as the tourists are directed to a version of the past that filters the war through fiction, the residents themselves discuss the war only in its aftermath, as an occasion for reconciliation. The fact that division was never something that they sought makes reconciliation the only form of heroism that is an unalloyed memory.

In the aftermath of the war, Hopewell faced the burdens of readjustment and reconstruction. Court records show an increase of violent crimes, although the numbers remain very small. J. F. Smithson, one of Hopewell's most prominent and litigious citizens, whose defense of suits for debt mark the grand jury reports during the war years, invoked the battle of Hopewell in his defense in yet another lawsuit:

> Because at the time of holding court defendant was residing with his family at a remote distance from the court and a large body of United States troops occupying the country between the court and defendant's then place [of] residence, whom he was informed had torn up the railroad and rendered it almost impossible for him to get to court and then at the holding of said Court such was the condition of the Country in consequence of military operations and the surrendering of the principal confederate armies as to induce defendant to believe that the court would not be held. (County Superior Court Minutes, October term, 1865)

His lawyer added that "at the time of rendering said verdict and judgment [against Smithson] the court had no legal authority to pass upon said case the court being held at that time under the constitution and laws of state adopted and passed after the state had seceded from the Government of the United States" (County Supreme Court, October term, 1865). Smithson soon afterward joined the bar himself and enjoyed a successful practice.

Meanwhile, the county itself was utterly impoverished; in November 1865, for example, the school fund consisted of $9.36 in Confederate money. The first presentments after the war record the enormity of the physical reconstruction of the region, as well as the emotional reconstruction required by the amnesty oath:

> We find by the ravages of War that we are destitute of a Court House and County Jail. . . . We also find and publish roads in bad condition generally. . . . We are satisfied after a deliberate investigation that there is no rebellion Spirit among our people now that having taken the amnesty oath they are willing to let by gones be by gones and that henceforward they are willing and expect to be true and loyal Citizens of the United States. In view of these facts we believe that we are entitled protection which the Constitution of the United States guarantees to its citizens against unlawful seizures. (County Superior Court Minutes, November term, 1865)

In the intense problematics raised by secession, war, and the Reconstruction, contemporary residents of Hopewell find their images of southerness and the urgency of unity. These images merge easily with the Baptist images of sacredness and, equally, with others' images of authenticity in the fact of sacrifice (even martyrdom) and defeat in the Civil War. More important to contemporary Hopewell, however, is the reconciliation that followed the war—at the time, perhaps, less a reconciliation than a mute endurance but today a testimony not only of survival but of triumph and modernity.

## "A Good One on the Boys"

The third narrative focuses on the election of 1892, when the county had made a full recovery from the devastation of the war years but was in the midst of depression. The narrative names a prominent citizen as the spokesman for the Democrats in a contest against an unnamed Alliance spokesman. The Alliance was also known as the Third party, or the People's party; it was the party of the Populists who held wide support among the small farmers of Hopewell County from the last decade of the nineteenth century until the 1920s. The county had its own political life by then; the influence of the earlier political dependence on Lynette and Harold counties had diminished with the end of the war. One index of the increasing local participation in politics is the development of local newspapers in the second half of the nineteenth century. The town's first newspaper was founded in 1870, and by 1893 it was joined by a second. When a town had more than one paper, it generally meant that each one represented the views of a particular party; newspapers were widely read and discussed. The older paper, the Hopewell *News*, was the Alliance's paper. Apparently, no copies are extant, although the Atlanta *People's Party Paper* is accessible. The *News* was survived by the second paper, the *Enterprise*.

The *News* was at one time (early 1880s) edited by the Baptist minister, the same man who figures in the Baptists' narrative about the minister and the railroad. This same man was twice elected to the state assembly. I was able to find only one published comment from a Baptist that—however indirectly—seems addressed to this man. It is a letter from a longtime church member, and appeared in the Baptist church's anniversary booklet:

[169]

I don't like "withholding more than is mete; it tendeth to poverty"; I
don't like much the annual choosing of a pastor; I don't much like
swapping off pastors too often; I don't like worshipping a preacher; I
don't like fairs, suppers, etc. to raise money for churches or missionary purposes; I don't like for Baptists to subscribe for a political
paper and leave off the Christian Index [a Baptist circular].

The Hopewell bicentennial booklet has this to say about the
Alliance: "These alliances were organizations of farmers who had
been hit very hard by the depression of 1889. They did little good
to relieve the farmers' plight, but developed into political organizations leading to the Third Party and finally the Populists." The
Populists, led by Tom Watson, were well mobilized in Hopewell
County by the mid-1890s. In 1894, for example, the local People's
party joined with other delegates to nominate Samuel Taliafero for
the state senate; the Atlanta *People's Party Paper* added that the
nomination "aroused considerable enthusiasm among the people's
party of Hopewell County. They claim that hundreds of good democrats will vote and work for Taliaferro" (September 7, 1894). In
fact, although the paper did not report the total vote cast, Taliaferro
lost in the county by only a very narrow margin (Atlanta *People's
Party Paper*, November 9, 1894).

The contest between the Populists and the Democrats seems to
have been fairly evenly drawn, but it is difficult to know who were
its supporters in Hopewell. We cannot know who the readers of the
*News* were, but the subscribers' lists of the *People's Party Paper*,
published in every issue, show no subscribers in Hopewell itself.
There were a handful farther south in the part of the county where
the greater concentration of poorer farms was.

The history of farming in Hopewell County is the history of
farming in the region in general. Hopewell was settled from two
directions by small farmers from the Carolinas and larger planters
from the coast. The land of Hopewell County was "fair to middling"
for cotton (Street 1955), never reaching the high production or the
high quality of areas farther to the south. But cotton was the reason
farmers continued to push back the Georgia frontier in the early
part of the nineteenth century. Until the advent of chemical fertilizers in the late 1850s (Flanders 1933: 98), agriculture continually

demanded new soil (Flanders 1933: 67–68). Hopewell is on the edge of Georgia's "black belt" or "slave belt," the wide band of counties across the middle of the state where plantation agriculture and slavery predominated. The southern edge of Harold County, Hopewell's neighboring mother-county, penetrated this region. There are no systematic records of agricultural production until the end of the nineteenth century, but cotton production in Harold County appears to have been twice that of Lynette (Flanders 1933). Sherman's report from the field suggests the extent of cotton farming: "I have burned a good deal of cotton, but will save enough to pay the expenses of the salute [one hundred guns at major Federal bases to celebrate the anticipated victory at Atlanta]" (United States War Department 1891). Addresses on federal army letters (for example, from Brigadier-General Jackson at "Mrs. . . . 's gin-house" on August 20, 1864 [United States War Department 1891: 981]) suggest that cotton production was sufficiently intensive that major farms had their own gins, although there is no indication of how many gins existed locally during this period. Probate records show gins assessed at one hundred dollars in 1865.

The midnineteenth century was probably the peak period for cotton production in Hopewell County. By then, chemical fertilizers and rail service made renovation of lands less expensive than relocation. For example, on the rail line that ran through Hopewell, carload lots of manure sold at two dollars a ton (Flanders 1933). By the late 1880s and early 1890s, cotton prices collapsed as a result of overproduction, creating economic disaster for some farmers and widespread political unrest. In 1899, when county reporting of cotton production began, the harvest was low. The crop peaked once more between 1909 and 1919. After 1920, production plummeted and remained low until it disappeared entirely in the early 1970s. In 1913, just after the height of the county's production, nineteen gins were active in the county, and four were idle. Gins steadily declined in number until they disappeared in the 1950s.

One local businessman's efforts to establish a gin in Hopewell during the good years early in this century is documented in correspondence that I found mouldering in the town's unused rail depot in 1973. The federal government attempted to control cotton prices by—among other things—restricting the licensing of new cotton gins. The Food Administration's reply to this man's application for a ginning license began:

> The Food Administration does not desire that any new gin plants be erected where there is at present sufficient number of gins to properly care for the 1918 crop. You will, of course, understand that a surplus of gins will only add to the manufacturing cost and will be a tax either to the producer or the consumer, and will naturally draw labor from the farms that is very much needed at this time. We hope that you will take a broad view of the situation. (Food Administration, Letter, April 15, 1918)

The letter included a short questionnaire requesting data on gin output at the five establishments closest to the businessman's proposed location. The applicant's reply was as follows:

| | | | |
|---|---|---|---|
| 1. | Hopewell | Bales ginned last season | 1654 |
| | | Bales ginned from 10/24–11/7 | 301 |
| | | Average per day 10/24–11/7 | 28 |
| 2. | Town A | Bales last season | 1067 |
| | | Bales 10/24–11/7 | 185 |
| | | Average per day 10/24–11/7 | 18 |
| 3. | Town B | Bales last season | 1148 |
| | | Bales 10/24–11/7 | 226 |
| | | Average per day 10/24–11/7 | 20 |
| 4. | Town C | Bales last season | 416 |
| | | Bales 10/24–11/7 | 139 |
| | | Average per day 10/24–11/7 | 20 |
| 5. | Town D | Bales last season | 1860 |
| | | Bales 11/7–11/20 | 311 |
| | | Average per day 11/7–11/20 | 24 |

*Source:* Applicant, Letter, April 24, 1918.

He concluded that "realizing the great necessity of a new gin outfit at this place, we desire to erect one to meet the requirements of this territory" (April 24, 1918).

If this man's figures are accurate, they give some indication of the distribution of cotton farming in the county. Together, the five gins he reported accounted for approximately 60 percent of the county's

1917 ginned crop (6,046 square bales out of a total 10,391) and five out of the county's thirteen active gins. The territory that he did not report is in the southern portion of the county and in the margins of the county closest to Harold and Lynette counties. These places were the areas of the largest farming operations (and where the "big houses" still stand, some in ruins), where farmers could perhaps afford to run their own gin operations.

The average Hopewell County farm was not large enough to earn high profits from cotton. The earliest acreage figures begin in 1924, when of the 32,671.0 acres harvested, roughly two-thirds (23,604.0 acres) were on farms of fewer than 100.0 acres (United States Department of Agriculture 1925: Table VII). The average farm in 1925 was 53.3 acres. By 1964 the number of farms (155) was 10 percent of what it had been forty years earlier (1526), but the size of the average farm had trebled (to 143.4 acres). For most of this century, cotton prices have been low; for example, in 1940 and 1945, years for which data on the market value of cotton happen to be available (United States Department of Agriculture 1945), the return per bale was roughly six dollars in 1940 and eight dollars in 1945. During the 1930s the average profit per bale was fifty cents in Mississippi (Davis, Gardner, and Gardner 1941). Georgia figures for those years are not available, but at the turn of the century, costs of producing an acre of upland cotton in Georgia represented five-sixths of its market value. The profitability of cotton farming depended primarily on yields, which appear to have fallen precipitously between the midnineteenth and early twentieth centuries. White (1849: 246) reported that the land in Lynette County produced 500.0 pounds of cotton per acre. By 1896 Watkins (1899) had placed the average yield per acre of upland cotton at 255.6 pounds. The plight of the cotton farmer becomes clear: costs per acre were rising relative to yields, and prices wobbled downward as production expanded across the South.

If cotton was an unreliable resource, it was better than other uses to which an acre of land might be put. The acreage under corn has always exceeded that of cotton in Hopewell County, but the value of corn was only half that of cotton (United States Department of Agriculture 1925–1964). Dairy farming survived the demise of other major forms of agriculture in the county, but the last dairy farm closed in the early 1970s.

Hopewell County had no cotton mills, so all cotton had to be transported elsewhere—usually to Atlanta—for processing. The rail line through the county made Hopewell a convenient market town. Other businesses associated with cotton were present in Hopewell, for example, a bag and tie plant, a gin (the applicant won his license), vehicles and farm implements sales, several general stores (Dun and Company 1928), and, later, a feed and seed store (Dun and Bradstreet 1950). Thus for some of its history, Hopewell was the center of its own small region, eclipsing its parent centers (Lynetteville and McDougall).

Hopewell County's farmers managed to withstand the Great Depression by their own system of mutual aid. Court records for 1929–1940 show virtually no foreclosures, and people held their farms with the help of neighbors and the churches. One person who remembers the Depression said that it "wiped out the castes. The bankers were as bad off as the ragged tail farmers. It was a pretty democratic thing." He recalled that the churches were active throughout the twenties and thirties in contributing to disaster relief and subsistence: "No one got real down and out."

The question of how wealth affected social status is difficult to answer at the local level:

> When the Indian lands were opened to settlers [in the 1820s], planters and small farmers moved in and began the cultivation of cotton. Here, it seemed, the small farmer was on an equal basis with the planter. But soon the natural leanness of the soil, soil exhaustion, transportation, and native ability crystallized society, and the small farmer was placed at a disadvantage. . . . [Nevertheless] the large number of professional men and merchants prevented the exclusive ranking of individuals by the criterion of land and slaves. There was no rigid social system in antebellum Georgia. (Flanders 1933: 127–128)

Indeed, the status distinctions among local farmers—very few of whom owned slaves before the war and very few of whom had farms of as much as a thousand acres (Flanders 1933: 131)—did fade and then regain their clarity at various times throughout the county's history. As Flanders's comment indicates, the earliest years of settlement were years of few social distinctions, as were the war years, but before the war, and after recovery, social boundaries appear to have been more clearly drawn. By the turn of the century, tenant farming accounted for roughly two-thirds of land tenure (United States Department of Agriculture 1925–1964); the tenants were the "ragged tail farmers" that one individual referred to above. Tenant farming declined steadily in relation to other forms of tenure from 1925, when the census records begin on this question, until it disappeared after World War II.

The collapse of tenant farming in the county appears to have marked a process of major social transformation; what is striking is contemporary residents' silence on tenants' presence or absence. I was unable to elicit descriptions of their conditions or way of life, although they were present in large numbers in the county until opportunities for wage labor increased in the city with the industrial boom following World War II. When I asked about the Third party, I was widely referred to a retired lawyer who has a reputation (well deserved) for his political acumen. He and another man, who had a long career in county affairs, attribute the Populists' strength to Tom Watson's charismatic appeal to farmers—"hero worship," in the words of one man, although he added that there were some "economic things" too. (See Key 1949: 106–129 for a discussion of charisma in twentieth-century Georgia politics.) "Folks were disgruntled with the Democrats," he said, "but the dissent was not very well crystallized. It was largely negative." The Populists were, in his words, "once powerful" in Hopewell County and won some offices, once defeating the Democratic mayor, displacing him for one term. Both men also ascribe the effectiveness of the Populists to their appeal to blacks. Watson is said (by one informant) to have gathered his original support from blacks, until the Democrats in South Carolina mobilized blacks to vote against him—then, the story went, he changed his stand. Both men cited corruption at the ballot box, as did the *People's Party Paper*, although accusing the other side. One man remembered what he called "a tale" from the 1880s and 1890s in Hopewell: Some white men locked some black men in a barn around a whiskey barrel, got them drunk, and brought them from poll to poll so that they would vote in each place. A local history (the book by an elderly resident, mentioned earlier) also refers to this or similar incidents:

The black people voted, or more correctly speaking, many of them were voted by unprincipled leaders on both sides. A common practice was for these manipulators to gather groups of blacks together the night before the election in the woods and dine and liquor them until they brought them the next day to the voting place. Stealing away by the opposition of some of the crowd was not uncommon. When voting they were supplied by pre-marked ballots. Registration and voting requirements were lax or nil, depending on the whims somewhat of the precinct managers. In some of the statewide elections, some rode trains, it was said, and voted in every town along the way, the train stopping long enough for the votes to be cast.

Today, the accounts of corruption and ballot stuffing are told as humorous tales; less so are the accounts of violence and enmity that apparently marked the county's political life in the 1880s and 1890s. The local paper (no date; in the collection of the Hopewell librarian) mentions a riot over the election of 1894, adding that no one knows the cause. The local history indicates that: "Election contests and rioting at the polls . . . was the usual rather than the exception. It was rather routine that the 'outs' would get the 'ins' indicted by the next succeeding Grand Jury for rioting or stealing an election. But by the time the trial would come up, the 'outs' would be 'ins' and the 'ins' would be 'outs' and little would ever come of it." One local man corroborated the extent of political fights. In the 1880s or 1890s, one wealthy and prominent citizen was attacked near the courthouse; his throat was slit and he barely escaped death. "[He] got real strong in the Baptist Church after that." (See Ayers [1984] for an analysis of violence, politics, and racism in the South.)

The local history contains a description of one election riot, although not the year. The judge named in the account was judge in 1880 but undoubtedly had a longer tenure:

Country precincts closed earlier than the one at the county seat [Hopewell]. The Democratic candidate . . . was a few votes ahead of the populist candidate . . . outside of [Hopewell] precinct. During the counting of [the rural] box, fighting broke out around the polling place where the votes were being counted, and Judge . . . , a Democrat and one of the election holders, refused to continue the counting until things quieted down. The hour grew late without order being restored, and finally after much bickering Populist partisans suggested that the count be postponed until morning and agreed that Judge . . . would take the ballot box home with him. Of course, there was a contest and the Hopewell box was thrown out, leaving the Democrat the winner, although it was rather conceded that had the county seat precinct been counted, the results would have been otherwise.

Close elections seem to have been common in those years. One man recalled that the general elections were considered less critical than the primaries (in which only whites were permitted to vote). He said that the Democratic party had factions based on personality. Campaigning was door to door—"soliciting votes," he called it. If someone was neglected on these rounds, he voted for the other side. The goal of each candidate was to speak personally to every registered voter. This system enabled candidates to assess their strength with great accuracy. My informant's great-uncle ran for sheriff in 1928 and predicted his victory by nine votes ("if things stay the way they are right now"), and he did.

The popularity of the Third party faded, according to both men, after Tom Watson's death in 1920. Indeed, Hopewell has had only seven mayors since 1923 and only one from 1959 until his death in office in 1986. The "colorful" electioneering of the past—as those who refer to it call it—is over. It is those years, amounting to a generation, to which the narrative refers. As in the other narratives, the profound conflict that divided the town has been effaced ("the 'outs' would be 'ins' and the 'ins' would be 'outs'"); in fact, the years of the nineties until World War II are virtually obscured by silence. Local records are absent because of fire in the courthouse. People who can give verbatim accounts of what their ancestors said to one another during the 1860s say they know nothing of this more recent period. From the determined lack of curiosity about the days of the Populists, I soon understood that it was bad manners on my part to ask about them in Hopewell.

In the fragmentary references to the days of the Populists, the most widely shared local images of identity can be understood. The distinctions between poor/rich, egalitarian/elitist, rural/urban, and insider/outsider seem to refer to the deeply felt conflict between the established Democrats and the Populists, who are today cast in the role of outside agitators. The contrasting images of this narrative simultaneously capture the Populists' program and efface it.

[177]

It identifies a particular social structure as being authentically local, and as should now be clear, these images merge easily with those whose meanings constitute the "edge" of the other narratives that have been the subject of these pages.

## History's Sacred Meanings

In this chapter, the question has been the principle by which historical knowledge is selected by people in Hopewell. The question arose in the context of the metaphors with which Baptists explain and understand salvation in their own lives. The metaphors, as Chapter 3 show, are social classifications, which are themselves carefully ascribed positive and negative value by Baptists and others in the community. Importantly, the Baptists and others alike share this symbolic "sociology" but make different sorts of claims with it—for Baptists, it is an idiom of their spirituality; for others, it is first an expression of the authenticity of their local identity. In this chapter, I try to make clear the local referents of Hopewell Baptists' spirituality, in the context of an ethnographic discussion of the general community's conceptions of the past. Local images of salvation and identity have common referents in the social divisions engendered by past crises in Hopewell.

The question of why Baptists have a special status—albeit an ambivalent one—in the town is not a question at all to the Baptists themselves. To them, it is the self-evident product of their salvation. The records of the county's earliest days illumine the question, as Baptists can be seen to have been placed in a state of political contradiction by their sectarian leadership. Thus the Baptists, whose local positions were influenced by the political interests of the aristocrats and the Troup party, could scarcely avoid disputes with their definitively nonaristocratic neighbors. Still the church managed to control its internal conflicts (Chapter 5) but could respond to external conflicts only by its own device of withdrawal. A conspicuous exception to this position was the activist minister, who not only led his Baptist congregation for many years but also served in the legislature and edited the Populist newspaper. The popular narrative about the train and the Baptist minister refers to the special ambivalence of the Baptists—literally running between two places—without referring to the controversy that produced that stance.

The second narrative, too, pushes Hopewell's greatest crisis— the war and the conflict that suffused all of the years before, during, and after—into the background in preference to the conciliatory reference to local residents and the Union victors. The emphasis on conciliation is reiterated in the version of the secession convention offered by one Hopewell citizen, a member of an old family there: He said that the county voted against secession at Milledgeville in January 1861, along with Lynette and Harold counties, but that they later reversed their votes to make the convention unanimous. Consensus within consensus, the local position yielded to give life to the larger ideal of southern unity. I could not corroborate his account in the records I was able to find, but it is a compelling example of what this chapter has been about. Its parallel is in the second narrative itself, in which the southern position yields to that of the nation reunified. But as I have suggested above, the recon- ciliation with the Union also made possible a reconciliation with groups that had been considered Union sympathizers during the war itself, that is, those who had opposed secession.

Finally, the third popular narrative refers to a generation of polit- ical turmoil, the local character of which is difficult to reconstruct. People acknowledge the period in the narrative, which has the Democrat effectively silencing the Populist by "putting one over on him." Whatever meaning the narrative had at the time of its first publication in 1893, it appears to have a wider meaning now. Im- portantly, the Populist is not named in the narrative, just as the Populists are not a part of Hopewell's presentation of its own past. When pressed, Populists are acknowledged as having filled an in- terlude in the local scene, but again, importantly, their cause is obliterated by the credit given to Tom Watson's personal charisma. In other words, the Populists are depoliticized in current memory and became a character type in the human drama.

In the Baptists' set of images of the saved—poor, agrarian, local, and southern—it is (somewhat ironically) the Populist idiom that persists. Perhaps the activist Populist minister, who guided the church through the Civil War and who became an editor-politician while still in the pulpit, was instrumental in the process of merging spiritual and local imagery. This is not to say that the church was actively political—that is impossible to know. Today, at any rate, Baptists disapprove of any political discussion from the pulpit; as I have mentioned, they actively disapprove of the Moral Majority on those grounds.

In their glorification of the novel that they say is about their town—a representation of the past—people in Hopewell conceal the past. The narratives do not quite conceal the past; they are doors left slightly ajar. Indeed, to lose the past altogether would be to make the suffering and the anguish of conflict—including the war, but not only the war—unbearable, unimaginable to the point of being absurd. This point returns the discussion to the question of what is the principle of selection in Hopewell's knowledge of the past. It is a double principle: conflict and its resolution. The resolution might not end the conflict, but it permits the conflict to be cancelled out: in the first narrative, the Baptists run to the train; in the second, the divided community unites; in the third, the Populists are silent. In the latter two cases, local people offered historical information that was explicitly a cancelling out of the underlying conflict. One person described the town as having been antisecessionist, portraying the delegates as being committed enough to consensus to change their votes. Another man depicted the electoral contests—bitter to the point of murder at the time—as an equilibrium ("ins" and "outs" evenly trading places). It is this cancelling out that permits and demands that the modern day be modern. The conclusion of the elderly resident's book is expressed as hope—a hope that I would argue also suffuses the last sentence of his book: "For those of the younger group, our narrative, we hope, may enable them to compare the transpirations of the beginning of the century with those of its ending. The results will no doubt be astonishing almost to misbelief."

The ahistoricism that so meticulously severs the present from the past is thus based on the same conception of order that precludes disputing among devout Baptists. Each is the result of the other, in a cultural sense. The elements of that conception are individualism, the personalization of the past, the conviction that personal relationships are not negotiable (nor is one's relationship to the past), and a strong affirmation of the moral value to be gained not only in harmony but in harmonizing. Harmony is the redemption of conflict. Sociology is the redemption of history. The principle of selection that guides Hopewell's knowledge of the past is, put positively, the possibility of resolving conflict. This same principle is the one that Baptists in Hopewell experience daily as their need for salvation: it is the experience of turning to prayer, that moment of acknowledging Jesus in the context of trouble—not just once but minute by minute—that epitomizes their sense of what it is to be Christian. Their sense of modernity, which is for them bound up in an ever-creative God, differs only by degree from the determined modernity of the rest of the town. The modern community—both sacred and secular—refer to the same local past. They are both "about" Hopewell. When Hopewell's Baptists pray for justice, they effectively release themselves from the burden of keeping the past with them. I have argued that their conception of order and the imagery with which they portray it originates in the development of Hopewell itself and that inseparable from the Baptists' faith is the community's conviction that their town's past might have mattered once but matters no longer.

# [5]

# Praying for Justice

The last chapter showed that the social categories that constitute Hopewell's "map"—the same categories in terms of which local Baptists apply their sociology of conflict—refer to old and unreconciled divisions in the town's past. More precisely, Chapter 4 argues that the contemporary residents' narratives of the past preserve the salience of these old factional lines. This chapter addresses the remaining piece of the ethnographic puzzle: How is it that the response to these divisions became—for the Baptists—an ethic of Christian harmony? How is it that conflict acquired its negative value in the local church community?

This chapter proposes that the contemporary equation of Christianity and harmony that is drawn so assiduously by Hopewell's Baptists began as a negotiated response to problems that were most pressing during the forty years between the first white settlement of the county and the Civil War. In other words, the local Baptists' rejection of adversarial disputing is not only local but a local tradition that developed in the first half of the nineteenth century. The scriptural and doctrinal idioms for expressing this tradition were already well established in Christianity generally. How and why did they come to take on their local character? Beyond Hopewell, law avoidance, or law aversion, was not unique during this period. Konig (1979) and Nelson (1981) described the rise and fall of consensual dispute resolution mechanisms among Massachusetts Congregationalists in slightly earlier periods. Consensus failed within those churches as the congregations were drawn into forms of social

[182]

participation beyond their local communities. Perry Miller (1965) and Strout (1974) suggested that throughout American history the polarity of order-in-law and order-in-nature has been a dominant theme. Of the early nineteenth century, Miller wrote:

> It is fair to say that into the post-Revolutionary period survived something of the old Puritan hostility to lawyers as being men sworn to advocate any case regardless of its merits. But by 1790 or 1800 . . . , the distrust had become basically suspicion of the law as by its very nature sophisticated, whereas the American people are natural, reasonable, equitable. A last echo of this legal pietism persisted as late as 1846 in the claim that the Gospel forbids brother to sue brother. (1965: 104)

Thus the local Baptists built their ethic at least in part out of elements that were available in the culture at large. Some of Hopewell's earliest white settlers might have imported some anabaptist ideas with them from south-central Pennsylvania, where, two and three generations earlier, they had settled with other German families in what remains Amish country (see Hostetler 1968). At least one of the major families to move to the county after the treaty with the Creeks was from Lancaster, Pennsylvania, the heart of the Amish region.

In the formation of the concepts of conflict that are at issue here, the fact that the social group involved is a religious one suggests some of its imagery and idiom but by no means all of it. At crucial points, the local Baptists invoked their American identity and, at a particularly critical juncture, their southern identity. These larger identifications were drawn into a strategy that transformed conflict so effectively that it no longer threatened the local church's survival but instead essentially guaranteed it. The stages in this process of transformation were defined by crises that inspired progressively refined responses. The data in this chapter derive from the minutes of the Baptist church association that included the Baptist churches from what became Hopewell County and neighboring Lynette and Harold counties (see Chapter 4). The local associations were relatively autonomous within the national church association. This one met annually to settle matters of business and discipline and, it seems, to encourage local church leadership in their efforts toward community revival. I call this local association simply "the association," although each group was in fact named for some local geographical feature or for a particular member church. We know virtually nothing of the founding of the association, except that it was one of many formed in the national effort on the part of Baptists to reach and rationalize grass roots membership.

From the very earliest days, the minutes contrast modes of authority to Baptist doctrine, which focuses so emphatically on unmediated individual relationships with God. The early minutes refer benignly to harmony as a sign of God's approval, but this harmony was tested many times during the first half of the nineteenth century. Nationally, Protestant churches responded—sometimes with division—to the national events whose local reverberations are explored in Chapter 4 and here. Marty (1977: 125) traced the allegiances of the Baptists during the American Revolution, when Northern Baptists allied with the crown (until 1775) against the Congregationalists, while Southern Baptists allied with Jefferson, Madison, and Mason against the "Episcopal establishment." Hopkins (1940) pointed to the major impact of the Civil War on Protestants nationally, and events leading up to the war included the schisms that produced the Southern Baptist convention and the Primitive Baptists. Wallace (1978: 459–467) mapped the impact of the Civil War on millennial fundamentalism in a northern town, Rockdale. The period about which Hopewell is most silent—the Populist era—was an epoch of major Protestant realignment (Szasz 1982: xi); the Great Depression, too, became divisive as social reform strained against the conservativism of the southern churches particularly (Szasz 1982: 106). In the pages that follow, the shadows—never the faces—of these developments dance across the records of the local church. The purpose of the chapter is to connect local historical consciousness to the sacred meanings of harmony in Hopewell.

## Baptists in and around Hopewell

The Hopewell church played a distinctive role in every period of the local association's history. The church was founded in 1825, after several years during which members met informally and irregularly in the homes of Baptist preachers who were among the county's earliest white settlers. For many years, until 1849, this church was Hopewell's only church. The church's own published history, written in celebration of the congregation's anniversary in the mid-1950s, is largely an account of memberships and the succession of ministers. Even this relatively bland record reflects some of the consequences of the association's early tumultuous years. Throughout the 1830s, internal disagreements divided churches in Hopewell and in the surrounding area; other churches were schismatic and suffered secessions. In the 1840s, too, regional issues severely divided the local association. In 1856 the local minister himself was excluded from the church in a case of what the minutes called "gross" (but unspecified) conduct (Baptist Association *Minutes* 1879: 27).[1] The Hopewell church also led the region's temperance movement, excluding members who drank alcohol or sold "ardent spirits." Importantly, Hopewell Baptists who are interested in their church's institutional past clearly identify not with these early days but with a later period, one romanticized in the published history and in people's memories—the postwar church of the 1880s. Yet it is in the early period, between the church's founding and the cataclysms of the war years and Reconstruction, that Christianity and harmony were welded together in the specifically local context of Hopewell. The process of drawing explicit connections between the Christian life and social harmony was an extended one that developed in three distinct phases. These phases were marked by regional disputes that were particularly deeply felt at the local level for reasons outlined in the previous chapter.

The discussion here traces the development of the new symbolism of Christian harmony in Hopewell. In tracing the outlines of this history, the minutes form a fortuitous record in that they make the fact of the embeddedness of local doctrine in the historical process clear. They also form a frustrating record, in that the discourse of the minutes omits direct reference to most of the sources and substance of the conflicts that so shaped local thinking. In other words, although we know that there were local issues divisive enough to make local churches struggle to contain and rechannel

---

1. Further references in this chapter, unless otherwise noted, are to the association *Minutes*, 1825–1901. Citations are to year and either page number or item number, depending on the density of references in any particular year.

the conflicts that surrounded them, we do not know precisely what they were.

In any event, the earliest years—three at most—of the association's records are marked by a studied harmony. The absence of dissension at the early conventions was taken as "demonstrative evidence of Divine approbation to this step [the founding of the association] in your Christian procedures" (1825a: 8). The idea of harmony as a sign of God's approval was never directly mentioned among the Baptists I knew in Hopewell. As we have seen, people might refer to their own struggle for harmony as a sign of their commitment to Jesus, but it was the struggle, not the result, that informed believers. As will soon be clear, this particular significance of harmony had to be abandoned as it became increasingly clear that the local association was not of one mind on any number of questions.

The association defined its purposes as threefold: maintenance of the gospel in a state of "purity"; "settling of the Churches upon the Apostolic plan"; and maintenance of a pure and "unblamable" ministry. In theory, church leaders could accomplish this business by submitting themselves to the Lord's will. In practice, the association was faced with the question of how to resolve disagreements and promulgate decisions without violating the very doctrine it was commited to defend. The founders were careful to justify their authority in terms of experience rather than some sacred mandate: "[W]e would [not] exercise authority over you, but . . . experience has proven that something of this kind is necessary [so that?— illegible] things may be done with decency and good order . . . ; believing it to be consistent with the word of God . . . and strictly necessary to prevent error" (1825a: 8). Indeed, authority became a central and critical issue for the association, since the association's jurisdiction required that it intervene in local churches in two domains: the interpretation of scripture and the licensing of preachers.

Early on, the association proferred authoritative judgments in response to queries submitted in writing and recorded in the minutes. Letters of inquiry touched on questions of doctrine, membership requirements, the technicalities of dismission and excommunication, and so on. Even when letters were relatively extensive in detailing the ramifications of some problem, the association sometimes answered simply yes or no; it rarely offered elaboration or justification. The lack of justification suggests the extent to which the association assumed its own legitimacy—or, perhaps, held to the position that God's will is not subject to human reasoning. The queries are interesting glimpses of community life around Hope-well in the very early days of white settlement as the churches acquired an important role as mediators of social credit (see Weber 1946a).[2] The minutes also regularly included sermons and "circular letters" that dealt with local church problems with varying degrees of directness.

The association was compelled to take more direct action in the licensing of preachers and the maintenance of doctrinal purity. In many cases, these two issues could not be separated, and an early statement by the association gives some sense of the very prob-lematic stances these needs entailed. A preacher qualified himself by being unable to resist the calling, which set him apart from—and above—other believers: "[He] will be electrified with love to God and man; having an impression of mind, that a dispensation of the Gospel is committed to him. . . . [He] will also at the same time have a discovery of his incapacity and fear to venture; having awful apprehensions that he may dishonor the Redeemer's cause here on earth" (1826: 6–7). The intensity of the calling could be measured by a new preacher's fervor, but his freedom from error was a more difficult matter to judge. In the 1820s, the association defined *orthodoxy* as being simply knowledge; *dissent* became "false knowledge." Knowledge was thought to be authored by God and error authored by men. The fact that knowledge was thought to be God's word and will simultaneously (since, in the case of God, *word* equals *will*) meant that knowledge was, by definition, right. What was right was also compelling. By means of this logic, the association was able to define its relationship to the control of preachers without raising the issue of human authority, until that issue was raised by a growing number of dissidents in member churches.

The first of the overt protests against the association's legitimacy and modes of control erupted in 1829, and they continued, with a

2. The full set of queries available in the minutes of the Baptist Association *Minutes* is presented in Appendix 1.

few lulls, until the Civil War. The minutes rarely reveal what the causes of the disputes were, but they give ample voice to the responses of member churches to the association's official role. Sometimes the debate extended beyond the association to sister groups in other parts of Georgia. The typical pattern of these disputes was one of rapid escalation. I infer that the opening round was in the form of some letter of complaint or a query from a member church, unable to contain its own debate. The association's response would take the form of an investigatory team, which would attend a church meeting and interview members. Orthodox members would be reconstituted as the church, and heterodox members—even if they were the majority—would be expelled. The association was very careful to characterize expulsion as its own withdrawal from impurity. Even so, member churches readily recognized the authoritative aspects of withdrawal. The first such dispute was greatly intensified by the volatile and allegedly heterodox preacher, who refused to allow the examining committee "or any other set of men under Heaven" to assess his church (1829: item 32). The idiom of his response—rejecting the authority of the association rather than debating the doctrinal issue—became typical. The association's attempts at conciliation took the form of pleas for "mutual forbearance" and "Christian communication" (1832: 3–4); there could be no compromise since the issue was presented as being one of God's will, not human contention.

Divisions in the churches and diminished memberships became so numerous by the mid-1830s that the association began to complain of "languidness" (1835: 7) and "coldness" (1836: 2) in its churches.[3] There was some effort to review the heterodox groups that had been expelled from the association, apparently in the hope of recalling some of them, but the result was only a reaffirmation of the original divisions. The spirit of tension sharpened severely over the question of "benevolent associations" in the second half of the decade. Some local Baptists objected to any church support for missionary groups, temperance societies, Sunday schools, and so forth on the grounds that they would blur the scripturally demanded separation between members of the church and "the

3. The table in Appendix 2 shows the membership of the Hopewell church from its founding in 1824 until the turn of this century.

world." The doctrinal objections to dunning church members for money or other forms of material support for these causes have a long tradition in this region. Indeed, clergy were not paid a salary until this century; the Hopewell clergy lived on donations from the church members until after World War I. In the context of the 1830s, however, the doctrinal objections spoke for other voices, as the battle against "benevolent associations" became the cry of anti-Cherokee forces and antiabolitionists, who feared that these groups would benefit from church-sponsored support. The association refused to bar benevolent associations, and significantly, its grounds were not doctrinal so much as libertarian: "freemen" ought to have the right to dispose of their "names or money" as they choose (1838: 5). This response marks a new phase in the history of local Christian symbolism, since it transforms the issue of authority from one of religious doctrine alone to include political doctrine in a postrevolutionary state:

> The Baptist denomination have always boasted of the freedom of conscience, which is allowed them in supporting the Gospel in the way which each member might feel inclined to do—Therefore, none are compelled to give or not to give, even to their own Pastors, but the case is left between them and their God, to be governed by his word. . . . [O]ur forefathers might as well have submitted to a grievous taxation, without a fair Representation, for Baptists now to yield up the rights of conscience to the domineering spirit of ecclesiastical usurpation. . . . Pure religion is better understood by being felt, than it can be by being defined. (1838: 5)

In this extraordinary passage, the association secularizes its imagery in an entirely new way. The new idiom represents a widening of local religious discourse, in that it later permits direct responses to regional and national events, such as the secession of the Southern Baptists from the national convention in 1845 (1845: 7) and the secession of the South from the Union (1861: 11). The secular assertions of equality were only functionally equivalent to the religious deference to the authority of Jesus. Symbolically, the secular image of equality, based as it was in political freedom, demanded that the association relinquish some of its role as overt arbiter of doctrinal matters. This is the significance of the statement that "pure religion is better understood by being felt, than it can be by being defined."

At this same moment, the association pulled back from some manifestations of its direct authority; the minutes of the late 1830s and early 1840s request that member churches stop sending queries to the leadership, except as a remote last resort (for example, 1843: 8–9). Presumably, the rise in church memberships that began in 1840 (Hopewell church was singled out for praise [1840: 6]) proved the efficacy of these innovations.

As the region and nation became increasingly caught up in the events that led to war in 1861, the voice of the association became increasingly fluent as a southern voice, as pleas were published for support against "Northern fanatics" (1840: 7), for "the necessity of separating from our Northern Brethren" (1845: 7), or, finally, as the association "pledge[d] ourselves as citizens to the defence and support of the Southern Confederacy" (1861: 11). On religious matters, the association's new voice was increasingly abstract, allegorical, and indirect. Indeed, for the first time in the mid-1840s, the association published an opinion that explicitly separated religion and politics on moral, if not doctrinal, grounds:

> And how is he rebuked, who by profession a preacher of righteousness, becomes a "noisy dabbler in party politics?" . . . He may become popular: but his is the popularity, not of the *preacher*, but of the *partizan*, and the homage which he receives is paid, not to his *piety*, but to his political *zeal*. And worse than all, his time is wasted, his spirituality destroyed, his feelings embittered, his usefulness diminished, and the success of his labors sinfully obstructed. (1844: 10; original emphasis and orthography)

In articulating the perils of piety and politics sharing the same breast, the association found the central image that remains current today. The difference today is that the proscription is general and abstract. In these early days, the proscription would have been specific, one designed to preserve the churches against a succession of schisms the leadership feared would be fatal. The published minutes began to reflect a new tone of other-worldliness, stressing the ideal of separation from the world to a greater degree than ever before. For example, in a circular letter exhorting Christians to refrain from drink and common social vices, the author included the following advice: "While many others [that is, self-proclaimed Baptists] are to be seen in the streets talking politics—telling their social jests or conversing about subjects which should be considered beneath the dignity of the children of God. . . . This is not yielding fruit to the glory of God" (1848: 6–7). Letters, too, stressed the need to abandon "undue attachment to the world" (1849: 7), the importance of evangelism (1851: 7), and the need for uniform rules of practice, or decorum (1850: 9). Circular letters finally ceased entirely in 1852, silencing that formerly authoritative counsel and giving way to a series of committee reports on the various concerns of the association.

The last great issue to divide the association before the Civil War was the leadership's attempt to print and promulgate an "abstract of faith."[4] Dissident churches resisted the claimed right of any group to form a synopsis of scripture and to offer it as the word of God; once again, it was the association's authority that was attacked. Also once again, there were expulsions and secessions. The debate was long and heated. It unfolded in the familiar pattern, except that the association found yet another way to assert its new proscriptions against politicking by claiming that conflict itself is heterodox: "[I]f any preacher . . . shall disturb the peace and harmony of this Association, by advocating the cause of such violators of compact and union, they shall be considered under the censure of this body and turned over, to answer for their conduct, to the church or churches of which he or they may be members" (1852: item 9). This was the most explicit attempt on the part of the association to suppress conflict. The earliest efforts had been to reduce the rate of conflict; next, they had been addressed to creating Christian modes of disputing. In this new context, conflict itself was rejected categorically as being unchristian.

The effect of the war on the association was to cement the equa-

4. The abstract of faith, reprinted many times (the one below is from 1850), is as follows (in the minutes, it is entitled simply "Faith"): "1. We believe in one only true and living God, and that there are three persons in the Godhead—the Father, the Son, and the Holy Ghost. 2. We believe that the Scriptures of the Old and New Testaments are the Word of God, and the only rule of faith and practice. 3. We believe in the doctrine of eternal and particular election. 4. We believe in the doctrine of original sin. 5. We believe in man's impotency to recover himself from the fallen state he is in by nature, by his own free will and ability. 6. We believe that sinners are justified in the sight of God only by the imputed righteousness of Christ. 7. We believe that God's elect shall be called, regenerated and sanctified by the Holy Ghost."

[191]

tion, then newly formed, between Christianity and silenced conflict. The minutes express solidarity for the southern cause, and the
record of the war years is filled with accounts of missionary and
other supportive efforts. In responding to the war first as southerners and second as Baptists, the association experienced a new form
of unity.[5] Earlier rallying points had been internal disputes; however, the war provided the organization with a focal point beyond its
own administration and mobilization. The war accomplished something that the association had not been able to accomplish on its
own: the conclusive bond of harmony, Christianity, and southernness. In the new spirit of union through common suffering and the
common need for redemption, some of the divisions over doctrinal
questions and issues of authority were resolved; others grew silent.
Indeed, with only one brief exception, conflict never again crossed
the pages of the minutes. Throughout the war and the painful years
of Reconstruction, the association never failed to meet, although
the minutes—always cryptic—became increasingly skeletal and
uninformative. The record of the years after 1865 was primarily
concerned with activities of the association within the church communities, for example, temperance, the establishment of prayer
meetings, Sunday school, the reiteration of the rules of decorum
(reprinted in every annual report), and the articles of faith. In 1868
advertisements for consumer goods (clothes, shoes, and so on) began to appear and continued. Dancing was unanimously ruled disorderly in 1870, and violation of the rule was sanctioned by "withdrawal" by the association. From 1866 until the available minutes
ceased in 1901, there were no signs of disputes or divisions, even
when, at the turn of this century, the region was severely divided
by the split between the Populists and the Democrats (see Chapter
4). Unlike Cherokee removal and the benevolent associations, populism as a cause seems not to have played in the arena of local
religious doctrine, at least not in the Baptist church. In a sense, this

5. Hopkins (1940: 11–15) notes the galvanizing impact of the Civil War on
American Protestants generally. Particularly after the Civil War, the churches split
to form two groups, the fundamentalists and the modernists. The modernists, who
preached a "social gospel," addressed what they saw as the excesses of capitalism
with a collection of programs for reform (Hopkins 1940: 323–324, May 1949, and
Miller 1958). The Baptist church in Hopewell—as this chapter shows—has consistently taken a strong conservative stance on the role of the church in social and
political issues. For general discussion, see also Eighmy (1972).

was a triumph. The separation of religious and political discourses had long been the goal of the association leadership. The final minutes reflect only the association's role as the facilitator of local business and everyday life.

As I have mentioned, contemporary Baptists do not refer to this early period. Instead, their church's past seems to begin after Reconstruction. In Hopewell, the postwar years were a period of revival. The first great revival came during the years 1891 to 1896 and was accompanied by a building program. The church itself was destroyed by wind or lightning (accounts differ) in 1892. The only indicator that disputes possibly occurred within the church during this period is a published reference to conferences that met each Saturday before the Sunday services (twice monthly): "At these conferences members in bad standing were given a chance to speak for themselves. If the church deemed it necessary, such members were excluded" (Baptist Church *History* 1956: 8). Unfortunately, there is no existing record of such exclusions, although church membership shows a period of decline beginning in 1895.

The church "took on new life" in 1920 (Baptist Church *History* 1956: 9), when the minister made the church a social center for the town at large: a playground, movies, a library, a tennis court, and a water fountain fulfilled the minister's declaration of purpose: "[T]he church ought to be a community center. It ought to be made useful to folks in order to get folks. It ought, somehow, to be the center of the clean and helpful social life of the community. It ought to be the center of the intellectual life of the community, and it goes without saying that it ought to be the heart, the beating, pulsing heart of the spiritual life of the community" (Baptist Church *History* 1956: 9). Again, in the midst of revival, the church building burned to the ground. Much of the contemporary pattern of weekday activity began during this period, when church members formed money-raising activities to build a new sanctuary. Women sold dinners on the days when court was in session across the street, the church ran a booth at the southeastern fair, there were sales of candy and cakes, and so on. The minister, perhaps in a show of sectarian pride, refused offers from the Methodists and Presbyterians to shelter the congregation's worship services during the rebuilding. Instead, he accepted a secular association, borrowing the school auditorium, empty on Sundays.

Baptists' accounts of revivals form a small genre of their own. In 1894 "Wash" Oliver, an illiterate preacher from Milner, Georgia, was leading a prayer meeting under a tent when a violent storm blew up and extinguished all the lanterns. He shouted his prayers over the storm, praying for the storm to end, which it did—bringing forth many new conversions. Oliver went on to preach in Hopewell to a crowd of farmers whose fields were parched by a long summer drought. He prayed for rain and "brought pouring rain out of a cloudless sky" and saved eighty seven souls. (Contemporary Baptists do not tend to link prayer so directly to events, nor do they encourage prayer for specific benefits.) The stories about "Wash" Oliver are interesting because they appear to associate his lack of social grace (his illiteracy) with heightened spiritual grace (rainmaking); this remains a popular theme. Another period of revival was in 1951, when a "continuous chain of prayer" spanned the entire week of revival; presumably this meant praying in shifts for almost two hundred hours. Other accounts tell of prayer meetings that had to adjourn before all the testimony could be taken, and so on. The association of revival with meteorological events and the literal conflagration of churches takes on a feeling of the apocryphal, although the weather and the destruction of the buildings can be verified. The church's historical records were burned in the two fires mentioned.

The local church history and the association's minutes overlap, but the relationship between them remains largely a matter of inference. It is clear that the local church's leadership was disproportionately active in the association and was important in its leadership during the early years of trouble. We can infer from that what the local church stood for over questions of association authority, benevolent associations, secession, and the ideology of conflict propounded by the association during its first forty years. At the same time, those positions were not unanimously held by the local community; one report, unverified and possibly untrue, suggests that church membership fell as low as seven during the late 1830s. Churches in neighboring towns, for example, in Harold County, divided. It would be unreasonable to presume that the Hopewell church alone would be free of dispute. The local church's legitimacy as an agency of social control was apparently greater than that of the association, however, since the local church continued to examine and exclude members publicly as late as the early part of this century, although no records remain to reveal what the offenses and procedures were. The only specific reference to exclusion comes much earlier, in 1864, when forty black members were excluded for running away from their owners during the war. The remaining twenty-three blacks were constituted into their own church, a block away from the white Baptist church, where it remains today. Thus we can infer that the divisions within the local church, although serious, came early and that the consolidation effected at that time (the early 1840s) remained viable, whereas that of the association was tested several times subsequently.

At each point in the sequence of events that the minutes outline, the same negative aspect of conflict is singled out for elaboration. In theory, conflict itself is not unchristian, but rather the authority it calls forth contradicts local understandings of Baptist doctrine. In practice, the association must continually push away the conflicts that its members confront it with in order to avoid being pulled into contradiction between its doctrinal claims about personal autonomy and its potential role as mediator or arbitrator. In the single dispute that is mentioned in the minutes following the war (in 1875), the full day spent hearing testimony about a slander of one church member by an adversary from another congregation is remanded back to the congregation for negotiation. Thus it is entirely reasonable to characterize the ultimate state of the association as one of consensus, but it is crucial to add that the consensus itself was restricted to the value placed on consensus.

## Christian Harmony and the Desire for Justice

We have retraced the outlines of the historical development of the negative value Hopewell Baptists place on disputing and adversarial confrontation in other forms such as in politics. The clearest link between this process of development and the local historical consciousness discussed in Chapter 4 is in the crisis over benevolent associations. The earliest resistance to "missionary societies" placed dissidents at loggerheads with the local Baptists' support for the Cherokees; at the end of the antebellum era, as we have just seen, the dissidents led the antiabolition movement. There is also a

[195]

more subtle connection between the historical events that shaped the local Baptist church and central ethnographic problem of this book, which is to account for the particular importance Hopewell Baptists place on conflict in proscribing it. Contemporary Baptist historical consciousness limits the rubric of "the past" to the period since the Civil War, virtually obliterating the period during which the local religious idiom took on its modern form. It is the selectivity of the local temporal dimension that underscores the connection between the modernity and the faith of contemporary Baptists. The active proscription of conflict is an everyday gesture toward the very sources of Hopewell's sense of community, yet one that simultaneously closes those sources—they are dry wells. In discussing the importance of historical closure, we could close with the conclusion, from Durkheim, that "religion is something eminently social" (1965: 22).

What remains is to explore one more theme, and that is the quality of justice Baptists claim to find in their faith. What is its nature? What is its Christianity? What desire gives it continued life in the enduring logic of the Hopewell church? These questions do not ask, what are the results of Baptists' ideas of justice? Such a question betrays the asker as a nonbeliever, since the notion of "result" in advance of some final judgment is moot. They ask, instead, about the shape of hope.

Whatever this justice is, it has a twin: harmony. It is the twin whose face we have been exploring. As we have seen, harmony is Christian because it became Christian in this specific locale at a particular historical moment. Harmony obviates the need for human authority, which is to say that harmony guarantees some fundamental equality for all believers. Equality clearly has secular referents as a key symbol, but it also has sacred referents, since all "brethren" are equal under God. We have been exploring the development of this logic, which connects harmony to Christian brotherhood through the image of equality. There is more to this logic, which if we were to stop here would evoke the civil religion that opened this book. What makes the Hopewell Baptists' harmony a very particular religious statement is a set of definitions that give harmony its moral content. First, as we have seen most clearly in the historical material, harmony implies by its very existence the absence of error in interpreting God's word. Thus a harmonious society can on some level be understood as the very image of God's will, although I never heard a contemporary Baptist put matters so directly. Second, harmony implies—again, by its very existence— the purity that we have seen developing in the early years of the association: purity derived from consistent withdrawal from hetero- dox elements. This is no contradiction to the modern idea of the life of a good witness, since witnessing categorically defines the liminal aspects of a believer's life in the world. Importantly, purity is not the same thing as unity, since consensus on the response to hetero- doxy does not necessarily or simultaneously define orthodoxy in any affirmative way. In fact, harmony has a somewhat negative cast, in that its meaning has more to do with the silencing of disputes than with the absence of disagreement. The early church record is clear on this point. Believers in those days would have felt very keenly the test of their faith that silencing their tongues constituted. To- day, believers readily state that Jesus helps them cope with trou- ble, not that he has effaced the impulses of anger or grief that trouble brings. These meanings—of harmony, freedom from error, purity—all give considerable focus to Baptists' sense of need for salvation, as well as their sense of focus in their faith.

Thus if the question is: what is Christian about harmony in Hope- well? the answer must lie in the direction of the faith that at once suspends self-interest and compels it. Just as Baptists celebrate the ability of spiritually mature individuals to set their own interests aside, in doing so, they illumine the very interests that seem on the point of vanishing. This point returns us to the personal sketches that opened the first chapter. The local understanding of the con- cept of being "born again" revises one's autobiography to begin at the moment of conversion—often the subject of public testimony— which is to say at a point of self-consciousness in crisis. Salvation is contingent on acknowledging one's own spiritual and perhaps phys- ical frailty. The liberation is as large as the burden.

As I understand Hopewell Baptists' thinking on the "born-again experience," the idea of salvation takes shape as a yearning, as desire. It is desired, surely, as the proof of faith. Such proofs are valued in individuals' quests for self-knowledge. Salvation is also desired as a form of freedom, and this connection brings us closer to

[197]

the heart of the particular justice believers say salvation will provide. The freedom local Baptists describe is, in general terms, freedom from the constraining judgments of other people: "Jesus lets me feel free to be me," as one teenager said. The longer statements of Martha Jean, Mack, or Lynn, or the many other people whose testimonies I heard in public or privately, amount to the same thing. Yet as their testimonies also suggest, freedom is not the same thing as the desire for freedom. This distinction is key. Freedom in some ultimate form would sever the very bonds these many individuals struggled for the strength to preserve. Faith is, indeed, referred to as spiritual *strength*. These men and women do not use their strength to break their social ties but to sustain them. The freedom that salvation promises is not invoked in its entire, full form but is instead invoked as a possibility that bathes in light the partnerships that are the heart of their social concerns. In framing a desire for freedom—and the desire for freedom is not freedom— believers articulate relationships, the idea of whose rewards they cherish. In the desire for freedom, more than in freedom, individuals simultaneously evoke their mutual separateness and their bonds. In their confirmed desire for freedom, the hypothesis that social life can be understood in terms of personal meaning is both confirmed and clarified.

When Hopewell's Baptists pray for justice, I believe that they pray for this clarity, which is the very particular harmony that has been the subject of this chapter. It is a harmony founded in and manifested in certainty. It is a harmony that would, in its own terms, guarantee the conditions of freedom. The conditions of freedom are understood as equality and the reserved expressions of authority we saw perfected in the midnineteenth century. The social categories whose constructions this book has examined acquire their meanings through symbolic claims that would make these categories, in part, rehearsals for this ultimate moment of judgment and reward. As we have seen, the meanings emerge out of sharply drawn contrasts among generic types of person and experience, and these are themselves contemporary references to Hopewell's historical experience. These prayers for justice require and plead that history remain silent, just as much as they require and plead for the silence of men and women whose desires for freedom bring them to prayer.

## Appendix 1: Queries to the Baptist Association

The following sets of questions and answers compose the full set of queries considered by the association. I include them to indicate the sorts of issues that concerned the membership.

1826, item 16. Querie: Shall a Minister of the Gospel be considered orthodox in the faith, who says he believes in the doctrine of Election, but does not think it right to preach it for it is discouraging to sinners. [Answer] We answer no. [No explanation]

1826, p. 2, item 17. Q.: Consistent with Gospel for all male members to have property assessed and dunned for support of clergy and church (?) [Answer] No.

1826, p. 3, item 18. Q.: What would [be] the most proper course to pursue with a member, who has a letter of final dismission from a church who offers the same for membership, but is refused by a member in the church, in consequence of a hurt given, yet the person applying, cannot see that he has given cause of hurt, and wishes to be heard? [Answer] We advise the Church to receive the letter, and then call the aggrieved brethren and deal accordingly.

1826, p. 3, item 20. Q.: How to give letters of dismission. [Answer] As final.

1826, p. 3, item 21. Q.: What shall be done with the excommunicant who refuses to give up his letter or credentials? [Answer] If all else fails, send names to Assoc. so names can be printed in minutes.

1826, p. 3, item 22. Q.: Whereas a matter of difficulty has arisen among us, in that a brother, (and he a Deacon,) though different of our members have often labored with him, and the church also, but he still holds and contends that God created man for the express purpose to fall, and that God never sent a judgement on any people for their transgressions, but to show forth his power; and further, that the Devil, together with the whole human race, does the Lord's will in all cases? We ask your advice. [Answer] We advise to have no fellowship with fatalism or universalism, and advise churches to withdraw from such as believe in either.

[199]

1827, p. 2, item 26. Q.: What shall be done with members holding letters of final dismission and will not give them up? [Answer recommends that they] be amenable to the church in whose vicinity he may reside.

1828, p. 2, item 11. Q.: How shall a church proceed with members who are reported to walk disorderly, but in such a way as not to be seen by a member of the church, but by others. [Answer] Cite him to the conference, and, on trial, give all testimony the weight which the church may believe to be deserving, and provided the testimony goes to the removing of fellowship, exclude them.

1828, p. 2, item 11. Q.: Is it right for a church to debar members from getting their letters [of dismission], let them live at what distance they may, if they are in full fellowship? [Answer] No.

1829, p. 2, item 12. Q.: What shall be done with a member that has taken a letter of dismission from a church of our order in any part of the Union, and continues to live in the bounds or convenient to any of the churches in this Assoc., and withholds said letter and lives immorally at the same time? [Answer refers to "similar case" in earlier minutes.]

1829, p. 2, item 13. Q.: Is it right to receive a member who has had a letter of dismission and has lost it, by one member of the church testifying that he has seen it, and that it was a good letter? [Answer] We believe it to be right, provided a new letter cannot be obtained.

1829, p. 2, item 14. Q.: [Query asks how to proceed with licensing a minister to preach.] [Answer] First encourage this gift in the home church, seek judgment of old and experienced ministers; do not flaunt the gift, travel with those ministers from whom one can learn.

1838, p. 2, item 9. Query: What shall be done with a member who was excluded on a charge of unsoundness of Faith; by a Church which has since then seceded from our Union, and now said member applies to a church which is still in our Union for membership. [Answer] Inasmuch as we view those Churches as having departed from Original Baptist usage, by setting up a new standard of fellowship, it is the sense of this body, that should such applicant fully satisfy the church of the soundness of his faith and the correctness of his christian deportment, that he should be received into her fellowship.

1847, p. 2, item 10. Query. What is the duty of Churches in reference to members applying for and obtaining letters of dismission, and holding said letters for years in the bounds of the church? [Answer] We recommend the churches to exercise their discretionary power.

1847, p. 3, item 21. Query. Have the Anti-missionary Baptists, by their non-fellowship resolutions, and by their resolutions to re-baptize applicants who have been baptized by our ministers, caused divisions among us contrary to the doctrines which we have learned from the Bible, or not? [Answer] We think they have. (Q.) If yea, we then wish to know if it is consistent with Bible truth and good christian order, to invite their preachers into our pulpits to preach, or should be avoid them? [Answer] We believe it is not consistent.
N.B. Passed unanimously.

1847, p. 3, item 22. Query found on the table. Is it right in the nineteenth century, for the Church to receive into, or hold in fellowship, a member who is a vender of spiritous liquors, except for medicinal purposes? [Answer] We believe it is not right.

1847, p. 3, item 23. Is it necessary that applicants for membership with us from the United Baptists, should be re-Baptized? [Answer] We think it is not necessary, if they were Baptized in order.

1856, p. 10, item 19. Query—Will it be right to retain a member who distills ardent spirits? Answer unanimous, as follows: Whilst we are not prepared to affirm that the making and selling of spiritous liquor are positively sinful in and of themselves, as they may possibly be used for medical, chemical, mechanical, and other useful purposes: But, should a brother make or sell ardent spirits under such circumstances as would induce a reasonable man, in the exercise of a prudent discretion, to foresee that drunkenness or intemperance will be the direct consequences of his act, then we hold such conduct altogether disorderly and unbecoming a Christian. And should such a brother persist after gospel steps taken to reclaim him from his error, then we should advise his expulsion.

*Source:* Baptist Association, *Minutes,* 1825–1865.

# Appendix 2: Membership of Hopewell Church, 1824–1895

| Year | Baptized | By letter | Dismissed | Excommunicated | Dead | Total Members |
|------|----------|-----------|-----------|----------------|------|---------------|
| 1824 | 13 | 14 | | | | |
| 1825 | 8 | 12 | | | | 59 |
| 1826 | 10 | 11 | 1 | | | 79 |
| 1827 | 27 | 10 | 15 | 2 | | 99 |
| 1828 | 0 | 1 | 9 | | | 89 |
| 1829 | 8 | 14 | 20 | | | 89 |
| 1830 | 1 | 8 | 4 | 4 | | 87 |
| 1831 | (no records available) | | | | | 74 |
| 1832 | 1 | 6 | 5 | 3 | | 73 |
| 1833 | 2 | 3 | 13 | 2 | | 63 |
| 1834 | 5 | 5 | 13 | | | 60 |
| 1835 | 3 | 8 | 9 | 1 | | 61 |
| 1836 | 0 | 3 | 5 | 1 | 2 | 57 |
| 1837 | 1 | 0 | 5 | | | 56 |
| 1838 | 8 | 7 | 3 | | | 51 (1 restored) |
| 1839 | 3 (?) | 11 | 6 | 13 | 3 | 52 (1 restored) |
| 1840 | 43 | 13 | 9 | | 1 | 100 (2 restored) |
| 1841 | (no records available) | | | | | |
| 1842 | 24 | 13 | 3 | 3 | | 135 |
| 1843 | 27 | 5 | 9 | 1 | | 156 |
| 1844 | 41 | 13 | 18 | 4 | 3 | 185 |
| 1845 | 10 | 6 | 13 | 1 | 1 | 186 |
| 1846 | 0 | 3 | 64 | 1 | | 124 |
| 1847 | 0 | 13 | 0 | 8 | | 129 (4 restored) |
| 1848 | 27 | 16 | 5 | 3 | 2 | 163 (1 restored) |
| 1849 | 1 | 3 | 14 | 1 | 3 | 150 |
| 1850 | 47 | 25 | 14 | 4 | 2 | 203 (2 restored) |
| 1851 | 26 | 11 | 8 | 1 | 2 | 229 |
| 1852 | 5 | 15 | 20 | 1 | | 222 |
| 1853 | (no records available) | | | | | |
| 1854 | 8 | 5 | 11 | 1 | 3 | 209 |
| 1855 | 0 | 6 | 7 | 7 | 3 | 196 |
| 1856 | 41 | 13 | 13 | | 4 | 234 (1 restored) |
| 1857 | 26 | 12 | 13 | 3 | 6 | 258 (2 restored) |
| 1858 | 4 | 5 | 22 | 3 | 2 | 240 (1 restored) |
| 1859 | 7 | 5 | 42 | 3 | 1 | 207 (1 restored) |
| 1860 | 0 | 6 | 18 | 1 | 1 | 193 |
| 1861 | 10 | 11 | 13 | 2 | 1 | 207 (1 restored) |
| 1862 | 1 | 4 | 1 | 0 | 2 | 203 |
| 1863 | 23 | 5 | 3 | 0 | 1 | 225 (1 restored) |
| 1864 | (no records available) | | | | | |

# Appendix 2—*continued*

| Year | Baptized | By letter | Dismissed | Excommunicated | Dead | Total Members |
|------|----------|-----------|-----------|----------------|------|---------------|
| 1865 | 21 | 4 | 10 | 20 | 8 | 220 |
| 1866 |  |  |  |  |  | 198 |
| 1867 |  |  |  |  |  |  |
| 1868 |  |  |  |  |  |  |
| 1869 |  |  |  |  |  | 218 |
| 1870 |  |  |  |  |  | 218 |
| 1871 |  |  |  |  |  | 184 |
| 1872 |  |  |  |  |  |  |
| 1873 |  |  |  |  |  | 194 |
| 1874 |  |  |  |  |  | 201 |
| 1875 |  |  |  |  |  | 202 |
| 1876 |  |  |  |  |  | 199 |
| 1877 |  |  |  |  |  | 200 |
| 1878 |  |  |  |  |  | 203 |
| 1879 |  |  |  |  |  | 200 |
| 1880 |  |  |  |  |  | 205 |
| 1881 |  |  |  |  |  | 200 |
| 1893 |  |  |  |  |  | 223 |
| 1895 |  |  |  |  |  | 305 |

*Source:* Baptist Association, *Minutes*, 1825–1901.

*Note:* Membership "by letter" means that an individual was a member in good standing at another Baptist church and joined the Hopewell church by presenting credentials. "Dismissed" refers to the reverse process, presenting a departing member in good standing with credentials so that he or she may join another church. Credentials are the subjects of some of the queries in Appendix 1. "Excommunicated" refers to exclusion from the Baptist order for some gross or persistent unorthodoxy.

# Postscript: Additional Comments

The central problem in this book has been to account for local conceptions of order in Hopewell and for the terms in which those concepts convey negative or positive value. The five chapters of the text have considered the concentric domains (so they are conceptualized in Hopewell) in which those attitudes take on form and meaning. Chapters 1 and 2 examine the individual and intimate circle, the church and God. The differentiation of these domains— and, again, the criteria of that set of differentiations—became problems in themselves in Chapter 3; Chapters 4 and 5 explain the secular and sacred referents of the local Baptist sociology. The order of the chapters is intended to show the embeddedness of contemporary patterns (and justifications) of conflict avoidance in a historical consciousness that silences cleavage and contradiction. It is the particular way in which these two aspects of the problem intersect in Hopewell (the specific issues with the specific conflict discourse) that have formed the argument presented here. I have indicated in the text points where other scholars have found related or parallel developments elsewhere in the United States.

What does such a study accomplish? In part it offers some ethnographic confirmation of the concluding pages of Weber's *Protestant Ethic and the Spirit of Capitalism*, in which he pointed to the heritage of the Puritans' "vocation" in a hollow sense of duty that the modern middle class brings to its workplaces: "The Puritan wanted to work in a calling; we are forced to do so" (1958: 181). It is at the end of this passage, summarizing the impact of Protestant asceticism on the development of capitalism, that Weber referred to the culmination of that development, with its material allure, as "an iron cage." Now, he continued, "the idea of duty in one's calling prowls about in our lives like the ghost of dead religious beliefs" (1958: 182). He also asked who will live in the iron cage in the future. The passage evokes Hopewell in several important respects: the sense of isolation that duty imposes not only in the affairs of the marketplace but also in matters of the heart; the sacredness of duty in connecting an individual's private role simultaneously to the social arena and to God. At the same time, Baptists in Hopewell would say that they have found a way to lighten the iron cage, or at least to enlarge it, by interpreting their material goods as indices of their capacity to support the church in a material way and in seeing their professional successes as opportunities to "serve the Lord." Their invocations of ascetic values do not describe their way of life but rather the contrast they see between their own values and those of the unsaved around them—the people with "dollar signs in their eyes."

From another perspective, this study demonstrates a set of interconnections among a set of broad social domains: religion, law, and order. The people I knew in Hopewell readily conceded the importance of law as a social control mechanism—even (unfortunately, they would add) a necessary one. Although their resistance to the idea of law in the context of interpersonal disputes has as its consequence a resistance to the interventions of the state in this particular quarter of their private lives, that is certainly not their motive. Instead, their resistance—as we have seen—is rooted in the logic of sacredness that obviates not only applications of human authority, but human authority itself. Human authority, apparently, is not made by God as a form of celebrating individual merit; there is always the implication that a person who sets himself above others does so illegitimately. Thus although their view of social control concedes the need for authority, that need is separate from their conception of order. Order is not a question of power in their view but a question of the sacred logic of absolute equality among all Christians (this would be their term for born-agains) and the goodness that the assurance of salvation can guarantee. All order and all meaning ultimately refer to this logic in their view. It should now be clear why and how it is that questions of legal ordering are very quickly transformed into questions of other sorts.

Although this specific claim refers only to Hopewell, wider patterns of remedial choice making among Americans suggest that parallel logics may be at work elsewhere. First, Americans' disputing behavior tends toward two poles: there is a certain amount of confrontation and litigation (and these activities certainly provide the idiom of disputing), but the majority of Americans do nothing about their grievances—they "lump" them (Nader 1980). Although studies of Americans with a wide array of disputes (for example, in housing or as consumers) show them to be inventive in pursuing satisfaction, what is more striking is the relative absence of disputing processes short of litigation—mediation and arbitration. It is true that many cities now have institutionalized mediation in neighborhood centers of various sorts; however, early evaluations of them tended to suggest that they were underutilized except when their dockets were provided by court referrals (in general, see Tomasic and Feeley 1982).

A second point of comparison between Hopewell and other American communities is provided by the work of Perin (1977) and Engel (1984). Perin examined the cultural significance of the nation's zoning categories. Her analysis makes it clear that planners, bankers, and residents alike hold a view of human nature that breaks down into a number of distinct genres, or types. The types are easily distinguished by income, occupation, and form of tenancy. These types also convey positive and negative value by their association with various indices of trouble—levels of noise and mess, financial reliability, and so on. As in Hopewell, such social categories reflect a sociology based on criteria of the likelihood of conflict, thus (as in Hopewell) simultaneously locating conflict and interpreting it. Engel's study examines conflict more directly. In "Sander County," the expectation of conflict clearly marks the boundary between insiders and newcomers from the insiders' perspective. Engel explored the significance of litigation from the cultural vantage point of these local social cleavages and their symbolic expression. Thus it appears that it is not only in Hopewell that people place particular importance on conflict and its meaning. These two points—the relative lack of indigenous forms of overt dispute processing and the view that conflict is the result of particu-

lar genres of human nature—are consistent in that the one rein-
forces the other. One does not fight what one cannot change. Conflict is not seen as the result of specific violations of one's rights but
as the result of the actions of defective social types.

Although the view of conflict explored in this book may have
parallels beyond Hopewell, there is still something distinctly local
about its character. Engel's study also suggests this point. A final
concluding theme, therefore, must be the importance of place in
culture. The conclusion of Blumin's social history of nineteenth-
century Kingston, New York, raises the question of the enduring
importance of place in modern America: "It remains to be proved
that in larger cities, and in a later era, continued growth and more
highly developed non-local communications and trade truly destroyed the sense and reality of local community in America" (1976:
222). The case of Hopewell offers testimony to the vitality of the
concept of community there and its importance as a dimension in
cultural analysis. The embeddedness of individualism in community (see Blumin 1976: 221, Varenne 1977) is no abstraction. We have
seen in Chapters 1 and 2 that the very terms with which people
define their most intimate relationships draw on signs and classifications that themselves refer to the modern and historical community. Personal values (in the sense of valuations) are expressed in
terms of authentic Hopewell, as we have seen in Chapter 3. Although the people themselves are virtually unaware of important
aspects of the town's past—and many newcomers would be totally
unaware—this analysis shows that the terms of cultural reasoning
derive most immediately from distinctly local experiences. These
experiences are conveyed across the generations and to new arrivals in the language people use to express merit and inadequacy.
Terms such as *city people* or *Yankee* have specific historical referents, but with the suppression of overt conflict, their salience now
is in their denotation of generic social types. The corollary of a
widespread pattern of ahistoricism and avoidance would seem to be
a view of human nature that subsumes conflict as a characteristic (or
typification) of certain groups. In this way, conflict can be explained
as being the product of nature rather than historical circumstance.

The people of Hopewell live full, ordinary lives and so are concerned on a daily basis with many things besides those discussed in
these pages. Perhaps the most basic conclusion to draw from this

study is its justification of a focus on conflict and its claim that conceptions of conflict are fundamental cultural facts in this social context. The central place that conflict holds for people in Hopewell—in their judgments of themselves and others—forms one axis along which Hopewell might be drawn into the wider ethnography of the United States and the cross-cultural literature, particularly of legal anthropology. Conflict may not play the same role everywhere in the United States—I have stressed the local dimensions of this study throughout—but the emergent evidence (sketched above) seems to suggest a general pattern. A second axis of comparison forms along the corollary—or so it is perceived in Hopewell— between human equality and the absence of human authority. Whether one's basis for insisting on equality is the Bible or the United States Constitution, the resulting social logic makes overt conflict problematic in that it invites the intervention of authority in the person of the third party. In Hopewell, the objections to authority are doctrinal; elsewhere, they are expressed in political or moral or other terms. Thus I would connect the Hopewell Baptists' perceptions of conflict to the widespread concern Americans express with allegedly excessive litigiousness in the United States generally. At the same time, this usage contrasts sharply with another view of the connection between equality and hierarchy, and that is an orientation toward courts that makes them agents of change. If I were to turn from Hopewell to America at large, I would begin at these junctures.

# Bibliography

As indicated in the Preface, the Note to Readers from Hopewell, and the Introduction, my concern in presenting the ethnography is to conform to anthropological ethical conventions by concealing the identities of individuals living and dead and the place I call "Hopewell." This commitment requires, too, that I conceal the identity of some of my published sources, because the people of Hopewell have written about themselves, as have others in the official and unofficial record. This book is the first scholarly work on the town's life. I welcome inquiries from other scholars whose research demands the precise referencing that I have had to omit from this volume. In addition to private collections of letters and other papers in the possession of residents of Hopewell, I consulted books and articles published privately in Hopewell and nearby towns, and the following local sources:

Baptist Association. *Minutes,* 1825–1901.
Baptist Church. *History.* 1956.
Centennial Souvenir Booklet.
The County *Annual.*
County Court of Ordinary. "Minutes, Book A." Unpublished.
County Superior Court. "Minutes, Book A." Unpublished.
Methodist Church. "Historical Papers." Unpublished.
Public Library. "Historical Collections." Unpublished.

Abel, Richard L. 1980. "Taking Stock." *Law and Society Review* 14(3): 429–443.

Bibliography

Atlanta *People's Party Paper*, September 7, 1894, November 9, 1894.

Ayers, Edward L. 1984. *Vengeance and Justice: Crime and Punishment in the 19th Century American South*. New York and Oxford: Oxford University Press.

Bailey, F. G., ed. 1971. *Gifts and Poison: The Politics of Reputation*. Oxford: Basil Blackwell.

Batteau, Allen. 1982a. "Mosbys and Broomsedge: The Semantics of Class in the Appalachian Kinship System." *American Ethnologist* 9(3): 445–466.

————. 1982b. "The Contradictions of a Kinship Community." In Hall and Stack 1982.

Bauman, Richard. 1983. *Let Your Words Be Few*. Cambridge: Cambridge University Press.

Baumgartner, M. P. 1980. "Law and the Middle Class: Evidence from a Suburban Town." Paper presented to the annual meeting of the Law and Society Association, Madison, Wisconsin.

Bellah, Robert. 1968. "Civil Religion in America." In McLoughlin and Bellah 1968.

Bentley, Carter. 1984. "Hermeneutics and World Construction in Maranao Disputing." *American Ethnologist* 11(4): 642–655.

Black, Donald. 1976. *The Behavior of Law*. New York: Academic Press.

Blu, Karen I. 1980. *The Lumbee Problem: The Making of an American Indian People*. Cambridge: Cambridge University Press.

Blumin, Stuart M. 1976. *The Urban Threshold*. Chicago: University of Chicago Press.

Bohannan, Paul, ed. 1967. *Law and Warfare*. Garden City, N.Y.: Natural History Press.

Bott, Elizabeth. 1957. *Family and Social Network*. London: Tavistock.

Brooks, R. P. 1913. *History of Georgia*. Boston: Atkinson, Mentzer.

Bryant, Carlene F. 1980. *We're All Kin*. Knoxville: University of Tennessee Press.

Buckle, Leonard, and Suzann Thomas-Buckle. 1982. "Doing unto Others: Disputes and Dispute Processing in an Urban American Neighborhood." In Tomasic and Feeley 1982.

Cain, Maureen, and Kalman Kulscar. 1981–1982. "Thinking Disputes: An Essay on the Origins of the Dispute Industry." *Law and Society Review* 16(3): 375–402.

Carrithers, David Wallace. 1977. Introduction to *Montesquieu: The Spirit of Laws*. Berkeley: University of California Press.

Cash, W. J. 1941. *The Mind of the South*. New York: Vintage Books.

Cobbett, William. 1964. *A Year's Residence in the United States of America*. Carbondale: Southern Illinois University Press.

Collier, Jane F. 1975. "Legal Processes." In B. Siegel, ed., *Annual Review of Anthropology*, vol. 4. Palo Alto: Annual Reviews, pp. 121–144.

Comaroff, John, and Simon Roberts. 1981. *Rules and Processes*. Chicago: University of Chicago Press.

Crèvecoeur, Michel Guillaume St. Jean de. 1964. *Letters from an American Farmer*. Garden City, N.Y.: Doubleday.

Curran, Barbara A., and Francis O. Spalding. 1974. *The Legal Needs of the Public*. Chicago: American Bar Foundation.

Danzig, Richard. 1982. "Towards the Creation of a Complementary Decentralized System of Criminal Justice." In Tomasic and Feeley 1982.

Davis, Allison, Burleigh B. Gardner, and Mary R. Gardner. 1949. *Deep South*. Chicago: University of Chicago Press.

Dollard, John. 1957. *Caste and Class in a Southern Town*, 3d ed. Garden City, N.Y.: Doubleday Anchor Books.

Dun and Bradstreet, Inc. 1959. *Reference Book*, vol. 366, bk. 2. New York: Dun and Bradstreet.

Dun, R. G., and Company. 1928. *Reference Book*, vol. 241. Brooklyn: Dun and Company.

Durkheim, Emile. 1965. *The Elementary Forms of the Religious Life*. Trans. J. W. Swain. New York: Free Press.

Eighmy, John Lee. 1972. *Churches in Cultural Captivity: A History of the Social Attitudes of Southern Baptists*. Knoxville: University of Tennessee Press.

Engel, David M. 1984. "The Oven-bird's Song: Insiders, Outsiders, and Personal Injuries in an American Community." *Law and Society Review* 18(4): 549–579.

Ervin-Tripp, Susan. 1976. "Speech Acts and Social Learning." In Keith Basso and Henry Selby, eds., *Meaning in Anthropology*. Albuquerque: University of New Mexico Press, pp. 93–122.

Favret-Saada, Jeanne. 1981. *Deadly Words*. Cambridge: Cambridge University Press.

Felstiner, William. 1974. "Influences of Social Organization on Dispute Processing." *Law and Society Review* 9(1): 63–94.

Fitchen, Janet. 1981. *Poverty in Rural America*. Boulder, Colo.: Westview Press.

FitzGerald, Frances. 1979. *America Revised*. Boston: Little, Brown.

Flanders, Ralph Betts. 1933. *Plantation Slavery in Georgia*. Chapel Hill: University of North Carolina Press.

Forrest, John A. 1982. "The Role of Aesthetics in the Conversion Experience in a Missionary Baptist Church." In Hall and Stack 1982.

Galanter, Marc. 1983. "Reading the Landscape of Disputes: What We Know and Don't Know (and Think We Know) about Our Allegedly Contentious and Litigious Society." *UCLA Law Review* 31(1): 4–71.

Geertz, C. 1973. *The Interpretation of Cultures*. New York: Basic Books.

———. 1983. *Local Knowledge: Further Essays in Interpretive Anthropology*. New York: Basic Books.

Georgia, State of. 1975–1976. *Official and Statistical Register*. Atlanta: Department of Archives and History.

Georgia General Assembly. 1859. *Journal of the House of Representatives of the State of Georgia at the Annual Session of the General Assembly Commenced at Milledgeville*, November 3, 1858.

Gibbs, James L. 1963. "The Kpelle Moot." *Africa* 33(1): 1–10.

Gluckman, Max. 1940. "Analysis of a Social Situation in Modern Zululand." Rhodes-Livingston Paper No. 28 (1958).

———. 1955. *The Judicial Process among the Barotse of Northern Rhodesia.* Manchester: The University Press.

———. 1967. *The Judicial Process among the Barotse of Northern Rhodesia,* 2d ed. Manchester: The University Press.

———. 1973. "Limitations of the Case Method in the Study of Tribal Law." *Law and Society Review* 7(4): 611–641.

Goldschmidt, Walter. 1974. "Social Class and the Dynamics of Status in America." In Jorgensen and Truzzi 1974.

Gorer, Geoffrey. 1948. *The Americans: A Study in National Character.* London: The Cresset Press.

Greenhouse, Carol J. 1982a. "Looking at Culture, Looking for Rules." *Man* 17(1): 58–73.

———. 1982b. "Nature: Culture:: Praying: Suing." *Journal of Legal Pluralism* 20: 17–35.

———. 1983. "Being and Doing: Competing concepts of Elite Status in an American Suburb." In George Marcus, ed., *Elites.* Albuquerque: University of New Mexico Press, pp. 113–140.

———. 1985a. "Mediation: A Comparative Approach." *Man* 20(1): 90–114.

———. 1985b. "Anthropology at Home: Whose Home?" *Human Organization* 44(3): 261–264.

———. 1986. "Fighting for Peace." In M. Foster and R. Silverstein, eds., *Anthropological Perspectives on War and Peace.* Basic Books.

Grindal, Bruce T. 1982. "The Religious Interpretation of Experience in a Rural Black Community." In Hall and Stack 1982.

Hall, Robert L., and Carol B. Stack, eds. 1982. *Holding on to the Land and the Lord.* Athens: University of Georgia Press.

Hawkins, Benjamin. 1848. "A Sketch of the Creek County in the Years 1798 and 1799." *Collections of the Georgia Historical Society,* vol. 3, part 1. Savannah: Georgia Historical Society.

Henry, Jules. 1974. "A Theory for an Anthropological Analysis of American Culture." In Jorgensen and Truzzi 1974.

Hill, Carole E. 1977. "Anthropological Studies in the American South: Review and Directions." *Current Anthropology* 18(2): 309–326.

Hill, Samuel S. 1966. *Southern Churches in Crisis.* Boston: Beacon Press.

Hopkins, Charles H. 1940. *The Rise of the Social Gospel in American Protestantism, 1865–1915.* New Haven: Yale University Press.

Hostetler, John A. 1968. *Amish Society,* rev. ed. Baltimore: The Johns Hopkins University Press.

———. 1984. "The Amish and the Law: A Religious Minority and Its Legal Encounters." *Washington and Lee Law Review* 41(1): 33–47.

Hughey, Michael W. 1983. *Civil Religion and Moral Order: Theoretical and Historical Dimensions.* Westport, Conn.: Greenwood Press.

Huizinga, Johan. 1972. *America: A Dutch Historian's Vision, from Afar and Near*. Trans. Herbert H. Rowen. New York: Harper & Row.

Jorgensen, Joseph G., and Marcello Truzzi. 1974. *Anthropology and American Life*. Englewood Cliffs, N.J.: Prentice-Hall.

Key, V. O., Jr. 1949. *Southern Politics*. New York: Vintage Books.

Koch, Klaus-Friedrich. 1974. *War and Peace in Jalémó*. Cambridge: Harvard University Press.

Koch, Klaus-Friedrich, Soraya Altorki, Andrew Arno, and Letitia Hickson. 1977. "Ritual Reconciliation and the Obviation of Grievances: A Comparative Study in the Ethnography of Law." *Ethnology* 16(3): 269–283.

Konig, David Thomas. 1979. *Law and Society in Puritan Massachusetts, Essex County, 1629–1692*. Chapel Hill: University of North Carolina Press.

Krakow, Kenneth K. 1975. *Georgia Place-Names*. Macon, Ga.: Winship Press.

Krutza, Vilma, and William Krutza. 1973. *Friendship Is . . .* Santa Ana, Calif.: Vision House.

LaBarre, Weston L. 1969. *They Shall Take Up Serpents*. New York: Schocken Books.

Leckie, George G. 1954. *Georgia: A Guide to Its Towns and Countryside*. American Guide Series. Atlanta: Tupper and Love.

Llewellyn, Karl N., and E. Adamson Hoebel. 1941. *The Cheyenne Way*. Norman: University of Oklahoma Press.

Loveland, Anne C. 1980. *Southern Evangelicals and the Social Order, 1800–1860*. Baton Rouge: Louisiana State University Press.

McLoughlin, William G., and Robert N. Bellah, eds. 1968. *Religion in America*. Boston: Houghton Mifflin.

Marty, Martin E. 1976. *A Nation of Behavers*. Chicago: University of Chicago Press.

———. 1977. *Religion, Awakening and Revolution*. Gaithersburg, Md.: McGrath Publishing Company—A Consortium Book.

Mather, Lynn, and Barbara Yngvesson. 1980–1981. "Language, Audience, and the Transformation of Disputes." *Law and Society Review* 15(3–4): 775–821.

May, Henry F. 1949. *Protestant Churches and Industrial America*. New York: Harper and Brothers.

Mead, Frank S. 1975. *Handbook of Denominations*, 6th ed. Nashville, N.Y.: Abingdon Press.

Merry, Sally Engle. 1979. "Going to Court: Strategies of Dispute Management in an Urban Neighborhood." *Law and Society Review* 13(4): 891–926.

———. 1982. "The Social Organization of Mediation in Nonindustrial Societies: Implications for Informal Community Justice in America." In Richard Abel, ed., *The Politics of Informal Justice*. New York: Academic Press, pp. 17–45.

Milledgeville *Federal Union*, January 15, 1861.

Miller, Perry. 1965. *The Life of the Mind in America*. New York: Harcourt, Brace and World.

Miller, Robert M. 1958. *American Protestantism and Social Issues, 1919–1939*. Chapel Hill: University of North Carolina Press.

Montesquieu. 1973. *Persian Letters*. New York: Penguin.

———. 1977. *The Spirit of Laws*. Ed. D. W. Carrithers. Berkeley: University of California Press.

Moore, Sally F. 1970a. "Law and Anthropology." In B. Siegel, ed., *Biennial Review of Anthropology 1969*. Stanford, Calif.: Stanford University Press, pp. 252–300.

———. 1970b. "Politics, Procedures, and Norms in Changing Chagga Law." *Africa* 40(4): 321–344.

———. 1978. *Law as Process: An Anthropological Approach*. London: Routledge and Kegan Paul.

Moseley, James G. 1981. *A Cultural History of Religion in America*. Westport, Conn.: Greenwood Press.

Nader, Laura. 1965. "The Anthropological Study of Law." *American Anthropologist* 67 (6, 2): 3–32.

———. 1968. "A Note on Attitudes and the Use of Language." In J. A. Fishman, ed., *Readings in the Sociology of Language*. The Hague: Mouton.

Nader, Laura, ed. 1980. *No Access to Law*. New York: Academic Press.

Nader, Laura, and Harry F. Todd, Jr., eds. 1978. *The Disputing Process—Law in Ten Societies*. New York: Columbia University Press.

Nelson, William E. 1981. *Disputes and Conflict Resolution in Plymouth County, Massachusetts, 1725–1825*. Chapel Hill: University of North Carolina Press.

Peacock, James L. 1971. "The Southern Protestant Ethic Disease." In J. K. Moreland, ed., *The Not So Solid South*. Athens: University of Georgia Press, pp. 108–113.

———. 1975a. "Weberian, Southern Baptist, and Indonesian Muslim Conceptions of Belief and Action." In Carole E. Hill, ed., *Symbols and Society*. Athens: University of Georgia Press, pp. 82–92.

———. 1975b. *Consciousness and Change*. Oxford: Basil Blackwell.

Perin, Constance. 1977. *Everything in Its Place*. Princeton, N.J.: Princeton University Press.

Phillips, Ulrich B. 1968. *Georgia and States Rights*. Yellow Springs, O.: Antioch Press.

Pitkin, Hanna Fenichel. 1972. *Wittgenstein and Justice*. Berkeley: University of California Press.

Postel-Coster, Els. 1977. "The Indonesian Novel as a Source of Anthropological Data." In Ravindra K. Jain, ed., *Text and Context: The Social Anthropology of Tradition*. Philadelphia: Institute for the Study of Human Issues, pp. 135–150.

Rosaldo, Michelle Zimbalist. 1984. "Toward an Anthropology of Self and Feeling." In R. Schneider and R. Levine, eds., *Culture Theory*. Cambridge: Cambridge University Press, pp. 137–157.

Rosen, Lawrence. 1984. *Bargaining for Reality*. Chicago: University of Chicago Press.

Rousseau, Jean-Jacques. 1952. "The Social Contract." In Ernest Barker, ed., *Social Contract: Locke, Hume, Rousseau.* London: Oxford University Press.

Schneider, David. 1968. *American Kinship: A Cultural Account.* Englewood Cliffs, N.J.: Prentice-Hall.

Sherwood, Adiel. 1837. *A Gazeteer of the State of Georgia,* 3d ed. Washington City, Ga.: P. Force.

Simkins, Francis Butler. 1963. *A History of the South,* 3d ed. New York: Alfred A. Knopf.

Singer, Milton B. 1977. "On the Symbolic and Historic Structure of an American Identity." *Ethos* 5(4): 431–454.

———. 1984. *Man's Glassy Essence.* Bloomington: Indiana University Press.

Smith, Timothy C. 1980. *Revivalism and Social Reform: American Protestantism on the Eve of the Civil War.* Baltimore: The Johns Hopkins University Press.

Snyder, Francis G. 1981. "Anthropology, Dispute Processes, and Law: A Critical Introduction." *British Journal of Law and Society* 8(2): 141–180.

Stack, Carol. 1974. *All Our Kin: Strategies for Survival in a Black Community.* New York: Harper Colophon Books.

Stein, Peter. 1980. *Legal Evolution.* Cambridge: Cambridge University Press.

Street, James, Jr. 1955. *James Street's South.* Garden City, N.Y.: Doubleday.

Strout, Cushing. 1974. *The New Heavens and New Earth: Political Religion in America.* New York: Harper & Row.

Sutton, Brett. 1982. "Language, Vision, and Myth: The Primitive Baptist Experience of Grace." In Hall and Stack 1982.

Szasz, Ferenc Morton. 1982. *The Divided Mind of Protestant America, 1880–1930.* University: University of Alabama Press.

Tindall, George B. 1967. *The Emergence of the New South, 1913–1945.* Baton Rouge: Louisiana State University Press.

———. 1972. *The Disruption of the Solid South.* New York: W. W. Norton.

Tocqueville, Alexis de. 1945. *Democracy in America.* 2 vols. New York: Vintage.

Todd, Harry F., Jr. 1978. "Litigious Marginals: Character and Disputing in a Bavarian Village." In Nader and Todd 1978.

Tomasic, Roman, and Malcolm Feeley. 1982. *Neighborhood Justice: Assessment of an Emerging Idea.* New York: Longman.

Turner, Victor. 1969. *The Ritual Process.* Harmondsworth, Eng.: Penguin Books.

———. 1974. *Dramas, Fields, and Metaphors.* Ithaca, N.Y.: Cornell University Press.

United States Department of Agriculture. 1925–1965. *Census.*

United States Department of Commerce. 1860. *Census.*

———. 1917–1975. *Cotton Production in the United States, Crop of 1917 through Crop of 1975* [separate publications].

United States Department of Commerce and Labor. Bureau of the Census. *Cotton Production 1906.* Bulletin No. 76.

[217]

————. *Cotton Production 1907*. Bulletin No. 95.

————. *Cotton Production 1913*. Bulletin No. 125.

United States War Department. 1891. *The War of the Rebellion: A Compilation of the Official Records of the Union and Confederate Armies*. Series I, vol. 38, 5 parts. Washington, D.C.: Government Printing Office.

Useem, Ruth Hill, John Useem, and Duane L. Gibson. 1974. "The Function of Neighboring for the Middle-Class Male." In Jorgensen and Truzzi 1974.

van Gennep, Arnold. 1960. *The Rites of Passage*. Chicago: University of Chicago Press.

van Velsen, J. 1969. "Procedural Informality, Reconciliation, and False Comparison." In Max Gluckman, ed. *Ideas and Procedures in African Customary Law*. London: Oxford University Press.

Varenne, Hervé. 1977. *Americans Together*. New York: Teachers College Press.

————. 1984a. "Collective Representation in American Anthropological Conversations: Individual and Culture." *Current Anthropologist* 25(3): 281–300.

————. 1984b. "The Interpretation of Pronomial Paradigms: Speech Situation, Pragmatic Meaning, and Cultural Structure." *Semiotica* 50(3/4): 221–248.

————. Forthcoming. "Meaning Community." In Hervé Varenne, ed., *Symbolizing America*. Lincoln: University of Nebraska Press.

Wallace, Anthony C. 1978. *Rockdale*. New York: W. W. Norton.

Warner, W. Lloyd. 1949. *Democracy in Jonesville: A Study of Quality and Inequality*. New York: Harper and Brothers.

————. 1952. *Structure of American Life*. Edinburgh: University Press.

————. 1961. *The Family of God*. New Haven: Yale University Press.

————. 1962. *American Life: Dream and Reality*. Chicago: University of Chicago Press.

————. 1963. *Yankee City*, abridged ed. Ed. W. L. Warner. New Haven: Yale University Press.

Watkins, James L. 1899. *The Cost of Cotton Production*. United States Department of Agriculture, Division of Statistics. Miscellaneous Series Bulletin No. 16. Washington, D.C.: Government Printing Office.

————. 1901. *The Cotton Crop of 1899–1900*. United States Department of Agriculture, Division of Statistics. Miscellaneous Series Bulletin No. 19. Washington, D.C.: Government Printing Office.

————. 1904. *The Commercial Cotton Crops of 1900–1901, 1901–1902, and 1902–1903*. United States Department of Agriculture, Bureau of Statistics. Bulletin No. 28. Washington D.C.: Government Printing Office.

————. 1905. *The Commercial Cotton Crop*. United States Department of Agriculture, Bureau of Statistics, Bulletin No. 34. Washington, D.C. Government Printing Office.

Weber, Max. 1946a. "The Protestant Sects and the Spirit of Capitalism." In H. H. Gerth and C. Wright Mills, trans. and ed., *From Max Weber: Essays on Sociology*. New York: Oxford University Press, pp. 302–322.

———. 1946b. "Religious Rejections of the World and Their Directions." In H. H. Gerth and C. Wright Mills, trans. and ed., *From Max Weber: Essays in Sociology*. New York: Oxford University Press, pp. 323–359.

———. 1954. *On Law in Economy and Society*. Trans. Max Rheinstein. New York: Simon and Schuster.

———. 1958. *The Protestant Ethic and the Spirit of Capitalism*. Trans. Talcott Parsons. New York: Charles Scribner's Sons.

———. 1963. *The Sociology of Religion*. Trans. E. Fischoff. Boston: Free Press.

White, George. 1849. *Statistics of the State of Georgia*. Savannah: W. Thorne Williams.

———. 1855. *Historical Collections of Georgia*, 3d ed. New York: Pudney and Russell.

Williams, Charles. 1982. "The Conversion Ritual in a Rural Black Baptist Church." In Hall and Stack 1982.

Wills, Garry. 1978. *Inventing America*. New York: Vintage.

Wittgenstein, Ludwig. 1958. *Philosophical Investigations*, 3d ed. Trans. G.E.M. Anscombe. New York: Macmillan.

Yngvesson, Barbara. 1979. "The Atlantic Fishermen." In Laura Nader and Harry Todd 1978.

Zaretsky, Irving I. 1974. "In the Beginning Was the Word: The Relationship of Language to Social Organization in Spiritualist Churches." In Irving I. Zaretsky and M. Leone, ed., *Religious Movements in Contemporary America*, vol. I. Princeton, N.J.: Princeton University Press, pp. 166–219.

# Index